CONTENTS

Canada: The State of the Federation 2010

Shifting Power
The New Ontario and What it Means for Canada

Edited by
Matthew Mendelsohn
Joshua Hjartarson and
James Pearce

Institute of Intergovernmental Relations
School of Policy Studies, Queen's University
McGill-Queen's University Press
Montreal & Kingston • London • Ithaca

The Mowat Centre

The Mowat Centre is an independent public policy research centre located at the School of Public Policy & Governance at the University of Toronto.

The Mowat Centre is Ontario's non-partisan, evidence-based voice on public policy. It undertakes collaborative applied policy research, engages in public dialogue, and proposes innovative recommendations on Canada's most important national public policy issues.

The Institute of Intergovernmental Relations

The Institute is the only academic organization in Canada whose mandate is solely to promote research and communication on the challenges facing the federal system.

Current research interests include fiscal federalism, health policy, the reform of federal political institutions and the machinery of federal-provincial relations, Canadian federalism and the global economy, and comparative federalism.

The Institute pursues these objectives through research conducted by its own staff and other scholars, through its publication program, and through seminars and conferences.

The Institute links academics and practitioners of federalism in federal and provincial governments and the private sector.

The Institute of Intergovernmental Relations receives ongoing financial support from the J.A. Corry Memorial Endowment Fund, the Royal Bank of Canada Endowment Fund, the Government of Canada, and the governments of Manitoba and Ontario. We are grateful for this support, which enables the Institute to sustain its extensive program of research, publication, and related activities.

L'Institut des relations intergouvernementales

L'Institut est le seul organisme universitaire canadien à se consacrer exclusivement à la recherche et aux échanges sur les questions du fédéralisme.

Les priorités de recherche de l'Institut portent présentement sur le fédéralisme fiscal, la santé, la modification éventuelle des institutions politiques fédérales, les mécanismes de relations fédérales-provinciales, le fédéralisme canadien au regard de l'économie mondiale et le fédéralisme comparatif.

L'Institut réalise ses objectifs par le biais de recherches effectuées par son personnel et par des chercheurs de l'Université Queen's et d'ailleurs, de même que par des congrès et des colloques.

L'Institut sert comme lien entre les universitaires, les fonctionnaires fédéraux et provinciaux et le secteur privé.

L'Institut des relations intergouvernementales reçoit l'appui financier du J.A. Corry Memorial Endowment Fund, de la Fondation de la Banque Royale du Canada, du gouvernement du Canada et des gouvernements du Manitoba et de l'Ontario. Nous les remercions de cet appui qui permet à l'Institut de poursuivre son vaste programme de recherche et de publication ainsi que ses activités connexes.

ISSN 0827-0708
ISBN 978-1-55339-200-2 (pbk.)

PREFACE

When I took over as director of the Institute of Intergovernmental Relations in March 2010, my predecessor as director of the Institute, Tom Courchene, had decided to partner with Matthew Mendelsohn and the Mowat Centre to organize the 2010 State of the Federation conference. This made sense to me because I have long believed that the place of Ontario in the Canadian federation has not received enough attention. The November 2010 conference, held in Toronto, considered Ontario's changing role in the federation and its implications for our national politics and economy.

The Institute is now publishing the book largely based on the conference, Shifting Power: The New Ontario and what it means for Canada. We thank the editors Matthew Mendelsohn, Joshua Hjartarson, and James Pearce.

The 2010 State of the Federation conference was dedicated to Al Johnson and Peter Leslie who had just passed away. The community of federalism scholars and practitioners had lost two significant personalities. This is not the place to review or summarize their careers but it is appropriate to point out that the State of the Federation series of conferences and books was started in 1985, when Peter Leslie was the director of the Institute. He held the position from 1983 to 1988.

Against the backdrop of current approaches to fiscal federalism, it is worth remembering that in the mid-sixties, Al Johnson, formerly deputy treasurer in Saskatchewan, was the chief architect of the federal participation in the federal-provincial Tax Structure Committee, one of the most extensive joint reviews of intergovernmental fiscal relations.

Thus, Matthew Mendelsohn and I are pleased to dedicate this book to Peter M. Leslie and Albert W. Johnson.

André Juneau
Director of the Institute of Intergovernmental Relations

CONTRIBUTORS

Randy Besco is a PhD candidate in Political Studies at Queen's University, Kingston

P. E. Bryden is Associate Professor of History at the University of Victoria

Tijs Creutzberg is a Partner of Ottawa-based consultancy, Hickling Arthurs Low

Peter Graefe is Associate Professor of Political Science at McMaster University

Joshua Hjartarson is the Policy Director at the Mowat Centre in the School of Public Policy & Governance at the University of Toronto

Rachel Laforest is Associate Professor and head of the Public Policy and Third Sector Initiative in the School of Policy Studies at Queen's University, Kingston

Roderick Macdonald is F.R. Scott Professor of Constitutional and Public Law at McGill University and President of the Royal Society of Canada

J. Scott Matthews is Associate Professor of Political Science at Memorial University of Newfoundland and Director of the Canadian Opinion Research Archive

Matthew Mendelsohn is the founding Director of the Mowat Centre in the School of Public Policy & Governance at the University of Toronto

James Pearce is a Policy Associate at the Mowat Centre in the School of Public Policy & Governance at the University of Toronto

Steve Penfold is Associate Professor in the Department of History at the University of Toronto

David A. Wolfe is Professor of Political Science at the University of Toronto and Co-Director of the Program on Globalization and Regional Innovation Systems (PROGRIS) at the Munk School for Global Affairs

Jennifer Wallner is Assistant Professor in the School of Political Studies at the University of Ottawa

Robert Wolfe is Professor in the School of Policy Studies at Queen's University, Kingston and an Associate in the Trade and Investment Program of the International Institute for Sustainable Development

I

Introduction

1

INTRODUCTION: ACCOMMODATION OF THE NEW ONTARIO AND CANADA'S NEW NARRATIVES

Matthew Mendelsohn

Le fédéralisme canadien est dominé depuis un demi-siècle par la prise en compte des aspirations du Québec et de l'Ouest du pays. Mais pour la génération à venir, c'est aux intérêts en mutation de l'Ontario qu'il devra s'intéresser. Un exercice qui s'annonce ardu car les intérêts ontariens, complexes et variés, ne peuvent se réduire à quelques demandes. D'où la nécessité d'élaborer de nouveaux discours favorisant cette conciliation. Le consensus laurentien est chose du passé et celui du Nouvel Ouest offre peu d'attraits à l'Ontario. Car s'il partage certains intérêts avec les provinces traditionnellement bénéficiaires de la péréquation, tout comme avec les productrices de ressources, l'Ontario a surtout ses propres intérêts en tant que province sans pétrole mais relativement prospère, désireuse de renforcer sa présence dans un monde interconnecté. Pour redéfinir le contrat social interrégional du pays sur des bases pancanadiennes sans imposer à l'Ontario un fardeau financier inéquitable, il nous faudra donc de nouveaux discours nationaux et des propositions stratégiques correspondantes.

For the first time since the confederation debates of the 1860s, the accommodation of Ontario's interests within the federation is likely to be the most important regional challenge facing the federal government in the coming decade. While efforts to accommodate the interests of Quebec and the West have dominated the national conversation for two generations, dealing with an evolving Ontario is the challenge for the current generation. It is a challenge for which neither the country nor the federal government are prepared – nor are Ontarians themselves.

This essay outlines the economic challenges facing Ontario, the evolution of Canada's political economy and Canada's experience with regional accommodation.

It argues that Ontario's interests are not being sufficiently integrated into federal decision-making and that a new national narrative is necessary to replace the defunct Laurentian Consensus and compete with the emerging and ascendant New West Consensus.

THREE ECONOMIC CHALLENGES

Ontario is currently facing three inter-related economic challenges which will make the accommodation of Ontario all the more difficult. The first challenge is fiscal. Ontario's deficit is large and concerted efforts will be required to align spending and revenue. But this effort takes place against the reality that Ontario's government already has the lowest per capita spending of any province, except PEI.

The second challenge is structural. Ontario is going through a once-in-a-lifetime economic restructuring, changing the basic economic assumptions on which Ontario's prosperity has been based. This new economic order has many features, including a weakened manufacturing sector, exchange rates unfavourable to Canadian exporters and a new global economic playing field shaped by a relative economic decline in the United States (by far Ontario's largest trading partner) and the rise of emerging markets in Asia and elsewhere. The details of this restructuring can be debated, but there is little question that Ontario's industrial base is significantly weakened, and the province's economic success is now forever dependent on its ability to compete in global markets.

Third, the operation of fiscal federalism exacerbates these fiscal and economic challenges. Despite changed economic circumstances, funds continue to be redistributed away from Ontario rather than toward it. This is no doubt news to many in the commentariat who bemoan – usually with a twinkle of joy in their eye – Ontario's descent to "have-not" status. That Ontario now has below average fiscal capacity but continues to redistribute funds to other parts of the country highlights the broken nature of the country's fiscal arrangements. Based on updates of Provincial Economic Accounts, the Mowat Centre estimates that in 2012-13, redistribution away from Ontario will be over $11 Billion, or about 2 percent of the province's GDP. This leaves Ontario with the lowest real fiscal capacity of any province (except for PEI), once federal fiscal transfers have been distributed.

In order to address the first of these three fiscal challenges, the Ontario government has signalled its intention to align revenues and spending over the medium term, mostly through restraint on the spending side (with revenues constrained in part by the second and third challenges). The second challenge is a significant one for many governments, but one for which there are limited tools. To the extent that there are tools to deploy in the face of economic re-structuring – monetary, trade and taxation policy – they lie more in federal than in provincial jurisdiction. The federal government also has far greater fiscal capacity to address the issue through spending decisions.

Meeting the third challenge depends entirely on the federal government. It alone can alter how funds slosh around this country, pouring out of Ontario and pooling elsewhere. Over the past decade, the federal government has given very little indication that it recognizes the problem or cares to address it.

THREE NATIONAL PROJECTS

A simplified history of the political economy of Canadian federalism could start with the National Policy of the late 19th century. The federal government made a choice to build a protected internal market, which allowed Ontario and Quebec to prosper by producing goods behind high tariff walls and selling them to Canadians in other provinces. Southwestern Ontario benefited from this first national project by attracting people from Atlantic Canada and profiting from the settlement of Western Canada. These regions understandably came to see federal policy as tilted toward Central Canada, with political and economic power concentrated in the hands of elites in the triangle of Montreal, Ottawa, and Toronto.

This first national project allowed Ontario to grow more prosperous than other regions and created the foundation for a second national project: the building of the Canadian welfare state in the post-war period. This project was designed to ensure that all Canadians, regardless of where they lived, had access to good-quality social programs such as health care, pensions, unemployment insurance, and public education. Prosperous Ontario was more than willing to have some of its wealth used to establish these programs, which strengthened the country and contributed to Canadians' national identity. Ontarians supported this project not only because they could afford it, but because forging a stronger, unified Canada was in the interests of the dominant, most prosperous player in the federation.

The policy architecture of this second national project – equalization, unemployment insurance, federal fiscal transfers for programs like health and education, regional economic development, etc. – was explicitly designed to correct for the structural inequities of the first, which had concentrated greater economic benefits in Central Canada, particularly in southwestern Ontario. The interplay of these two projects created a variety of well-known regional tensions, resentments, and demands.

But the third national project – the free trade agreements of the 1990s and globalization more generally – destroyed the foundations of this business model. The last 20 years have seen the dismantling of the first national project, which favoured Ontario, but no structural change to the policy architecture of the second. Canada's basic business model is broken and many of Canada's regional tensions today stem from the fact that we have not acknowledged that the foundations of the post-War model have collapsed.

Ontario's receipt of its first-ever equalization cheque in 2009 represented hard evidence that Canada's former "business model" (wherein the federal government's policies helped Ontario's manufacturing sector to prosper and in return Ontario redistributed much of its wealth to poorer regions that then buy back Ontario's manufactured goods) is now defunct. While many might cheer its demise, Canadians' continued success in the 21st century is contingent upon redefining a new Canadian business model in ways that work better for Ontario.

The terms of trade have turned against Ontario, while the policies that redistribute money away from Ontario persist. Whatever once remained of Macdonald's National Policy was undone by the Free Trade Agreement with the United States over two decades ago. Whatever one's retrospective views on the merits of free trade, at the time, the Agreement was rejected by most of Ontario and supported by a Quebec-West coalition. It had an enormous effect on Ontario, the manufacturing heartland, dislocating the political and economic assumptions of the previous half century without a clear replacement. The inter-regional redistributive framework inherent to the National Policy is still largely in place, but the political economy on which it was based has vanished over the past two decades. What remains is the fact that Ontarians continue to pick up the bill.

Canada's inter-regional, post-war social contract is collapsing. It is increasingly being made irrelevant by globalized patterns of trade, a commodity super-cycle, a global geopolitical re-ordering, and both immigration patterns and demographic changes that moderate the relevance of traditional national unity narratives. Most Canadians in Markham and Mississauga have no sense that they should get less from the federal government than do those in the Maritimes for historical reasons.

CANADA'S SUCCESS IN ACCOMMODATING REGIONAL INTERESTS

Regional politics in the second half of the 20th century were largely about the accommodation of Quebec, while the 80s and 90s added Western accommodation to the inventory of regional and national unity themes. These regional demands emanated from activist provincial governments in Quebec and Western Canada, but were also furthered by complementary or parallel efforts from the federal government to respond to dissatisfaction with the federation in Quebec or the West.

⋅ Quebec has largely achieved the agenda it began to lay out in the 1960s. Quebec is, for the most part, autonomous within the federation, supported by large fiscal transfers from elsewhere in the country, and recognized to be acting as a nation within Canada. Many in Quebec may reject this nationalist agenda, but responding to the ambitions of Quebec's political class has been the dominant agenda of the federation for much of the last five decades. There may be specific areas of federal policy or powers that some in Quebec continue to find problematic, but the agenda of the Quiet Revolution has been largely realized. The issues facing Quebec today have little to do with federalism. On the contrary, the federal architecture which provides financial support to Quebec from the rest of Canada has allowed Quebec to avoid confronting directly some of its most important economic, social and demographic challenges.

Western Canada's ambition has been to exploit, control, and profit from its natural resources. Many in Western Canada may reject this agenda (particularly those who chafe at the recent re-definition of "Western Canadian" interests through the lens of the oil patch), but dealing with this ambition has been the second main theme of Canada's national unity narrative since the 1980s. The main goals of the Western Canadian economic agenda that were laid out several decades ago, including increased political power in Ottawa, have likewise been largely fulfilled.

On occasions when the interests of Alberta and Quebec have aligned, as they did in the 1980s, the provinces were able to successfully drive forward the third national project of free trade and weakened federal government, opposed by Ontario. This third project was just as important as the first two, but while Quebec and Alberta are generally happy with the outcome of the trade liberalization project, neither has demonstrated any interest in fundamentally renegotiating the fiscal framework that continues to redistribute funds away from Ontario.

Canadians have very little recent experience thinking about a distinct set of Ontario interests. Not only has the federal government been more able to identify the interests of regions outside of Ontario, Ontarians themselves are probably more able to articulate the regional interests of others than their own. Canadians including Ontarians simply have more experience thinking through the accommodation of Quebec or the West – and to a lesser extent Atlantic Canada – than they do about the accommodation of Ontario.

Ontarians supported the accommodation of Quebec, Albertan, or Maritime demands because it strengthened national unity. This was in fact the strategic choice that Ontario made throughout the second half of the 20th century: support a strong federal government and encourage a minimization of regional grievances to build a strong Canada. A strong Canada led to optimism about the future of the Ontario economy and this economic optimism was a defining element of the Ontario psyche. "National unity" was Ontario's mission statement because if Canada was doing well, Ontario did even better. This investment in inter-regional redistribution paid off enormously in terms of a stronger, more united Canada, with policies that reflected the values of Toronto and southwestern Ontario more generally. If Ontario had a core mission statement beyond national unity, it was that Ontario was and should remain prosperous.

National unity remains important to Ontario, as does the success of other regions. The growth and diversification of provincial economies across the country is good for Ontario. Economic growth in Quebec is crucial to Ontario, as is the strength of the Western resource sector, where Ontario's financial sector invests and its professional services firms find clients. Ontario, more than any other province, has interests everywhere in the country, much like it always has. What has changed is that the province is less willing or able to sacrifice or suppress those interests.

The accommodation of Ontario's interests within the federation will require first an articulation that such a set of interests exists, distinct from the national interest itself, followed by a set of policy proposals. This articulation has yet to happen. The policies would relate to fiscal transfers, income support, poverty, the urban agenda, resource development, infrastructure, and monetary policy, amongst others. Global trends and local circumstances dictate that these policy interests will be more complex than the much simpler narratives that emerged in Quebec around autonomy and language or in Western Canada around control of natural resources and political power in Ottawa.

NEW NARRATIVES TO DEFINE NEW INTERESTS

Ontario's interests in the federation are complex and diverse. New narratives will be required to articulate these interests and to make sense of the evolving country.

Some have talked about the end of the Laurentian Consensus – a narrative that defined the federation through the prism of Montreal, Ottawa, Toronto, and the southwestern Ontario communities along the St. Lawrence and Great Lakes Basin. John Ibbitson has written a compelling piece in the *Literary Review of Canada* which popularized this thesis and added to it by suggesting the Laurentian Consensus has been displaced by a new diverse coalition, dominated by Western Canada. There is one important addition to this interpretation that must be highlighted: the Laurentian Consensus has not been displaced solely by what could be called "the New West Consensus" (i.e., an interpretation of Canadian interests through the lens of the natural resource sectors of Alberta and Saskatchewan). Rather, competing definitions and narratives are emerging to replace the largely defunct Laurentian Consensus, with the New West Consensus clearly in the lead and clearly ascendant with the current federal government.

While today's federal government may see issues through the lens of the Western Canadian resource sector, it is far-fetched to think that this vision encompasses the whole of the Canadian reality, or that it will endure for the foreseeable future. There is no one dominant national narrative that will be uncontested over the medium term. We are likely experiencing a period of contested narratives and mythologies. This is good. Canadians in Saskatchewan are telling the story of Canada through the assumptions of the New West Consensus and are no longer outsiders looking in at an economic and political story being dictated by Toronto and Montreal.

But "The West" has not replaced Ontario, nor has the New West Consensus replaced the Laurentian Consensus. Instead, we are experiencing the de-centring of wealth and power along with the emergence of competing narratives telling the story of Canada with different interests in mind. Ontario's is the most poorly articulated of these narratives. The absence of a clear Ontario voice in the national discourse weakens the conversation and undermines our ability to move past the regional and national unity debates of the 20th century to reconstruct a balanced Canadian consensus that works for all of Canada's regions.

THE POLITICS OF ACCOMMODATING ONTARIO

Articulating a distinct set of Ontario interests along with policy proposals to advance them will not be easy. For two decades, Ontario governments have struggled to do so, usually offering complaints but not a coherent vision of Ontario's interests within the federation.

By contrast, while many Western Canadians reject the New West Consensus and many in Quebec reject the nationalist narrative, it cannot be denied that control of natural resources in Alberta and greater provincial autonomy particularly around language issues in Quebec were core to these provinces' political agendas for decades. Nothing so simple is available to Ontario.

Since the economic restructuring that began in the early 1990s – as a result of globalization – successive Ontario premiers dealing with the nuts and bolts of budget-making and intergovernmental relations have questioned whether the federal-provincial fiscal framework still made sense. They understood that the interests of Ontario and Canada were not always identical and that Ontario's return on investment in inter-regional redistribution had become poor to non-existent.

In the years immediately following the implementation of the Free Trade Agreement, Bob Rae raised concerns about structural inequities in federal fiscal transfers. Many dismissed his complaints as a tactical ploy, from a profligate social democrat, to shift blame for Ontario's ballooning deficit to the federal government. When Mike Harris later raised the same concerns, he was dismissed as a stingy neo-conservative unwilling to offer up a slice of Ontario's largesse to his poorer neighbours.

The fact is that Ontario's fiscal situation is constrained by outdated federal-provincial fiscal relations. The Ontario public is finally beginning to understand what Rae and Harris (and more recently Dalton McGuinty) learned while in government: national social programs designed to redistribute wealth from Ontario created for an era of protected internal markets are unsustainable in a country where Ontario's comparative wealth is only average and where the province's businesses compete globally. Ontarians are at last coming to understand that their provincial government spends less than other provinces on the public services its residents need, while redistribution away from Ontario to other parts of Canada continues despite the increased natural resource wealth elsewhere in the country. Yet neither Ontarians nor federal political parties have a proposal to offer the country to address these challenges.

However, despite itself, Ontario has stumbled into a position of power. It has become ground zero for federal electoral competition. The next federal election will be won or lost in Ontario. The Conservatives, New Democrats, and Liberals all have a realistic hope for success across Ontario and in the Greater Golden Horseshoe more specifically. With so many contested seats available in the province and voters with very weak partisan attachments, it is shocking that the three parties have given so little attention to articulating a vision for Ontario.

A NEW CANADIAN NARRATIVE THAT MAKES SENSE FOR THE NEW ONTARIO

The federal Conservatives and NDP are perfectly happy to battle it out over the New West Consensus. The building of pipelines, the decline of the manufacturing sector, discussions of Dutch disease, musings about a carbon tax, reform to environmental assessments, changes to immigration policies to favour short-term workers to fill job shortages in the resource sector –these are all issues over which the NDP and its Quebec base and the Conservatives and their base in Alberta and Saskatchewan fundamentally disagree. They are also really just proxy skirmishes over the New West Consensus.

The debate reinforces their ideological and regional bases and squeezes the political centre of the electorate, where their chief historic rival – the Liberal party – has resided. It makes the demise of the Liberals even more likely. It also seems to force Ontario to choose: are you on the side of Quebec or Alberta? In favour of the oil sands or opposed? To the commentariat, it simplifies the choice even more: Are you part of the old wealth-consuming east or the new wealth-creating west?

However, the essays in this book show that this is a false choice. Ontario is neither part of the prosperous oil producing coalition nor of the less prosperous, traditional equalization-receiving provinces. Ontario is a relatively prosperous province without oil, competing in North America and the world for workers, markets, and investment. It has in fact moved away from its industrial base and the assumptions of the old Laurentian Consensus – but its lack of oil means that its interests will not consistently align with those of the New West Consensus. And it has yet to articulate a replacement for the Laurentian Consensus

On the one hand, Ontario's financial and business services companies benefit heavily from their relationship with the natural resource sector, as they always have. But on the other hand, the increase in the value of the dollar has contributed to havoc in Central Canada's industrial sector. Ontarians know that a booming Western Canada enjoying a sustained commodity super-cycle alongside a struggling Quebec and Maritimes is not a recipe for a healthy Canada. A strong resource sector, as well as a principled, redistributive fiscal architecture are both in Ontario's interests. Picking sides holds no appeal to most Ontarians.

This means that Ontario is actually becoming more rather than less important. Its demographic, political, and economic weight are able to tip the balance of power in the emerging debates about energy, the environment, and the future of the Canadian economy. Ontario remains the essential province, without which a stable majority national government is not possible.

In reality, the New Ontario will not choose between the Laurentian and New West Consensuses. Ontario no longer embraces the Laurentian Consensus, given the realities of free trade and globalization. Nor does Ontario embrace the New West Consensus, given that a world seen through the lens of impacts on the oil patch is not a world in which Ontario lives. To Ontarians, water is a far more important natural resource than oil.

Ontario is gradually grappling with its own emerging narrative, one that has more promise for the country than the moldy Laurentian Consensus or the regionally limited New West Consensus. Ontario's fortunes will be shaped by several global trends, including growing urbanization, heightened competition for immigrants, a more prominent role for diaspora networks, prosperity driven by advances in science and technology, adaptation to changing climate patterns, and increased global conflicts around water security and food security. Policy responses to these trends will all be part of the new Canadian narrative.

A New Canada narrative is still inchoate as a formal competitor of the Laurentian or New West Consensuses, but it renews Canada's value proposition to immigrants and young Canadians in a way that makes sense for the 21st century and makes sense for Ontario. This new emerging narrative must offer a realistic answer to the three economic challenges identified at the beginning of this introduction. None of the existing narratives have provided any credible answers. The irony of Ontario's emerging sense of regional interest is that it creates the foundation on which to establish a new national narrative to compete with the New West Consensus.

OVERVIEW OF THE BOOK

The essays in this volume were originally presented in November 2010 for the annual State of the Federation Conference held in Toronto and co-hosted by the Mowat Centre and the Institute of Intergovernmental Relations. They were revised and submitted during the summer of 2012.

The first section focuses on Old and New Ontario and places the themes of the book in historical and geographic context. Josh Hjartarson argues that key elements of the Laurentian Consensus are now contested by alternative understandings of the Canadian federation. More importantly, the political economy of the Old Ontario has collapsed, producing new narratives to help us understand the Canadian story. The old concepts – centre/periphery, rich/poor, industrial/agrarian – may no longer be relevant as new concepts are emerging. How the New Ontario positions itself in this evolving landscape will be a key determinant of the policy architecture for the New Canada.

J. Scott Matthews and his colleagues explore the evolutions in public opinion against the backdrop of Ontario's changing place in Canada. They find that there has been a weakening of inter-regional differences in political attitudes on a wide range of issues. Regardless of their region, Canadians across the country are becoming more similar in their political values and attitudes. However, regionalism persists as Canadians across the country continue to exhibit strongly regionalized sentiments to questions of federalism, intergovernmental politics, and federal treatment of one's province. Ontario's historic exceptionalism with respect to these issues (its stronger confidence in, and greater identification with, the federal government compared to other provinces) has virtually disappeared. Old Ontario's traditional role as the ballast in the federation, ensuring that regional sentiments and grievances didn't overwhelm the whole, has now dissipated. Ontarians are now just as likely as other Canadians to be concerned about the fairness of the federation.

P. E. Bryden provides a historical perspective on Ontario's exceptionalism, both old and new. According to Bryden, Ontario has always had a unique place in the federation due to its size, strength, and central place at the geographic, economic, and cultural heart of Canada. However, she concludes that although the New Ontario is evolving, its sense of exceptionalism is not. Bryden argues that this exceptionalism has not always been good for Canada, has usually been resented elsewhere in the country, and that these are unlikely to change anytime soon.

Steve Penfold reminds us that Ontario's interests have long been wrapped up with many surrounding regions. Many of Ontario's interests, old and new, have been entwined with US interests (especially those of nearby states like New York, Ohio, and Michigan) every bit as much as with other Canadian regions. The understanding that Ontario's interests and sense of self go beyond the Canadian border continues to evolve alongside shifts in the global movement of people, goods, and ideas. In other work presented at the *State of the Federation* conference and not included in this volume, Natasha Sawh highlighted the role of diaspora networks to the future of Ontario. Ontario's connections to these global flows are growing stronger and creating deeper linkages with Asia and Latin America in particular. Other regions of Canada are now competing with other countries in terms of importance for Ontario's sense of self and for its future.

The essays by David Wolfe and of Tijs Creutzberg both engage with the issue of Ontario's new economy and the role of government in facilitating and supporting Ontario's transition toward sectors where it has a comparative advantage. Wolfe argues that place-based approaches to economic development are required, along with investments in the unique assets of these places, including the research networks found in the public, private, and academic sectors. Creutzberg complements this analysis by arguing that governments should be more intentional in their choices about strategic sectoral investments, with a focus on those areas that have the capacity to develop into globally competitive industrial sectors. These essays highlight the fact that Ontario cannot rely on its traditional manufacturing base for future prosperity, but also document the significant areas where Ontario has the assets, skills, and capital to produce goods and services that meet a global demand.

Peter Graefe and Rachel Laforest argue that Ontario has not done a good job pursuing its social policy objectives through the intergovernmental arena. They highlight how, in a number of policy areas including social assistance, immigration, childcare, and poverty reduction, Ontario has yet to formulate a coherent strategy to confront modern social risks. Given that the federal government has vacated the space, Ontario's traditional posture of advocating and complaining, but waiting for the federal government to act, is no longer appropriate. Ontario must be more pro-active in pursuing its own independent social policy agenda to respond to modern social risks in Ontario where the failure of federal policy is so apparent.

For the past half century or more, the Ontario public has been the most vocal defender of a strong federal government and suspicious of the parochial concerns of provincial governments. It has been Ontario leaders who have often been at the forefront of arguments in defense of national standards. Jennifer Wallner's piece makes a compelling argument: in Canada, we can achieve robust national systems without any role for the federal government. Wallner contends that national standards can co-exist with devolution, a finding that may be attractive to those in Ontario who remain committed to the nation-building project but at the same time are sceptical that federal involvement in social policy can further Ontario's interests.

Roderick Macdonald and Robert Wolfe advance the intriguing argument that place-based federalism, so important to our understanding of Canada, is becoming less relevant. Governments will increasingly engage citizens in unmediated ways and allow individual citizens more power to design and operate their own programs and policies. What this means in practice is that Canadians will be treated equally regardless of where they live, rather than as representatives of territorial units. Individual Canadians will be able to exercise greater autonomy without having their preferences mediated by provincial governments who claim to speak for a region. For Canadians living in Ontario, such an outcome would further the national project and individual interests, but without the regional shakedown of Ontario that comes with so many federal spending decisions.

This volume concludes with two papers produced at the Mowat Centre. The first describes why Canada's system of fiscal transfers fails Ontario and how this system contributes to Ontario's economic, social, and fiscal challenges. It also outlines realistic proposals for reform. The final paper examines the roles and responsibilities of the federal and provincial governments and identifies where uploading, devolution, and greater clarification are needed. These two papers contain an agenda for fiscal federalism and more generally, for intergovernmental relations that would reflect Ontario's new interests.

ACKNOWLEDGEMENTS

The editors of this volume would like to thank all of the contributing authors for their patience and dedication to this project. We would also like to thank André Juneau, Nadia Verrelli and Mary Kennedy from the Institute of Intergovernmental Relations for their ongoing commitment to the State of the Federation series, and their support in completing this volume. Special acknowledgement should be paid to Pauline Craig and Linda Swanston for their copy-editing efforts, to the peer reviewers whose criticism and advice improved the final product and to Mark Howes of the Publications Unit at the School of Policy Studies, Queen's University for his patience.

A special thank you goes out to the staff of the Mowat Centre who contributed their time, talents and administrative efforts to organize the initial conference on which this book is based, and, ultimately, to the completion of this book.

II

Ontario: Old and New

2

ONTARIO AT THE GREAT LAKES BORDER/LAND: AN HISTORICAL PERSPECTIVE

Steve Penfold

Ce chapitre situe le « nouvel Ontario » dans un contexte historique élargi en examinant les liens de longue date entre la province et les États-Unis. Puisant aux derniers travaux sur l'histoire des Grands Lacs et des zones frontalières, l'auteur y traite deux principaux thèmes. Tout d'abord, il décentre l'histoire de l'Ontario au sein du Canada en retraçant les résonances et connexions transfrontalières qui ont façonné la province, ces liens multiples et variés (économiques et infrastructurels, environnementaux et sociaux) ayant suscité des échanges en matière commerciale et familiale, d'immigration et de loisirs. Examinant ensuite le rôle médiateur de la frontière dans ces échanges, il soutient que les liens transfrontaliers régionaux ont été tributaires des différents régimes de réglementation qui ont façonné la place occupée par l'Ontario dans la vaste région des Grands Lacs, mais sans jamais la déterminer entièrement.

When Oliver Mowat was Premier of Ontario – long before his name was attached to the centre that organized this volume – there was already something called "The New Ontario." But it was not the New Ontario that the Mowat Centre speaks of today; a region-state within a continental free trade economy or one province in an increasingly decentred federation. The New Ontario that was emerging as Mowat left provincial politics in 1896 rested upon the Canadian Shield. At Confederation, most Ontarians thought of the Shield as a barren landscape, a barrier to agricultural settlement, or something to be bypassed on the way to a new colonial society in the West. Over the course of Mowat's tenure, however, the Shield was reimagined as the potential site of a great economic future based on the exploitation of new resources like nickel and pulp. While much of the development of this New Ontario would take place after Mowat left office, his government lay some of the groundwork for this redefinition, by building roads, subsidizing railways, and setting up new institutions like the Bureau of Mines. The development of this old New Ontario, however, shared at least one important thing with our current New Ontario; it was deeply connected to the United States. The stirring of development in Mowat's New Ontario was unambiguously tied to American capital and markets, even in the presence of massive tariff barriers that shaped the precise nature of the trade (Nelles 1974).

Mowat's New Ontario was only one expression of a much broader and more diverse set of north-south relationships. Indeed, Ontario's history has always been intimately intertwined with continental developments and cross-border connections. These links have been multiple and plural, spanning economic, political, social, cultural and environmental history. My interest in these questions, and in the two New Ontarios, flows from teaching about the history of the Great Lakes region, a framework that breaks down the usual national containers and considers a different set of geographies. Indeed, while Canadian developments are important to this history, we spend more time in Michigan and Chicago than in Manitoba and Saskatoon. There are many frameworks that could accommodate this "Great Lakes" approach. The Great Lakes region might be defined as a species of continentalism, or in simple geographic terms as an economic region. Environmental historians might look to the watershed or basin of the Lakes themselves as the key geographic container. I draw on all these ideas in the Great Lakes course, but the main analytic inspiration is borderlands history. If many historians have traditionally stopped their analyses at a national border, borderlands historians look for connections and resonances across the line.[1] The framework is not without limitations. Some critics worry that it too easily ignores the power of the nation-state, while others criticize its sometimes excessive post-modern obsession with hybridity (Wilson and Donnan 1998; Greer 2010). The framework also entails some geographic complications; because it is based on relationships rather than lines on a map, a borderlands space can be fuzzy and contextual. This feature is both an analytic strength and a conceptual challenge, particularly in the Great Lakes region, where the United States often looms much larger in Ontario than Ontario does in the United States. Scholars of Ontario face another, more practical problem; in North America, most borderlands scholarship emerged around the US.-Mexico border, a line where contrasts of political economy, culture, development and race made for tense, yet analytically rich relationships. From this perspective, the 49th parallel – where people have often crossed easily and mingled seamlessly – seemed decidedly unsexy. Recently,

---

[1] For a good general discussion, see Morehouse 2004.

however, a few scholars, both American and Canadian, have begun to construct a history of the Great Lakes region as a borderlands space.[2]

On its surface, a borderlands approach to Ontario runs against many familiar narratives of Canadian history. It might, for example, appear to conflict with a "bordered history" of the province that begins with the American Revolution and traces the making of a "divided ground" in the region (Taylor 2006). A borderlands history of Ontario might also seem to cut across a more national story of the province as political centre, economic heartland, and cultural metropole – as the nucleus, in other words, of a transcontinental federation or of an east-west economy. Finally, it might run against histories that stress the rights and obligations of Canadian citizenship, the particularities of national politics, or the seemingly endless rounds of intergovernmental and cross-provincial negotiations that characterize a complex federal state. Yet a borderlands history need not deny the power of such explanations. Mowat's Ontario was forged by a long, complex, and fundamentally powerful, history of boundary-making and nation-building. The creation of Upper Canada (that later became Ontario) in 1791 was only one step in a much larger process in the region, as clearer and more fixed lines of sovereignty and jurisdiction replaced an older and more fluid geography of imperial rivalry and aboriginal influence (Adelman and Aron 1999; Taylor 2006). Over time, the terms of political geography were set by an international border and many lines of internal jurisdiction that eventually divided the Great Lakes into two nations, eight states and one province. Mowat himself had witnessed one of the last acts in this long process, the settling of the boundary with Manitoba in 1889, which solidified Ontario's control over the northern lands that came to be the first New Ontario. Meanwhile, many economic developments reinforced the process of border-making. By Mowat's time, Ontario stood at the centre of national development schemes that ran east-west, with mounting tariff walls with the United States and transcontinental railways forging deep and real connections to the rest of the country. Indeed, Mowat himself briefly joined a Liberal government in Ottawa that continued and reinforced these policies (initiated by John A. Macdonald's Conservatives), abandoning the party's earlier free trade and small government views in favour of protectionist tariffs and accelerated railway development. The effect of such policies was staggering. By 1913, as the Rowell-Sirois Commission famously put it so many decades ago, an "economically loose transcontinental area" had been transformed into "a highly integrated national economy." (Royal Commission on Dominion-Provincial Relations 1940, 68). Ontario – or, more accurately, "Montario," the industrializing corridor between Windsor and Montreal – stood at the centre of a real and meaningful set of east-west economic, political, and human connections.

---

[2] Bukowczyk et al. 2005, *Permeable Border,* is an excellent introduction to this collective project.

But these "national" dynamics have too often attracted over-heated rhetoric that severs Ontario's history from its ongoing cross-border and continental relationships. Indeed, at moments when the east-west impulse came up for serious discussion – 1911 and 1988 among others – its proponents spared few efforts in extolling its mythical importance. "We faced geography and distance and fought them to a standstill," George Foster told Parliament in 1911. "The plains were shod with steel, the mountains tamed and tunnelled, our national arteries were filled with the rich blood of commerce, our industries grew, our workmen multiplied, our villages became towns and our towns became cities." For Foster, linking (as did many Conservative speakers in 1911) the issue to British imperialism, reciprocity was a parting of the ways, "One the broad highway that we began to construct in 1867 running transversely across this continent with its east-west lines and ending, for our market, in the grand old mother country. And what is the other way? It is the way ... leading off this old and well-beaten highway down amongst unknown obscurities and hazards, but ending in the United States..." (Stevens 1970, 21, 34). Almost eight decades later, John Turner famously made the same point in a more directly nationalist way. "We built this country east and west and north," he told Brian Mulroney in a televised debate, "We built it on an infrastructure that deliberately resisted the continental pressure of the United States. For 120 years we've done it. With one signature of the pen, you've reversed that, thrown us into the north-south influence of the United States...."

There's no denying the rhetorical power of such claims. Turner's statement induced a number of nationalist high fives in my undergraduate common room and perhaps a few cups of tea were raised in more dignified endorsement of Foster's earlier words. But these claims are less satisfying as analysis, making one historical plotline into the whole story of Canadian development. In fact, at no point was the path leading to the United States obscure or unknown, and if Canada actually attempted to build "an infrastructure that deliberately resisted the north-south pressure of the United States" it never closed off other trajectories of development. Borderlands scholars would point out that such east-west dynamics need to be balanced against cross-border connections, with the power and import of each being judged less in grand rhetorical flourishes than in the specifics of the historical moment. Additionally, they would broaden the connections past political economy to social history, charting multiple forms of cross-border connection in family, leisure, and migration. The effect is often analytically paradoxical; on the one hand, borderlands history mutes the power of the border as an analytic container, on the other hand, it can actually focus greater attention on the border, moving it from assumed margin to analytic centre. In this sense, we can follow Ontario's borderlands history in two ways: first, to decentre Ontario's history within Canada, charting the long-standing cross-border resonances and connections that have shaped the province over time; second, to analyze the way those cross-border regional connections have always been dependent on shifting border regimes, which shaped but never determined Ontario's place in the broader Great Lakes region.

George Foster probably knew that his two path argument was better rhetoric than history. He was facing, after all, a government-sponsored measure, not some radical plan from the left field of Canadian politics. At the height of National Policy protectionism, east-west connections were never the whole story, even in Ontario. In the reciprocity election of 1911, the Liberals won only 13 seats in the province, but they garnered over 40 percent of the popular vote, only slightly below their national figure and only a small (3.8 percent) drop from 1908. Moreover, the National Policy tariff had the well-known effect, if not the intention, of spurring a branch plant economy, on the theory (to paraphrase a 20th century premier of Quebec) that it was better to import American capital than export Canadian jobs.[3] By 1914, 317 branch plants operated in Ontario. Continental forces also unleashed Mowat's New Ontario on the Canadian Shield. Mowat's successors in the premier's chair engaged in an ongoing war with the United States over where processing would occur – in Innisian terms, over who would capture the forward linkages – but there was never any question of where most of Ontario's pulp, timber, and minerals would end up. Even Ontario's "manufacturing condition" (on its face, a kind of provincial National Policy that required lease holders to process resources in the province as a condition of mining or cutting on Crown land) hardly sought to create an east-west trade, aiming instead to ensure processing in Ontario before commodities were exported to the United States. In 1916, an astonishing 87 percent of Canada's newsprint was shipped across the line (Nelles 1974; Traves 1979, 29). This New Ontario had important institutional consequences. By the 1920s, as Rowell-Sirois pointed out, resource revenues and northern development projects armed Ontario to think of provincial interests more than national ones, "In the successful development of these new frontiers, the importance of a national economic integration ... declined and the material basis which had bolstered political unity in the past was measurably weakened." (Royal Commission on Dominion-Provincial Relations 1940, 112). We could easily imagine something along these lines being written today.

In many ways, these developments expressed wide-ranging continentalist relations as much as the more geographically narrow borderland dynamics, but the links and connections were particularly intense along the border. By 1916, Windsor had 26 branch plants to Toronto's 94, but the border city was barely one-twentieth the size of the provincial capital. Indeed, borderland economic links were deep – in the early decades of the twentieth century, David Smith reports, "companies incorporated in Michigan comprised the single largest source of foreign capital in the province" (Smith 2005, 4). If those branch plants eventually became symbols of American economic domination, in the early days they represented a wide range of relationships, from complete corporate control to loose, almost non-existent

---

[3] The original quotation, from Alexandre Taschereau, is: "I'd rather import American capital than export French Canadians." (Frenette 1999, 567).

relations. The early history of Ford of Canada represents a good example of the latter, a kind of informal borderlands transfer of technology and ideas, more than a relationship of headquarters and subsidiary (Roberts 2006; Anastakis 2004). This well-known cross-border integration of the auto industry – accelerated but not created by the Auto Pact of 1965 – seems an almost perfect symbol of Ontario's dual role as both heartland and hinterland. For all its centrality in Canada's political economy, Ontario's key manufacturing sector remained very much an extension of America's Great Lakes industrial core.

Economic links were facilitated by many forms of physical connection. Even the railways – the quintessential institutions of east-west connection and technological nationalism – were usually more anxious to build to Detroit and Buffalo than to Manitoba. Railroad gauges were standardized in the few decades after 1860, facilitating much smoother cross-border connections. The Grand Trunk Railway built lines to Chicago in the 1880s, and long before that, the Great Western Railway had linked Detroit and Buffalo across the natural east-west conduit of the Niagara Peninsula (den Otter 1997). Toronto's dreams of forming the hub of an east-west railway network – connecting the wheat economy of the West to Ontario's manufacturing and transatlantic trade – was always balanced against its ongoing integration into Chicago's metropolitan railway system (Cronon 1991). These railway links sat in the middle of a much longer trajectory of cross-border connections. Looking back, ferries ran across rivers as early as 1800; steamboats connected main lake ports just after the War of 1812; bridges provided links for pedestrians and horses; canals on both sides formed an integrated transportation network (for all the rivalry between the Welland and Erie canals, for example, they were built and functioned in symbiosis – see Larkin 1994, 2005). Looking forward from the railway to the car, we might note that Ontario's first superhighway, the Queen Elizabeth Way, linked Toronto not to Montreal or Manitoba, but to the US border. Today, North America's busiest highway, Highway 401, serves a dual purpose as the transportation spine of "Montario" while funnelling traffic to the Windsor-Detroit border (van Nostrand 1983; Davis 1986). From the perspective of federalism and institution-building, moreover, the effect of the automobile had a noticeably decentring effect; car culture both required significant infrastructures (highways, local roads, bridges) and generated significant revenues (licensing, gasoline taxes). Both sides of this dynamic reinforced province-building and connection with the United States. Indeed, Canadian drivers could not cross the country on a single connected road until after the Second World War, as provinces showed little interest in pan-national highway building, except where it garnered them funds that could be applied to local demands (Monaghan 2002).

The Lakes themselves provided a fluid space and often a direct conduit for the borderlands economy. The border was drawn through the Lakes and rivers of the region, making the existing natural barriers into a physical threshold between sovereign jurisdictions. But in practice, the lines were fluid and frequently crossed. In Mowat's New Ontario, great booms of timber simply floated across the upper lakes bound for mills on the Michigan and Wisconsin coasts. Smuggling represented a quirkier – but no less important – example of water-borne borderland trade, as smugglers took advantage of the natural geographic connections of the region to pass commodities back and forth across the line. The most famous twentieth century example, of course, was rum-running during US prohibition, an "industry" that was at once a product of the border and operated in defiance of it. The water-borne trade was so extensive, in fact that the United States threatened to reverse the century-long disarming of the Lakes (Siener December 2008). More than any other industry, the commercial fishery highlighted the fuzzy lines of the "fluid frontier" (Cooper 2000), as boats on the water followed an unofficial working geography. "The belief is widespread," one American fisheries official complained in 1898, "that wherever the Lakes exceed 6 miles in width each country has jurisdiction only to a distance of three miles from its shores, leaving a neutral area of high sea between, to which fisherman from both sides are privileged to resort in common." (Bogue 1993).

But to fully appreciate Ontario's place in a borderlands region, we need to move beyond political economy to social history and from technological connections to human ones. Aboriginal groups were key participants in building borderland links, reaching across the line to forge political coalitions, share cultural resources, and to maintain relations of family and kin (Hele 2008). Non-native people also engaged in borderlands migration. At the time of Mowat's Ontario, Canada was a nation of emigrants, with many more people flowing out than in, although this is hardly the stuff of national mythmaking. By 1900, over one million Canadians, a figure equivalent to one fifth of the national population, lived in the United States (Ramirez 2001). At Windsor-Detroit, Sarnia-Port Huron and along the crossings in the Niagara Peninsula, Ontarians crossed the line in massive numbers for land and later industrial jobs. The Great Lakes states received the majority of Canadians before 1890 and a significant minority (40 percent) in the first four decades of the twentieth century (Faires 2005, 82-3). As Mowat left politics, fully one-quarter of Detroit's population had been born in Ontario. The emigration stream was notably diverse. Canadians are often proud of our "North Star" status as a terminal point on the Underground Railroad. At the time, however, many African Canadians actually traveled the other way, both for abolitionist and reform activities, and for simple reasons of resettlement. Indeed, in 1870, one-sixth of Detroit's "black" population was Canadian born (Cooper 2000; Faires 2005). It is no surprise, then, that it was the outgoing not the incoming that impressed many Ontario observers. "If matters go at the present rate," complained one Toronto newspaper, "one half of Canada will be in Illinois and the Far West before long. The whole people appear like swallows in autumn – preparing for emigration" (Faires 2005, 92).

These movements were the product of economic opportunity in the Great Lakes and Midwestern states, but were often structured by kin and family connections on both sides of the border, producing a net outflow in the aggregate, but a whole series of back-and-forth movements on the ground. Historian Nora Faires tells the story of George Gilboe, who was born in Essex County, Ontario in 1846 but had migrated across the border at least five times before middle-age, in addition to multiple movements within each jurisdiction. For Gilboe, according to Faires, these movements did not represent some grand story of international migration; rather, they placed Gilboe within a series of smaller and less dramatic steps among kin-connections on both sides of the line and between different economic opportunities in a single, transborder space. The transborder world of the Gilboes continued into the next generation, as George's children divided between settlement in Ontario and Michigan (Faries 2005, 93-4).

A whole range of leisure and consumer connections followed from this "human-borderlands," from shopping and bar-hopping to visiting and tourism. The borderlands formed a kind of "convenience zone" (Ontario Legislative Assembly 1991, 8) for shoppers that shifted and transformed in response to diverse economic developments on both sides of the line. Today, most Ontarians are intimately familiar with cross-border shopping, but fewer realize that the practice is long-standing. As early as 1833, Buffalo merchants took out advertisements in St. Catharines newspapers, a practice familiar to present day consumers (Larkin 1994, 5). In the 1950s, Americans crossed to Canada for cheap groceries and cut-rate dinners in Windsor steakhouses (*New York Times* 1951, 18). By the 1980s, cheap gas and cigarettes, among other products, pulled Canadian shoppers across the line in ever larger numbers, though the lower Canadian dollar always represented an inducement to stay at home (Ontario Legislative Assembly 1991).

Cross-border shopping, moreover, represented only one slice of a broader practice of borderland consumerism. In 1915, summer boats carried 271,000 people on recreational trips between Toronto and Lewiston and any attempt to control the flow raised howls of protest from amusement parks, tourist promoters, and others. On Lake Erie after 1910, the ferry *Canadiana* shuttled Americans across the water to the Crystal Beach Amusement Park, which became an extension of Buffalo's summertime leisure space. "The Crystal Beach Amusement Park *was* summer," one Buffalonian remembered (Klug 2010; Wolcott 2006, 66). Park promoters actively courted American youth, by various means including setting up discount-ticket booths in Buffalo neighbourhoods. In 1956, Buffalo youth carried the city's brewing racial tensions to the Park, causing what newspapers (in a fit of exaggeration) called a "race riot" (Wolcott 2006). Victoria Wolcott probes the way the incident played out within American race politics, with southern newspapers happily highlighting the North's problems, but the *Globe and Mail* found the borderland dynamics somewhat more perplexing. "The international border – so often the subject of after dinner speeches – facilitates in every way the easy entry of Americans into Canada," the newspaper editorialized. "Those who come in peace, we welcome. However, we do not welcome hoodlums like those who rioted at Crystal Beach. What precautions are taken at the Niagara border points against their entry, we do not know. We suspect very little. It should not be difficult, however, to tighten these precautions ... This, we are sure, is what the Americans would do, were the circumstances reversed."(*Globe and Mail* 1956, 6).

The *Globe* editorial showed little interest in race, but the issue was often a borderlands flashpoint, serving (at an ideological level) as a key marker of national difference and (on the ground) as one aspect of borderland politics. Race issues point to both profound differences and similarities between Ontario and the rest of the Great Lakes region. As several historians have pointed out, Ontario has a long history of racism, including many Jim Crow policies and practices, from separate schools to discrimination in housing and public accommodation (Walker 2010; Mathieu 2010). Yet Canadians often subscribed to what Constance Backhouse describes as the "ideology of racelessness" (Backhouse 1999, 13-14), the belief that Canada had no race problem, usually expressed in a morally superior attitude toward the United States. The result was a sort of Canadian Jacques Crow, a peculiar combination of legal discrimination, informal prejudice, and racial denial. In Ontario, this constellation of contradictory racial views was partly sustained by demographic and geographic difference. The migration of millions of African Americans to northern cities after the First World War completely changed the actual and symbolic racial geography of American Great Lakes cities, but had little effect in Canada. In 1900, Windsor's population was about 3 percent "black" while Detroit's was only a bit higher at 4 percent. By 1970, however, the Windsor percentage had declined to less than 1 percent, while African Americans represented almost 45 percent of Detroit's population. Instead, Windsor's swelling industrial population combined international immigrants and internal migrants (rural Ontarians, Maritimers, etc.).

This demographic and geographic difference shaped the racial politics of the borderlands, helping Ontarians subscribe to the Canadian ideology of racelessness and practice racial discrimination at the same time. Take the example of Windsor's Emancipation Day, which commemorated Britain's act of abolishing slavery in 1833. For many years, the event was popular with Windsorites and a big draw for African Americans from Detroit. In the aftermath of the 1967 Detroit race riot, Windsor's municipal council became concerned about the uncontrolled flow of African Americans into the city, eventually refusing to issue a permit for the event. The matter went to the Human Rights Commission, but the event itself never recovered its former glory. Herb Colling examines these events as part of his cross-border narrative of the 1967 Detroit riot (Colling 2003). His book is filled with informants who deny the importance of race in the Windsor area and raise their eyebrows at the racial problems across the water, but the racist reaction to the potential disruption on Emancipation Day undermines Windsor's raceless myth. Race marked both difference and similarity: Windsorites saw Detroit as racially different but feared problems would flow across the line. From a borderlands perspective, however, the most relevant point might be the way the riot reshaped leisure across the border. Colling points out that, after the riot, some Windsorites stopped visiting racially charged sections of Detroit, a development that suggests a borderlands space could be uneven and shaped by internal racial boundaries.

Borderlands leisure had been controversial before the 1960s. Dan Malleck reconstructs Ontario concerns about Americans crossing the border to drink during prohibition. In 1927, the Liquor Control Board of Ontario (LCBO) commented that "Ontario must not be made a beer garden for non-resident groups; at the same time the Board welcomes to Ontario and desires to give service to legitimate tourists and travellers from the United States and elsewhere" (Malleck 2007, 158). Once the United States repealed the 18th Amendment in 1933, the problem was reversed – Ontario retailers worried that Canadian drinkers would travel to the more permissive regime across the line. One Niagara Falls hotel keeper worried that "if they cannot indulge in dancing while partaking of their meals they will go to the American side and patronize hotels there" (Malleck 2007, 162). Eventually, the LCBO acceded to this borderlands reality by allowing highly restricted "dine-and-dance" establishments. In a parallel study, Holly Karibo has reconstructed one fascinating example of borderlands leisure – the "sex tourism" along the Detroit-Windsor border that thrived in the decade or so after the Second World War. Windsor served as a brothel suburb of Detroit, with incoming Americans met at bridge and tunnel exits by men and women handing out business cards with directions to nearby bawdy houses. The *Windsor Star* noted the connection to the official industrial economy, pointing to the "prostitutes and bootleggers vying for the payroll cash made available by the automobile industry ... [in] Michigan and Ohio." (*Windsor Star*, 14 March 1950, cited in Karibo 2010, 363). If, at one level, this cross-border sex trade "produced a cultural space where sexuality was exchanged as an international commodity," Karibo makes clear that it was equally based on proximity and permeability. "You see," noted one *Windsor Star* editorial, "[Windsor] is so much closer to Detroit than Michigan is." (Karibo 2010, 369).

Commuting was the third aspect of the human borderlands. Even in Mowat's Ontario, Windsorites trickled across the line, but by the 1920s, the industrial boom of Detroit increased the flow considerably – one government official estimated that as many as 15,000 Canadians from the Windsor area (with a population of about 90,000) worked across the line (Klug 2010, 412 n. 13). Labour unions often complained, but Detroit business elites and many Canadians recognized this movement as a common sense practice of an integrated borderland economy. Indeed, when the US border service interfered with this flow, protest was loud and vociferous. In April 1927, the American government began requiring commuters to secure proper immigration papers (before this, Canadians had not been required to obtain passports or visas before crossing). This innovation led to large demonstrations and massive editorial condemnation on the Canadian side. The *Globe and Mail* objected that "a hard and fast regulation is taking place of a custom of generations standing," providing an example of the widespread belief that legitimate border practices flowed as much from custom and common sense as law and regulation (Klug 2008, 89).

Beliefs and editorials do not always set policy, however, so borderlands relationships were often fragile and dependent on an unpredictable border regime. Yet even there, matters were complex; the border is a historical not a natural object, subject to shifting diplomatic and political forces over time. Initially a product of the American Revolution, the actual line through the Great Lakes was not rigorously surveyed until much later (after the War of 1812) and then not finally and formally settled until 1842. Yet drawing the border on a map hardly determined its meaning on the ground. By Mowat's time, the border had become a customs line but not a human boundary. Bruno Ramirez relates the story of the Canadian government official John Lowe, who crossed from Sarnia to Port Huron in 1883. The only border officials he met worked on customs, and they took their jobs quite literally. Lowe was asked about the goods he was carrying, but almost nothing about his identity, his destination, his "calling," his reasons for traveling, or any other information we now consider standard in the modern border-crossing regime. Over the next three decades, this open human border was closed. The American government became increasingly concerned about "backdoor immigrants" – Asians and Europeans who arrived in Canada with the intent of crossing to the United States – and by the First World War, a more modern legal and administrative structure was fully in place. Indeed, after 1894, the American government stationed officials at Canadian ports of entry and required US-bound immigrants landing in Canada to undergo American inspection (Ramirez 2001, 42; Lee 2002). Over time, the trend was to deepen and intensify border surveillance, especially at land-based entries. From a small staff of twenty at Detroit in 1916, immigration inspectors increased to 115 by 1931 (Klug 2008).

These border-making developments were the backstory to the problem faced by commuters, but in a borderlands space, real border enforcement could only be built on conflict and exceptions. Klug notes that, after protests over the 1927 innovations, American officials "transformed commuter aliens into *residents* of the US during the day and *visitors* to Canada at night," going so far as to list American workplaces as their putative residence (Klug 2008, 90). This bizarre legal fiction hardly resolved the broader issue. Immigration officials worked at the intersection of border and borderlands. They were at once obliged to monitor and control the border but not "obstruct or unnecessarily delay, impede, or annoy passengers in ordinary travel" (Klug 2010, 399). In practice, then, they made quick distinctions between "alien" and "legitimate" traveller, generally by relying on all too human clues; "persons whose appearance, talk, carriage, etc. show clearly that they are native US citizens are promptly admitted without unnecessary annoyance," the district director of the Immigration and Naturalization Service wrote to his superior. "[E]very person with the slightest accent is taken aside for complete questioning unless such passenger can show in line that he has proper credentials to enter." Yet if gatekeepers obviously had tremendous power, travellers fought back and shaped border practices. Attempts by American officials to sort travellers on the Windsor side, for example, were cancelled after a massive public backlash (Klug 2010, 403).

If there are few borderlands historians who would deny the historical power of Ontario's bordered history, the relationship between the two frameworks remains a central analytic problem. In many ways, the structure of the border and the human connections of the borderlands interacted and shaped each other, with borderlands migration, commuting, and leisure pressing back on policy and politics. Ordinary shoppers, commuters and immigrants created regulatory challenges for government officials and enforcement problems for border inspectors who, in turn, shaped and reshaped their institutions to meet new problems. But the border, while complex, is a regulatory line, tied to stable government institutions, which are influenced by interest groups and everyday activities, but are nonetheless able to coordinate regulatory activities, consolidate legal regimes, and control information. By contrast, borderland activities are often informal, uncoordinated, and everyday. As David Thelen noted some years ago, "Most people created borderlands life in face to face networks that assisted members with their everyday lives" (Thelen 1992, 440).

This tension is particularly clear in ongoing efforts to build collaborative institutions across the border. In the cultural realm, local elites and voluntary organizations have initiated a series of cross-border festivals, from Cleveland's Great Lakes Exposition in the 1930s through the Windsor-Detroit Freedom Festival in the 1960s, to the Niagara Region's joint commemoration of the War of 1812. More recently, scholars, government officials, and tourist organizations in Toronto and Buffalo have participated in cross-border exchanges coordinated by the School of Architecture at the University of Buffalo (Schneekcloth and Shibley 2005). Such efforts, however, were ad hoc and tied to particular personalities; as a result, the binational links created were often fragile. The 1812 Celebration, for example, lost funding on the Buffalo side, and so the American wing went dormant. Scholars at the University of Buffalo recognized that "a major challenge is the fact that the binational region, Niagara, exists only as a mental construct not yet widely shared. It lacks any unifying structure or official agency." (Shibley et al. 2003, 28). Borderlands practices, then, did not necessarily produce stable borderlands identities or institutions.

The same tension runs through the extensive cross-border collaborations related to water. The border drew lines across the water, creating multiple jurisdictions on top of a shared, if fluid, space. Fish, waste, and pollution travelled across the line in blissful ignorance of international or jurisdictional boundaries. These problems led to some of the most stable and coherent, but also difficult, cross-border collaborations. After 1912, the International Joint Commission (IJC), set up under the 1909 Boundary Waters Treaty, exercised various powers over shared water resources, but over time its most important function related to research and monitoring through "references" by Great Lakes governments (Hagen 2009; Read 1999). Through these references, which often led to binational technical advisory boards for research purposes, the IJC became a forum for considerable political, bureaucratic, and scientific collaboration and cooperation – the 1964 Lower Great Lakes Pollution Reference alone involved the efforts of 12 agencies of the two national governments, four states, and Ontario, culminating in the Great Lakes Water Quality Agreement (GLWQA) of 1972, which set water quality standards and empowered the IJC to monitor compliance in an ongoing fashion. However, in many ways a more important result was the creation of an "epistemic community" of technical experts and scientists from across the region (Suker 2001; Rabe 1997).

Binational collaboration by the public, however, has proved more elusive. To take a recent example, in the late 1980s, anti-pollution efforts focused on key "Areas of Concern" around the Great Lakes. The IJC set up "Remedial Action Plans" to bring federal, state, and provincial officials together to target particularly degraded or contaminated areas for intensive remediation efforts. The process integrated citizen representatives and public input through Binational Public Advisory Councils (BPAC). The results were uneven. Along the St. Clair River, an active Canadian BPAC focused the work of local citizen activists, leading to the founding of the Friends of the St Clair River. But the sister organization on the US side was much less active. Moreover, other BPACs proved fragile and subject to shifting funding and bureaucratic priorities. Since the IJC has no regulatory power, mobilizing political will on the ground was often key to real progress. Indeed, the GLWQA itself was partly the result of increased local action in the late 1960s. Growing environmental concern motivated several groups on the ground, from tourist interests and conservationists to citizen groups and municipal governments (Read 1999). But, as in the cultural realm, such mobilizing was often ad hoc and impermanent. In this sense, the borderlands produced collaboration among experts, but divided ground continued to shape public activism (Suker 2001; Rabe 1997). Here are the limits of the borderlands in policy terms – a shared space but not a shared political identity.

And this tension between shared space and divided ground leads us back to the new New Ontario. In the post-9/11 world, long line-ups at the border testify both to the profound connections and to the divisions between Ontario and the United States. America remains a magnet; at fourteen border checkpoints, Ontarians cross for work, to trade, to shop, to visit family, and for many other reasons. From the grand to the mundane, Ontario has deep connections to its southern neighbour – many of these relationships have intensified in recent decades. Yet the line-ups – which stretch for hours at the busiest times – testify to the profoundly important role the border plays in structuring, impeding, and shaping those connections. Surveying the Canadian border service's website, where wait times can be conveniently checked in advance, may indicate either a flow or a trickle – the border is permeable but unpredictable, a conduit and a barrier. This tension is long-standing. It has been worked out in different ways at different times and for different groups in different ways. In Mowat's Ontario, the border was a customs line but was open to people; the wide open human border closed in the early twentieth century, but left large holes for some Ontarians; the postwar years saw tariffs gradually coming down. In our New Ontario, the long-standing tension between connection and division plays out in terms of free trade and security. From the beginning of Ontario's history, in multiple ways, the province has been linked to, and separated from, its American neighbours.

REFERENCES

Adelman, J., and S. Aron. 1999."From Borderlands to Borders: Empires, Nation-States, and the Peoples in Between in North American History." *American Historical Review* 104 (3):814-842.

Anastakis, D. 2004. "From Independence to Integration: The Corporate Evolution of the Ford Motor Company of Canada, 1904-2004." *Business History Review* 78 (Summer):213-53.

Backhouse, Constance. 1999. *Colour-Coded: A Legal History of Racism in Canada, 1900-1950* (Toronto: University of Toronto Press).

Bogue, M. 1993. "To Save the Fish: Canada, the United States, the Great Lakes, and the Joint Commission of 1892" *Journal of American History* 79 (4) 1429-1454.

Bukowczyk, J. 2005. "Migration, Transportation, Capital and the State" in *Permeable Border: The Great Lakes Basin as Transnational Region, 1650-1990,* eds Bukowczyck, J., N. Faires, D. Smith, R. W. Widdis, 29-77. Pittsburgh: University of Pittsburgh Press.

Colling, H. 2003. *Turning Points: The Detroit Riot of 1967, a Canadian Perspective.* Toronto: Natural Heritage Books.

Cooper, A. 2000. "The Fluid Frontier: Blacks and the Detroit River Region, 1789-1854." *Canadian Review of American Studies* 30 (2):129-49.

Cronon, W. 1991. *Nature's Metropolis: Chicago and the Great West.* New York: W.W. Norton.

Davis, D. 1986. "Dependent Motorization: Canada and the Automobile to the 1930s." *Journal of Canadian Studies* 21 (3):106-32.

Den Otter, A. 1997. *The Philosophy of Railways: The Transcontinental Railway Idea in British North America.* Toronto: University of Toronto Press.

Faires, N. 2005. "Leaving the Land of Second Chance" in *Permeable Border: The Great Lakes Basin as Transnational Region, 1650-1990,* eds Bukowczyck, J., N. Faires, D. Smith, R. W. Widdis, 78-119. Pittsburgh: University of Pittsburgh Press.

Frenette, Y., with M. Paquet. 1999. "French Canadians" in *Encyclopedia of Canadian Peoples*, ed Magocsi, P.R., 538-86. Toronto: University of Toronto Press.

Globe and Mail. 1956. Keep them Out. 1 June.

Greer, A. 2010. "National, Transnational, and Hypernational Historiographies: New France Meets Early American History." *Canadian Historical Review* 91 (4):695-724.

Hagen, J. 2009. "The Dynamics of Bi-national Environmental Regime Formation in the North American Great Lakes Basin" PhD diss., Tufts University, Boston.

Hele, K., ed. 2008. *Lines Drawn Upon the Water: First Nations and the Great Lakes Borders and Borderlands.*Waterloo: Wilfrid Laurier University Press.

Karibo, H. 2010. "Detroit's Border Brothel: Sex Tourism in Windsor, Ontario, 1945-60." *American Review of Canadian Studies* 40 (3):362-78.

Klug, T. 2008. "Residents by Day, Visitors by Night: The Origins of the Alien Commuter on the U.S.-Canadian Border during the 1920s." *Michigan Historical Review* 34 (2):75-96.

---. 2010. "The Immigration and Naturalization Service (INS) and the Making of a Border-Crossing Culture on the US-Canada Border, 1891-1941." *American Review of Canadian Studies* 40 (3):395-415.

Larkin, J. 1994. "The Canal Era: A Study of the Original Erie and Welland Canal within the Niagara Borderland" *American Review of Canadian Studies* 24 (3):299-314.

Larkin, J. 2005. "Mr. Merritt's Hobby: New York State Influence in the Building of Canada's First Welland Canal." *New York History* 86 (2):169-93.

Lee, E. 2002. "Enforcing the Borders: Chinese Exclusion along the U.S. Borders with Canada and Mexico, 1882-1924." *Journal of American History* 89 (1):54-86.

Malleck, D. 2007. "An Innovation from Across the Line: The American Drinker and Liquor Regulation in Two Ontario Communities, 1927-44." *Journal of Canadian Studies* 41 (1): 151-71.

Mathieu, S. 2010. *North of the Color Line: Migration and Black Resistance in Canada, 1870-1955*. Chapel Hill: University of North Carolina Press.

Monaghan, D. 2002. *Canada's New Main Street: the Trans-Canada Highway as Idea and Reality, 1912-1956*. Ottawa: Canada Science and Technology Museum.

Morehouse, B. 2004. "Theoretical Approaches to Border Spaces and Identities" in *Challenged Borderlands: Transcending Political and Cultural Boundaries eds*. V. Pavlakovich-Kochi, B. Morehouse and D. Wastl-Walter, 19-39. Burlington, VT: Ashgate Publishing.

Nelles, H.V. 1974. *The Politics of Development: Forests, Mines, and Hydro-electric Power in Ontario, 1849-1941*. Toronto: Macmillan.

New York Times. 1951. Detroiters Buying Meat in Canada and Saving 20 to 30 Cents a Pound (22 January).

Ontario Legislative Assembly. 1991. *Report on Cross-Border Shopping* (Toronto: Standing Committee on Finance and Economic Affairs).

Rabe, Barry. 1997. "The Politics of Ecosystem Management in the Great Lakes Basin." *American Review of Canadian Studies* 27 (3): 411-36.

Ramirez, B. 2001. "Canada in the United States: Perspectives on Mingration and Continental History." *Journal of American Ethnic History*, 20 (3): 50-70.

---. 2001a. *Crossing the 49th Parallel: Migration from Canada to the United States, 1900-1930*. Ithaca, New York: Cornell University Press.

Read, J. 1999. "Addressing a Quiet Horror: The Evolution of Ontario Pollution control Policy in the International Great Lakes, 1909-1972." PhD diss., University of Western Ontario, London.

Roberts, D. 2006. *In the Shadow of Detroit: Gordon McGregor, Ford of Canada, and Motoropolis*. Detroit: Wayne State University Press.

Royal Commission on Dominion-Provincial Relations. 1940. *Report, Volume I* (Ottawa: King's Printer).

Schneekcloth, L., and R. Shibley. 2005. "Imagine Niagara." *Journal of Canadian Studies* 39 (3):105-20.

Shibley, R., L. Schneekcloth, and B. Hovey. 2003. "Constituting the Public Realm of a Region: Place-Making in the Bi-National Niagaras." *Journal of Architectural Education* 57 (1):28-43.

Siener, W. 2008. "A Barricade of Ships, Guns, Airplanes and Men: Arming the Niagara Border, 1920-1930." *American Review of Canadian Studies* 38 (4):429-450.

---. 2008a. "Through the Back Door: Evading the Chinese Exclusion Act along the Niagara Frontier, 1900 to 1924." *Journal of American Ethnic History* 24 (3): 34-70.

Smith, D. 2005. "Structuring the Permeable Border: Channelling and Regulating Cross-Border Traffic in Labor, Capital and Goods." In *Permeable Border: The Great Lakes Basin as Transnational Region, 1650-1990,* eds., Bukowczyck, J., N. Faires, D. Smith, R. W. Widdis, 120-151. Pittsburgh: University of Pittsburgh Press.

Stevens, P. 1970. *The 1911 General Election: A Study in Canadian Politics.* Toronto: Copp Clark.

Suker, A. L. 2001. "Managing Transboundary Water Resources: An Analysis of Canadian American Interlocal Cooperation" PhD diss., University of Texas at Austin, Austin.

Taylor, A. 2006. *The Divided Ground: Indians, Settlers, and the Northern Borderland of the American Revolution.* New York: Alfred A. Knopf.

Thelen, D. 1992. "Of Audiences, Borderlands, and Comparisons: Toward the Internationalization of American History." *Journal of American History* 79: 432-53.

Traves, T. 1979. *The State and Enterprise: Canadian Manufacturers and the Federal Government, 1917-1931.* Toronto: University of Toronto Press.

Van Nostrand, J. 1983. "The Queen Elizabeth Way: Public Utility Versus Public Space." *Urban History Review* 12, (2).1-23.

Wolcott, V. 2006. "Recreation and Race in the Postwar City: Buffalo's 1956 Crystal Beach Riot." *Journal of American History* 93 (1):63-90.

Walker, B. 2010. *Race on Trial: Black Defendants in Ontario's Criminal Courts, 1858-1958.* Toronto: University of Toronto Press.

Wilson, T., and H. Donnan. 1998. "Nation, State and Identity at International Borders." In*Border Identities: Nation and State at International Frontiers*, eds. Thomas Wilson and Hastings Donnan, 1-30.Cambridge: Cambridge University Press.

3

ONTARIO EXCEPTIONALISM: OLD IDEAS IN THE NEW ONTARIO

P. E. Bryden

Si de nouvelles réalités ont évidemment donné naissance au « Nouvel Ontario », rien n'a changé au sentiment d'une province occupant une place à part dans le système fédéral. Ce sentiment d'exception remonte presque aussi loin que la création même de l'Ontario, sinon davantage, mais l'interprétation de ses fondements a évolué au fil du temps. Reposant tour à tour sur la taille, l'histoire ou le pouvoir économique de la province, il aide à comprendre les diverses stratégies ontariennes dans la dynamique fédérale-provinciale. Ce chapitre retrace l'évolution de la notion d'exceptionnalisme dans les relations intergouvernementales de l'Ontario, et s'intéresse en particulier aux décennies du « vieil Ontario » comprises entre la fin de la Seconde Guerre mondiale et celle du XXᵉ siècle.

Change is in the air these days. Or, more accurately, the idea of change has acquired a certain cachet in the opening years of the 21ˢᵗ century. It probably began in the United States. Back in 2007 Barack Obama built his nomination, and then his presidential campaign, around the idea of change; he had millions of Americans chanting "Yes we can." The enthusiasm and idealism of that mantra had far-reaching effects, buoying Obama into the White House and at the same time shifting the political discourse of the Western world. Change is good, we all decided, and necessary, and, in the connected world that social media has created, can happen extraordinarily rapidly.

Even Ontario has changed. No longer the "big brother" of Confederation, Ontario has repositioned itself within the federal family. Now we have a "new Ontario," different from the old in both quantifiable and intuitive ways. The changes that have occurred in Ontario are rooted in economics. For the first time since the program's inception in 1957, Ontario was the recipient of equalization payments in 2009. Used to being the standard against which the other provincial claims were measured, the relative decline in Ontario's taxing capacity that led to "have-not" status was considerable. And the shift did not go unnoticed; newspapers across the country noted first the likelihood of, then the inevitability of, and then Ontario's actual shift onto the other side of the federal ledger book with fervor rarely directed towards issues of fiscal federalism (Lecours and Béland 2010). It was a "fiscalamity" (Courchene 2008) requiring the implementation of a "fairness" campaign on the part of Queen's Park that would address the inherent inequities in our system of federal transfers (Ontario 2011). But beyond the very obvious change we have seen in Ontario's economic rank within the federation, there has also been a more subtle change in the way Ontarians perceive their position. There was a time, not particularly long ago, when the people of Ontario identified more closely with the nation than with the province; they were Canadians first, Ontarians second (Wiseman 1997, 435). While this remains true in the broadest sense, as recent Mowat Centre polls have shown, there is no longer the same certainty or complacency about their place in the federation (Mendelsohn and Matthews 2010). What is beginning to emerge, apparently, is a "more self-interested, self-absorbed, and even just more selfish Ontario" (White 1998, 13), where there is increasing concern about protecting the provincial, rather than the national, interest. This is a louder, more muscular Ontario than observers have seen before. As Matthew Mendelsohn has explained, the new Ontario is less interested in appeasing other provinces and "less confident in its economic future" than it was in the past, but at the same time "has global ambitions" that will have serious ramifications for the political balance of the whole country (Mendelsohn 2010, 27).

But the major transformation that Ontario seems to be undergoing is doing little to make Ontario a province like the others. Despite joining the rest on the have-not side of the equation, despite increasingly identifying provincially rather than nationally, despite shifting toward a similarly aggressive approach to intergovernmental relations, Ontario remains distinctive within the federation. Those who live elsewhere probably continue to believe, as they always have, that central Canadians make more money, have more services, garner more attention, get more perks, and have more influence than people living anywhere else. Even those who live in Ontario, however, believe that it is a province different from the others. Not only does it have more in common with the broader Great Lakes region, and therefore is more integrated into the North American economy than other Canadian provinces, but it also, increasingly, has more in common with the rest of the world (Courchene and Telmer, 1998). Ever more diverse, increasingly a destination for the world's diasporas, Ontario has embraced, and been embraced by, the world outside Canada's borders in ways that the other provinces can only imagine. Moreover, even when confronted with the reality of a national economy driven by the resource sectors in the east and west of the country, public attitudes continue to picture an Ontario-centric economy. Thus, when viewed both from within and from without, an image of an Ontario has been constructed that is seen as bigger, bolder, and richer than other Canadian provinces. Whether this is true or not has little bearing on the persuasiveness of the perception. It is comforting both for those on the peripheries and those at the centre to believe, and to either ridicule or celebrate, this image of Ontario as different from the rest.

It is this very perception – this sense of Ontario exceptionalism – that has had a profound effect on the role Ontario has historically played within the federation. An idea generally applied to America, exceptionalism nevertheless has a resonance in discussions of Ontario. Rooted in ideas of difference or uniqueness, it is a concept dependent upon comparison to other states. In the case of Ontario, the difference that is emphasized is less historical than it is contemporary; rather than focusing on the uniqueness of Ontario's roots, as is the case with American exceptionalism (Lipset 1996, 18), it is the insistence that Ontario must play a different role in the federation that defines its distinctiveness. That role is certainly based on a history of both political and economic dominance, and therefore a unique position among Canadian provinces, but the key facet of Ontario's exceptionalism is its usefulness in understanding intergovernmental behavior (Tyrell 1991, 1032-1035). The provincial actors – from the premier to the ministers to their bureaucratic advisors – have long behaved as though Ontario occupies a unique place within the Canadian federation. Moreover, Ontario exceptionalism continues to shape the province's – and therefore the nation's – future, even as Ontario becomes less and less exceptional within the Canadian federation. The reasons for this sentiment in Ontario have changed dramatically over the last 150 years, but what remains the same – and remains important – is a profound sense of Ontario's exceptional place within the federation.

In the years prior to the Second World War, Ontario loomed large across the nation. The story of its exceptionalism was thus cast in terms of size – Ontario had the highest population of any of the provinces, and controlled the economy in ways that were only increased with the implementation of Macdonald's National Policy. Designed to create the circumstances under which a national economy could flourish, the Conservative prime minister's program included high tariffs to protect infant industries, a commitment to complete a transcontinental railway, and a plan to populate the territory around the rail lines. In reality, the scheme appeared to benefit Ontario disproportionately. The industries were predominantly in southwestern Ontario, the railway ensured that goods produced in Ontario could be transported to both western and eastern markets, and the immigration scheme ensured that there would be people willing to buy those goods (Dales 1979). At the beginning, Ontario seemed to be uniquely advantaged compared to other provinces, where local economies either stagnated or declined in the late nineteenth and early twentieth centuries.

Ontario's status of one of the original four made it different from other provinces. When battles were waged for provincial jurisdiction – usually in the courts in those early days – Ontario often led the pack. Premier Oliver Mowat wore his mantel of

"Father of Provincial Rights" easily, testing the limits of federal power at every opportunity. The cases dealing with the extent of federal jurisdiction over natural resources, the powers of the lieutenant governor, and the territorial boundaries of the province were important in defining the extent of both federal and provincial jurisdiction, but also played a significant role in setting Ontario apart from its provincial counterparts (Armstrong 1981). While all provincial premiers might be in favour of securing more power and carving out a bigger piece of the federal pie, it was to Ontario they looked for leadership. Mowat played a key role in the first interprovincial conference of 1887, co-hosting his colleagues with Quebec premier Honoré Mercier. He also waged fierce battles in the courts. The victories that Mowat won, and there were many, were shared by all provinces, as the interpretation of provincial jurisdiction in s. 92 of the *British North America Act* gradually widened in concert with a narrowing of the judicial understanding of federal powers under s. 91 (Saywell 2002, 57-149). Mowat was thus not the "Father of Ontario Rights" but of "Provincial Rights" and the province itself was clearly becoming exceptional within the provincial community. By the end of the nineteenth century, Ontario was central not in geography so much as in identity.

Mowat set the tone for the first seventy-five years of Ontario history. The jousting between provincial and federal leaders continued. Subsequent premiers were quick to emulate his vigorous defense of provincial rights in the hopes of also repeating his success at the polls. Sometimes, the barbs were clearly partisan; James Pliny Whitney, a Conservative premier during Wilfrid Laurier's prime ministership, called the Liberal justice minister "the most infantile specimen of politician" he had ever met, and Mackenzie King called another Conservative premier, Howard Ferguson, a "skunk" (Armstrong 1972, 94). On other occasions, however, the participants in the battle were of the same political stripe. Some of the most heated exchanges occurred between Mitch Hepburn and Mackenzie King, both Liberals but with very different ideas about government and jurisdiction. At an intergovernmental meeting described as "the god damndest exhibition circus you can imagine," Hepburn attacked the Rowell-Sirois Report recommendations for transferring tax power from the provinces to the federal government. "We are not behind you, we are ahead of you," he told King and his ministers. "Don't smash this confederation and stir up [a] possible racial feud in your efforts" (Saywell 1991, 460-1). The intergovernmental relationship was a vitriolic one in the years before the Second World War, with the participants on both sides of the divide frequently resorting to invective. But after the success of Mowat's appeal to the courts, and the early twentieth century rulings of the Judicial Committee of the Privy Council that ruled so often in favour of the provinces, successive generations of Ontario premiers had some basis for considering themselves equal to the prime minister.

Since 1945, Ontario has pursued quieter strategies in intergovernmental affairs, but ones that have positioned the province as no less exceptional than was the case during Mowat's Ontario. The postwar focus in federal-provincial relations has been on Ontario's capacity – and willingness – to articulate the national interest, surely an exceptional role for a province to undertake. That there was so little questioning of the role, either from provincial counterparts or, in most cases, from the federal government itself, serves to underline the extent to which Ontario exceptionalism has been accepted and even endorsed by the rest of the country. Under the Conservative dynasty of George Drew, Leslie Frost, John Robarts and Bill Davis, the Ontario government consistently advanced first alternatives to the intergovernmental policies emanating from Ottawa, and then ultimately initiated discussion on matters of common interest, earning a reputation for being the "big brother" of Confederation or the first among equals. Throughout it all, there were few voices questioning the exceptional place, and exceptional responsibilities, of Ontario within Confederation.

George Drew won the election of 1943 in Ontario in part on a platform of "cooperation with the Dominion Government" (Drew 1943a), but also with a commitment to stand up to a federal government that was widely regarded as being dominated by Quebec. He did this by urging King to call an intergovernmental conference on reconstruction "at the earliest possible date" in order to establish "the basis upon which the Dominion and Provincial Governments will cooperate," but he also sought allies in other provincial capitals (Drew 1944). Ultimately, he hoped "to consolidate the people of the various sections into one great Canadian unit" thereby adding to Ontario's "prestige and our influence in the international world" (Drew 1943b). It was a strangely national vision for a provincial premier to be taking, but when that premier was in Ontario, this exceptional perspective was simply the norm. Having made trips to lobby colleagues in other provinces, and directed his civil servants to undertake fact-finding missions of their own, it was alarming to learn over Christmas 1943 that the King government was in the process of designing its own policies for reconstruction, without provincial consultation or input. Drew led the provincial attack, demanding that together they reach "some understanding in regard to the present and future constitutional relationship of the various governments" (Drew 1944). King was unmoved by these entreaties, choosing instead to move forward unilaterally on family allowances, and stalling on the calling of an intergovernmental conference – despite increasingly shrill missives from Drew – until the summer of 1945.

Drew lost some allies when he complained that the federal family allowance scheme was going to be funded by Ontario taxpayers and was nothing more than a sop to the fecund families of Quebec, adopting a strategy in keeping with Ontario exceptionalism but not a particularly effective one. He was soon back on track, however, threatening to call a meeting of premiers to deal with the issue of postwar planning if the federal government continued to do nothing (Drew 1945a). By the time the Dominion-Provincial Conference on Reconstruction was finally convened, Drew had positioned himself as something of an alternative to federal authority. Other premiers, including Saskatchewan's Tommy Douglas and Maurice Duplessis of Quebec treated Drew as a quasi-official spokesman for the provincial position, urging him to press King on the timing and the content of the conference. Following the August preliminary gathering, when the federal delegation unveiled the Green Book proposals, Drew's group returned home to draft their counterproposals, again positioning Ontario as the spokes-province for provincial side. Appalled with the Green Book suggestion that provinces should continue to "rent" their direct tax fields to the federal government following the end of war – a situation that everyone had received assurances would never happen – the Ontario Treasury committee, headed by minister Leslie Frost, found a "compromise." Proposing "a plan which would be more favourable to Ontario [than the federal plan] and at the same time not unattractive to the 'have not' provinces" (Ontario, n.d), the Ontario scheme envisioned both a return of the rented tax fields and an equalization payout of some sort. As Drew claimed in a speech to the Canadian Club in the fall of 1945, this was a proposal that was "not only in the interests of the people of Ontario but it is also in the best interests of the whole of Canada" (Drew 1945b).

Ontario's alternatives to the Green Book plan for reconstruction gained no more support than the federal plan itself, and the conference finally adjourned in May 1946 without a decision having been reached. What was significant was not the success of Ontario's strategy, but the fact that Drew was beginning to chart a new course in intergovernmental relations – one based on articulating alternatives to the federal proposals and policies – that was just as rooted in a sense of Ontario exceptionalism as Mowat's court challenges of the nineteenth century. Drew underlined Ontario's pre-eminence within the federation by assuming the responsibility to press for the reconstruction conference in the first place, and then by being the only provincial premier to table an alternative to Ottawa's scheme. While he did not secure widespread provincial agreement on the Ontario proposals, no one suggested that he had been out of line in proposing his own Green-ish Book on reconstruction and recovery.

One of the chief participants in Drew's new intergovernmental strategy was his provincial treasurer, Leslie Frost. When Drew decided to make the move to federal politics, beating John Diefenbaker in the leadership race, Frost was the one who took the helm in Ontario. His experience in Treasury was certainly important – and he continued to serve in that capacity until 1955 – but it was his familiarity with the cut and thrust of federal-provincial relations that would serve him particularly well during his twelve years in office. Like those before him, he was content in the knowledge that Ontario was a province unlike the others, and that Ontario's exceptional status created heavier responsibilities. And like Drew, Frost positioned himself as something of an alternative to the federal authority. Wartime Tax Agreements had turned into the Tax Rental Agreements, negotiated every five years and characterizing the ad hoc approach that was taken to both tax- and cost-sharing in the wake of the failure of the Green Book proposals. Ontario and Quebec had both exercised their prerogative and demonstrated their uniqueness by refusing to participate in the 1947 tax agreements; by 1952 however, Ontario was coming around to the benefits of entering into an agreement with the federal government (Perry 1989, 383-4).

Perhaps, as some have argued, this was a sign of Ontario's shift into complacency, content now to support the federal government in whatever it proposed (Ibbitson 2001, 79-112). A closer examination of what was going on in Frost's government points to different motivations. In the months leading up to the conclusion of the 1952 round of fiscal negotiations, Frost and his team worked assiduously on their colleagues in Quebec, first seeking to understand the terms by which they would agree to some form of tax sharing, and then conveying that information to the federal government. What Frost and Duplessis agreed upon was a joint strategy for renting their corporate and personal tax fields at the same, higher, rate, and demanding that other fiscal conditions be met. Was this simply a return to the old days of battling the federal government, this time not in the courts but in the treasury departments of the nation? It might seem that way, except for Frost's comments to Prime Minister St. Laurent; Ontario wasn't the issue, he claimed, as it could "accept the terms of your tax rental proposal of last December or continue to collect its own taxes in its own way without substantial financial difference either one way or the other." The problem was Quebec, which did "not, even for a short period, favour the rental of its corporation tax." The threat of Quebec once again remaining outside the tax-rental agreement, this time alone was, " not a good thing for national unity." Frost urged the Prime Minister "to revise your proposal to make it possible for all the provinces to march together in substantial harmony" (Frost 1951). In the end, Quebec again remained outside the tax rental agreements that the rest of the country accepted. Once again an Ontario premier had put himself in an exceptional position in terms of the intergovernmental relationship; Frost was not basing his fiscal decisions exclusively on what would be the most beneficial for Ontario, or even leading the other provinces in taking a provincialist stance, but rather was considering what was good for national unity. It was both extraordinary and exceptional.

"Old Man Ontario," as Frost was called, stepped down from the premier's chair in 1961. He had guided Ontario through an unprecedented period of expansion, and had also settled into his role in the federal landscape. Not the prime minister, but also not quite the same as the other premiers, Frost was free to advocate national unity or press the federal government into action, as he did in 1955 when he opened the national dialogue on health insurance (Bryden 2009, 78). Not just a critic, Frost shifted the Ontario government into speaking for an alternative national vision than the one advocated by St. Laurent's Ottawa. Frost's successor as premier, John Robarts, made Ontario's transition complete. Under Robarts, Toronto began to usurp much of Ottawa's position within the intergovernmental family. Pearson's brand of cooperative federalism perhaps facilitated this, but it was Robarts' confidence and Ontario's exceptionalism that made it happen.

The intergovernmental agenda was especially crowded in the 1960s. Social policies that had been discussed for decades – like a national pension scheme and national health insurance – were finally being negotiated seriously. Robarts had first attempted to control the pension debate, crashing a meeting of health ministers called by federal minister Judy LaMarsh in the fall of 1963, and then offering Ontario's home-grown private pension plan as an alternative to the nascent Canada Pension Plan that the federal government was proposing. The honour of truly hijacking the federal initiative, however, had to go to Quebec's premier Jean Lesage, whose surprise unveiling of the Quebec Pension Plan left the assembled premiers shaking their heads in disbelief and wondering aloud whether they could sign onto the QPP instead of the CPP (Morin 1976, 7-11). Joking aside, the Quebec approach was characteristic of a long-standing strategy of simply going its own way, paying little heed to Ottawa's plans or to national unity. Robarts may have lost his place as the unofficial voice of the federal alternative during the pension negotiations, but in recognizing that the playing field had shifted somewhat he was able to respond. As one of the senior civil servants in Robarts' administration noted, "in the next few months, Ontario must demonstrate not only tactical but strategic initiative in the conduct of federal-provincial fiscal affairs as a contribution to profound changes in the character of Canadian federalism" (Macdonald 1965).

The tactical and strategic initiative that Robarts undertook was in the field of constitutional arrangements. Quebec's Quiet Revolution and the beginnings of separatist murmurings precipitated an elevated level of concern in the rest of Canada. Pearson had responded quickly by announcing the establishment of a royal commission on bilingualism and biculturalism, but that had done little to quell the rising tide of discontent in Quebec. Ontario's Confederation-year project was to figure out what Quebec wanted, and to do so Robarts called the Confederation of Tomorrow Conference for November 1967. The prime minister and all the premiers were invited to come to Toronto to begin a dialogue on constitutional change in Canada in light of the sentiment in Quebec. It was an unprecedented move on the part of a provincial premier, and Pearson was not shy about saying so. He informed Robarts that it was not "wise or desirable" for a premier to "initiate a Federal-Provincial Conference that could be awkward or untimely for one of the other provinces, or unhelpful to the country as a whole" (Pearson 1967). Robarts didn't care, and proceeded with his plans for the conference, exercising an increasingly common practice in Ontario to behave more like the federal government than like its provincial counterparts.

Provincial civil servants fanned out across the country, soliciting opinions on the matter of constitutional change prior to the opening of the conference. Some premiers clearly thought Ontario had overstepped its bounds in so blatantly usurping the federal role, but all, nevertheless, participated: the federal government quite pointedly, did not. The Confederation of Tomorrow Conference was not designed to solve any problems, merely to identify the contours of those that already existed. It did this in a friendly environment, without the usual acrimony characteristic of intergovernmental meetings that Ottawa convened. There was a sense that the premiers were more conciliatory, more willing to work together on a solution to their collective concerns without the watchful glare of a federal delegation. As Ontario's deputy minister of intergovernmental affairs, Don Stevenson, noted after the delegates had returned home, "the conference was noteworthy because of the spirit of compromise that was evoked with regard to an approach to" constitutional questions (Stevenson 1967).

Intergovernmental relations in John Robarts' Ontario were certainly not bilateral, and perhaps more closely resembled a trilateral relationship. Positioning the province as something that was neither federal nor provincial, Ontario became a linchpin, an interpreter, a transitional entity in the dialogue across governments in 1960s Canada. When Bill Davis took the reins of power following Robarts' decade-long tenure, his job was clear and the constitutional agenda had been set. The Confederation of Tomorrow Conference had opened Pandora's box, and the constitution would dominate the intergovernmental agenda for the remainder of the century. Beginning with the three-part constitutional conference that culminated in the failed Victoria Charter of 1971, and ending sometime after the collapse of the Charlottetown Accord in 1992, Canadians clung to a constitutional roller-coaster for more than 25 years. Ontario's strategy was set in the 1960s; to play neither a purely provincial nor a purely national role, but to exist in the space in between the two levels of government.

Reconciling Ontario's actions with this exceptional in-between role is not always intuitive. Ontario's betrayal of its provincial colleagues in supporting Prime Minister Trudeau's threat to amend the constitution unilaterally, for example, might be misunderstood as a shift toward explicitly supporting Ottawa; it should be seen, rather, as an effort to facilitate conversation. When Trudeau argued that the federal government did not need the agreement of the provinces before requesting that the British Parliament amend the *British North America Act*, he drew a line in the sand and essentially put an end to any further negotiations with the provinces. Bill Davis' decision to support that move was both a reflection of the long-standing commitment on Ontario's part to secure the patriation of the constitution, and a way of keeping the lines of communication open between Ottawa and the so-called "gang of eight." Ontario politicians and bureaucrats alike worked to build agreements, however small, on the constitution. Lobbying in England, Ontario representatives learned that there was both "a strong anti-Trudeau bias" among British MPs, but also that the absence of any "Tory pro-package presence" had undermined support for Trudeau's constitutional proposals even further (Segal 1981). Ontario's Attorney General, Roy McMurtry, who was among those in London canvassing opinion, thought that it was becoming "increasingly apparent that the Federal Government's proposals are not as generally accepted by either Canadian citizens or their political representatives in Provincial Legislatures as political changes of this magnitude ought to be" (McMurtry 1982-1983, 47). When the Supreme Court ruled on the reference question posed by the provinces, declaring unilateral patriation legal but contravening convention, the Ontario reaction was sanguine. The Davis team had "always known" that the threat of unilateral patriation "was a departure from general precedent in order to break a logjam" (Stevenson 1981). And in that it was a successful gambit, it did so. Phone lines began to buzz as bureaucrats floated the possibility of a compromise between the two positions, and politicians began to slowly lay some of their cards on the table. And Ontario was in the centre – the bureaucrats beginning to pull together the provinces, and Davis engaged in conversations with Trudeau that indicated he still had a "fair bit of flexibility on the charter, on timing, and some room for change on the amending formula" (Stevenson 1981). When agreement was finally reached, it was marred by the refusal of Quebec to sign, and more importantly by Levesque's profound sense of betrayal. But even with an incomplete victory, the Ontario team was still pleased to have been able to broker the elusive deal at all. Even in its partial failure, Davis's intergovernmental strategies were like those that had held the office before him. Seeking to occupy an exceptional place in the federal system, in an effort to secure a constitutional agreement that had been elusive for so long, the Ontario government could only work so much magic. It was a partial victory that would have been familiar to Robarts in his efforts to open the constitutional conversation, to Frost in his efforts to bring Quebec into the fiscal fold, and even to Drew with his alternative scheme for postwar reconstruction.

But with no question that the *Constitutional Act, 1982* was incomplete, Peterson's Liberal government in the mid-1980s was just as keen as its Conservative counterparts to secure a constitutional agreement that worked for everyone. With Mulroney in Ottawa and Bourassa in Quebec City, perhaps it was time to bring Quebec into the constitutional fold. Governments across the country prepared for such a prospect. The Quebec Liberal party issued a modest list of the five conditions that they considered necessary for a Quebec government to sign onto the *Constitution Act, 1982*. The Ontario civil service beefed up its constitutional office with the addition of advisors Peter Hogg and Ian McGilp. Mulroney made clear from his electoral campaign onward his intention to resolve the differences between Quebec and the rest of Canada (Monahan 1991, 45-7). After quietly ascertaining whether governments in other provincial capitals were interested in accommodating Quebec's conditions, and a great deal of private and not-so-private informal negotiation, Mulroney hosted the premiers at the fateful meeting outside of Ottawa at Meech Lake.

At both the initial meeting, and over the course of the three years that governments were given to ratify the Meech Lake Accord, Ontario's premier David Peterson played a key role in working to secure the passage of the amendments. At Meech Lake itself, Bourassa said that Peterson had been instrumental "in forging the unanimous agreement on Quebec's demands" (Monahan 1991, 100). A number of circumstances contrived against easy acceptance of the accord, including the very public and vitriolic attacks by former Prime Minister Trudeau and the change in government in other provincial capitals. In Ontario, where the 1987 election was fought largely on the issue of free trade, Peterson was returned with a majority government and the electoral security with which to defend the Meech Lake agreement. Changes of government in Newfoundland, New Brunswick, and Manitoba, however, had particularly devastating effects on the future of the accord.

Throughout it all, Peterson adopted the familiar Ontario approach to intergovernmental issues. Acting out of neither purely provincial nor purely national interests,

Peterson was adamant that "delaying the passage of the accord while an attempt is made to hammer out appropriate changes in areas not directly related to the reconciliation of Quebec, can put that spirit of reconciliation in great danger" (Stevenson 1987). He also worked to keep the constitutional conversation going, especially in those provinces where government changes had called into question the commitments that previous premiers had made. Ontario's Ministry of Intergovernmental Affairs paid close attention to the situation in both New Brunswick and Manitoba, preparing for frequent meetings between leaders and offering to convey as much intelligence as possible in the interest of securing agreement on the accord (Dutil 1988; Cameron 1988; Careless 1988). And at the end of the day, when some final act of compromise seemed necessary to bring all the provinces on board, Premier Peterson offered to reduce the number of Senate seats that Ontario was guaranteed under the constitution (Monahan 1991, 224-5). Throughout the entire process of agreeing to, and ratifying the Meech Lake Accord, Ontario's politicians and bureaucrats acted in exactly the same manner as three generations of Conservative administrators before them; Ontario was not a province like the others, and as such had an exceptional role to play in the constitutional process.

In the end, it did not work. The clock ran out on the Meech Lake Accord when neither Manitoba nor Newfoundland managed to ratify it before the three-year deadline. Perhaps this was the beginning of the end, too, of the old Ontario. Throughout much of the postwar period, successive Ontario government had pursued their own interests under the cloak of making the federal system more functional. When it came to big questions of constitutional reform, Ontario had consistently shifted more clearly towards nation-building and brokerage-politics. What the Mulroney government in general, and the Meech Lake Accord in particular, made clear was that there was no longer any space for a nation-building Ontario. As the Deputy Minister of Intergovernmental Affairs in Ontario said, "the federal government has adopted the role of broker of provincial and regional interests" and "in this environment, Ontario often becomes a reference point for unfavorable comparison and sometimes an object of attack" (Gagnier 1989).

Thus having failed to achieve the constitutional accord, and now pushed out of the role of broker, the Ontario strategy in intergovernmental affairs began an inexorable shift towards a protection of self-interest in the 1990s and beyond. Bob Rae's NDP government in the 1990s faced the problem head-on; if Ontario was perceived elsewhere in the country as that "inherently wealthy place [that] would continue to bankroll Canada" (Rae 1993), then the premier would undertake a "cost-benefit analysis of Confederation" to determine precisely what Ontario's "fair share" should be (Cameron 1994, 110). When it came to the dollars and cents of the federal system, Rae was vocal in his critique of the raw deal he saw Ontario as getting. "Ontario has been shafted and is being shafted within the federal-provincial system," he complained, pointing to the reductions in federal transfers as just "the tip of the iceberg" (Jalsevac 1993). The premier claimed that the "discriminatory treatment" from Ottawa had cost the province $23 billion over a three-year period

(Payne 1994). The calls for "fairer" treatment were loud and clear from the provincial capital, part of an important shift away from the standard postwar approach to intergovernmental relations and a move toward the "new Ontario."

The idea of "fairness" in one way or another has dominated Ontario's intergovernmental rhetoric since the 1990s, and has had a profound effect on the development of a "new Ontario." But there remains one key link between the old and the new Ontario, despite an altered view of the federal-provincial relationship, a rapidly transforming economy that has grown in ways not always advantageous to Ontario, and several transformational changes to the government in power – the sense that Ontario remains exceptional. While perhaps not the economic engine of the nation anymore, or the province best positioned to broker deals between provinces and nation, Ontario remains confident in its exceptionalism, even if it has come to be defined in different ways. In the nineteenth century, Ontario politicians saw the province as exceptionally blessed – with farmland and economic institutions and national political power – and while this was initially the inspiration for spirited battles with the federal government, by the middle of the twentieth century it had become a justification for a kind of intergovernmental generosity. Ontario would use its vaunted position to broker better deals, interpret the goals of one region for the benefit of the rest of Canada and, in general, articulate a national vision from the provincial capital. Even when it became clear that this approach offered few real advantages for either the provincial economy or its intergovernmental reputation, the idea of exceptionalism was so deeply imbedded in the Ontario psyche that it was impossible to drop completely. Refusing to be "taken for granted any longer" (Maychak 1991) meant a return to some older strategies in the new Ontario; provincial good fortune in terms of size and clout meant, not that Ontario would contribute more, but that it deserved more out of the federation. Exceptionalism, with its various definitions and bases, remains the key to understanding Ontario's strategies and goals within the intergovernmental framework.

As we look toward the future, it appears that an Ontario that began by presenting itself as the keystone province, and then shifted to articulating and translating national policy, might naturally move on to a vision that is supranational. As scholars of the new Ontario have demonstrated, the extent of international connections with Ontario, the global diasporas that call Ontario home, and the increasingly continental vision of Ontario politicians all suggest that we have moved into an era in which Ontario exceptionalism will seek a new stage. As a province that is not like the others, is it not possible that Ontario will shake off the provincial constraints with which it has been burdened, and move towards establishing extra-Canadian associations? Whether the province will be more successful in presenting an alternative international policy than it has been in articulating an alternative national policy, however, is anyone's guess.

REFERENCES

Armstrong, C. 1972. "The Mowat Heritage in Federal-Provincial Relations." In *Oliver Mowat's Ontario,* ed. D. Swainson, 93-118. Toronto: Macmillan.

Armstrong, C. 1981. *The Politics of Federalism: Ontario's Relations with the Federal Government, 1867-1942.* Toronto: University of Toronto Press.

Bryden, P. E. 2009. "The Liberal Party and the Achievement of National Medicare." *Canadian Bulletin of Medical History* 26(2):75-92.

Cameron, D. 1988. Letter to Hershell Ezrin. 1 September. F-2093-17-6-45, file: Meech Lake 1988. David Peterson Papers, Archives of Ontario.

Cameron, D. 1994. "Post-Modern Ontario and the Laurentian Thesis." In *Canada: The State of the Federation 1994,* eds. D. M. Brown and J. Hiebert, 109-132. Kingston: Institute of Intergovernmental Relations.

Careless, A. 1988. Letter to Peter Sadlier-Brown, re: Next Moves on Meech Lake Accord. 14 December. F-2093-17-6-45, file: Meech Lake 1988. David Peterson Papers, Archives of Ontario.

Courchene, T. J. and C. R. Telmer. 1998. *From Heartland to North American Region State: The Social, Fiscal and Federal Evolution of Ontario.* Monograph Series on Public Policy, Faculty of Management. Toronto: University of Toronto.

Courchene, T. J. 2008. "Fiscalamity! Ontario: From Heartland to Have-not." *Policy Options* June: 46-54.

Dales, J. H. 1979. "'National Policy' Myths, Past and Present." *Journal of Canadian Studies* 14, (3):92-94.

Drew, G. 1943a. "George Drew, Speaking Over a Province-Wide Network." 8 July. George Drew Papers, Private collection (in author's possession).

---. 1943b. Letter to Horace Hunter. 21 September. Office of the Premier: George Drew, letterbooks (RG 3-18). Archives of Ontario.

---. 1944. Letter to William Lyon Mackenzie King. 6 January. Box 3, file: Inter-provincial Conference, 1945. Department of Finance Papers: Dominion-Provincial Conferences, 1935-55 (RG 6-41). Archives of Ontario.

---. 1945a. Telegram to Tommy Douglas. 15 February. Reel M-9047. George Drew Papers. Library and Archives Canada.

---. 1945b. "Speech by Premier George A. Drew before the Canadian Club, Toronto." 1 October. Volume 27, file: Prime Minister no. 18, Canadian Club. Department of Finance Papers (RG 6-15). Archives of Ontario

Dutil, P. 1988. Letter to Anne Ritchie, re: Meech Lake and Manitoba: The Outlook. 3 August. F-2093-17-0-30, file: Oct. 1988. David Peterson Papers, Archives of Ontario.

Frost, L. 1951. "Draft Outline of Statement to the Right Honourable Louis St. Laurent." 14 August. Box 6, file: Dominion-Provincial Conference, Abbott, Hon. Douglas. Aug. 1951. Office of the Premier: Frost Premier's Correspondence Papers (RG 3-24). Archives of Ontario.

Gagnier, D. 1989. Speaking Notes. F-2093-39-0-49. Ministry files, Ministry of Intergovernmental Affairs, June-Dec. 1989. David Peterson Papers, Archives of Ontario.

Ibbitson, J. 2001. *Loyal No More: Ontario's Struggle for a Separate Destiny*. Toronto: Harper Collins.

Jalsevac, P. 1993. Ontario "Shafted," Rae to tell PM. *Windsor Star,* 21 July, A10.

Lecours, A. and D. Béland. 2010. "Federalism and Fiscal Policy: The Politics of Equalization in Canada." *Publius: The Journal of Federalism* 40(4): 569-596.

Lipset, S. M. 1996. *American Exceptionalism: A Double-Edged Sword* New York: WW Norton and Company.

Macdonald, H. I. 1965. Memo to John Robarts, re: Meeting of Ministers of Finance and Tax Structure Committee. 20 December. Box 394, file: Fed-Prov. Tax Sharing – Tax Structure committee – Dec. 65, Treasury. Office of the Premier: Robarts General Correspondence Papers (RG 3-26). Archives of Ontario.

Maychak, M. 1991. Ottawa Snubbing Ontario, Rae Says. *Toronto Star,* 29 November, A13.

McMurtry, R. 1982-1983. "The Search for a Constitutional Accord – A Personal Memoir." *Queen's Law Journal* 8:28-73.

Mendelsohn, M. 2010. "Big Brother No More: Ontario's and Canada's Interests are no Longer Identical." *Literary Review of Canada* October: 27-9.

Mendelsohn, M. and J. S. Matthews. 2010. The New Ontario: The Shifting Attitude of Ontarians toward the Federation. Mowat Centre Note February 1-8. Toronto: Mowat Centre.

Monahan, P. J. 1991. *Meech Lake: The Inside Story*. Toronto: University of Toronto Press.

Morin, C. 1976. *Quebec versus Ottawa: The Struggle for Self-Government, 1960-72*. Toronto: University of Toronto Press.

Ontario, Ministry of Intergovernmental Affairs. 2011. "Fairness for Ontario." At http://www.ontario.ca/en/your_government/mia/ONT05_024650 (accessed 29 January 2011).

Ontario, Taxation and Dominion-Provincial Co-ordinating Committee. No date. "An examination of the Financial Proposals of the Government of Canada with Ontario's Alternative Plans." Box 4, file: Dom-Prov Re: Taxation and D-P Coordinating Cttee, 1942-1945. Office of the Premier: Frost Premier's Correspondence Papers. Archives of Ontario.

Payne, E. 1994. Ontario Won't be Neglected Anymore, Rae Warns a New Federal Government. *The Ottawa Citizen,* 9 November, A2.

Pearson, L. B. 1967. Letter to John Robarts. 26 January. MU 5311, file: Correspondence, 1965-1971. George Gathercole Papers. Archives of Ontario.

Perry, J. H. 1989. *A Fiscal History of Canada: The Postwar Years*. Toronto: Canadian Tax Foundation.

Rae, B. 1993. "Join Us to Make Canada Work Again." Speech to the Provincial Renewal Conference, Toronto, 8 November.

Saywell, J. T. 1991. *"Just Call Me Mitch": The Life of Mitchell F. Hepburn*. Toronto: University of Toronto Press.

Saywell, J.T. 2002. *The Lawmakers: Judicial Power and the Shaping of Canadian Federalism*. Toronto: University of Toronto Press.

Segal, H. 1981. "London and Patriation Situational Review" 16 April. Box 83, file: FP-4-1-1, PM – Amendment to the Constitution of Canada, vol. 1, Jan.-April. William Davis Papers, central registry files (RG 3-49), Archives of Ontario.

Stevenson, D. 1967. Memo to file, "Follow-up on the Constitutional Questions Raised…," 4 December. Box 444, file: Confederation of Tomorrow Conference, Ontario Government, Nov.-Dec. 1967. Office of the Premier: Robarts General Correspondence Paper (RG 3-26). Archives of Ontario.

Stevenson, D. 1981. "Chronology of Steps Leading to Constitutional Agreement on November 5th, 1981." Donald Stevenson Papers, Private collection (in author's possession).

---. 1987. Letter to Robert Carman. 24 September. F-2122-3-0-447. Herschell Ezrin Papers, Archives of Ontario.

Tyrell, I. 1991. "American Exceptionalism in an Age of International History." *American Historical Review* 96(4):1031-55.

White, Randall. 1998. *Ontario Since 1985.* Toronto: Eastendbooks.

Wiseman, Nelson. 1997. "Change in Ontario Politics." In *Government and Politics of Ontario: Fifth Edition,* ed. G. White 418-441. Toronto: University of Toronto Press.

4

OLD HABITS DIE HARD: "NEW" ONTARIO AND THE "OLD" LAURENTIAN CONSENSUS

Joshua Hjartarson

On a longtemps utilisé l'adjectif « laurentien » pour définir le Canada en tant que pays dont le pouvoir politique, économique et culturel se concentrait dans les collectivités riveraines du fleuve Saint-Laurent et du bassin des Grands Lacs. Puis, avec le déclin de la base industrielle du Canada central, certains ont prétendu que l'Ouest avait économiquement et politiquement supplanté l'Ontario. Une hypothèse rejetée dans ce chapitre au motif que l'Ontario est loin d'avoir été éclipsé, même s'il a perdu son rang de tête. En fait, il joue désormais un rôle semblable à celui des autres provinces en défendant ses propres intérêts. Or, à long terme, l'égalité et la concurrence interprovinciales sont sans doute plus avantageuses pour la fédération que la domination d'une même province. C'est ainsi que sur le plan politique et administratif, l'Ontario doit aujourd'hui investir dans la défense de ses intérêts autant d'efforts que l'ont toujours fait les autres provinces du pays.

INTRODUCTION

Much has been written on Ontario's transition from Canada's political heartland and manufacturing hub to underachiever and "have not" province. According to some observers, Ontario has now been relegated to the periphery of Canadian political and economic life and will remain so for the foreseeable future. As contemporary conventional wisdom goes, Ontario's economy has been ravaged by globalization, the petro dollar, and free trade. It is on the verge of becoming a northern extension of the Rust Belt in America's Northeast and Midwest. Its role as an agenda setter in Canadian politics has been displaced by the West and more specifically, by Alberta.

The rumours of Ontario's demise are greatly exaggerated.

This chapter rejects the "decline" hypothesis as hyperbole at best. Ontario is indeed in the midst of an economic transition and there are certainly other influential voices and agendas on the national stage. However, rather than supplant Ontario's influence, these agendas have risen to compete with Ontario's traditional vision of the federation. This new competition is likely to become a permanent reality in Canada.

The result is a new imperative for Ontario that may bring the province to reconsider its traditional vision of the federation. Historically, Ontario could count on its large population and economic girth to automatically translate into favourable national policies. The province could afford to play a more passive role on some key national discussions and to trade specific interests for the greater good of the federation. However, Ontario's continued passivity on issues that are now at the core of its interests is a luxury that the province can no longer afford.

Ontario needs to be more instrumental in defining and defending its interests in the federation, particularly in the context of its multiple, strong, regional voices. Being more instrumental requires building policy capacity on intergovernmental issues that are now core to its interests and adopting the mindset and (occasionally combative) tactics of its provincial counterparts. It requires ignoring the inevitable grousing of commentators who will complain that Ontario is now playing the same game as other provinces. It requires cultivating an awareness within the bureaucracy and across the general public that Ontario, like the other parts of the country, has interests too. All of this needs to be supported by a new narrative that rejects the Rust Belt terminology and focuses on the *new* Ontario as a leading global player in finance, trade, and commerce.

This chapter begins by examining the Laurentian Consensus and its legacy. It then critiques the hyperbolic arguments of Ontario's decline. Finally, it concludes with an assessment of Canada's contemporary political economy and provides recommendations on how Ontario can begin to adjust to a new set of realities.

THE LAURENTIAN CONSENSUS

It is often said, usually with derision, that Toronto is the centre of the Canadian universe. From confederation to the 1990s, there have been elements of truth to this statement. Many students of Canadian political economy have observed that throughout this period national public policies were built to ensure the prosperity and preserve the privileged position of the Laurentian system – the cities based around or near the St. Lawrence watershed.

Some have gone so far as to say that national policies were the product of a "Laurentian Consensus": a consensus among the political, academic, business, and cultural elite (from cities within the St. Lawrence River watershed including

Toronto, Ottawa, and Montreal) focused on consolidating the commercial and industrial base from Montreal and Toronto.

> Indeed, the concept of the commercial empire of the St. Lawrence, rooted in an understanding of the ambitions of central Canada, has been widely employed as a way of explaining the development of British North America and certain of the chief ends that Confederation was meant to serve (Cameron 1994, 112-3).

There were three defining characteristics of the Consensus:

First, the suite of federal interventions in the economy, from monetary policy to investment in infrastructure, was conducted with the Laurentian system in mind. "Issue after issue, decade after decade, the Laurentian Consensus shaped the public policy arc of this country" (Ibbitson 2011). Natural resources from elsewhere in the country would be exploited to feed the industrial base centred in and between the Laurentian cities, much to the chagrin and resentment of peripheral regions. The national railroad, the Canadian Pacific Railway (CPR), was one expression of the desire to secure a protected market for a nascent industrial base headquartered in Montreal and Toronto. High tariff barriers were another.

A second defining characteristic of the Consensus was the accommodation of French Canada and the Quebec vision of Canadian duality. From pre-confederation to the 1990s, the regimes of Lower and Upper Canada found ways to make coexistence, mutual respect, and political partnership profitable. To most Canadians living outside of these two provinces, national political debate was shaped by the dialogue and accommodation between Quebec and Ontario.

After the Quiet Revolution, Montreal gradually declined as a commercial centre. Business and capital migrated westward to Toronto. Bay Street supplanted St. James Street as both the financial capital of the country and the lightning rod for resentment from Canada's other regions. The Laurentian Consensus (and the resentments it provoked) became more and more synonymous with Ontario and the Toronto/Bay Street elite, and increasingly cast Montreal's English speaking community in a secondary role. As Cameron notes,

> ... prior to the decline of Montreal as the Canadian centre of commerce and finance, it was possible for westerners to speak generically of central Canada. It was not just the "goddamned" CPR that was castigated, it was the financiers and bloated capitalists on St. James Street and Bay Street. St. James Street is now called Rue St. Jacques and has disappeared from the lexicon of occidental infamy, and Montreal has ceded its place of pre-eminence in national commerce and finance to Bay Street and to Toronto (1994, 113).

However, the new predominance of Ontario in the Consensus made accommodating Quebec's ambitions while preserving the federation an important priority. This brings us to the third characteristic of the Consensus: Ontarians strongly identified with Ottawa and the federal government. This was part commercial – the desire to keep the economic union together and functional – and part affinity and pride in the national project. Ontarians felt genuine patriotism for the country being built, with English and French partnership at its core.

In addition to accommodating Quebec, Ontario's position contributed to a willingness to underwrite the general prosperity of the country through the regional redistribution of sizable portions of its wealth. Ontarians were always prepared to "pay more" into the federation than they "got back" in the form of federal spending in the province. In practice, this meant that the federal government collected taxes from the Ontario tax-base and re-distributed them to the other parts of the federation directly through programs like Equalization, regional development, and other transfers, programs, and spending decisions.

Similarly, as long as Ontario was reasonably assured that the federal government would maintain the framework conditions that were supportive of Ontario's prosperity (such as manufacturing-friendly monetary policy, large-scale infrastructure projects like the CPR, and tariff walls), the province could afford to be more muted in its public pursuit of narrow provincial interests for the sake of national unity.

Interregional redistribution of resources away from Ontario was tolerable to the province's political and business elites and considered to be part of the cost of doing business. So long as the tariff and trade barriers remained, transfers to other parts of the country could be expected, at least indirectly, to fund the purchase of goods produced in Ontario.

According to Ontarians, this redistribution was the price of national unity. Resource transfers helped keep the country together and were the cost of a privileged place in the federation. Provincial acquiescence on issues such as the distribution of seats in the House of Commons, federal employment supports, military procurement, and others, would keep regional antagonisms in check.

As Bob Rae said in 1993, Ontario is "the part of Canada that dare not speak its name" (Cameron 1994, 109). This mindset became embedded in the operating culture of the Ontario Public Service and in the approach of successive Ontario governments' to intergovernmental relations. It is now part of the *modus operandi* of intergovernmental relations in Canada.

However, this old approach is incompatible with the *new* Ontario. In fact, it is a substantial drag on Ontario's economic ambitions, which are now firmly rooted in the global (as opposed to national) economy. We are now at a place where, as Chantal Hébert suggested in the *Toronto Star*, Ontario can no longer afford to give up "an inch of influence on the national stage" (Toronto Star, 13 July 2007).

WESTWARD HO! THE HYPERBOLIC DECLINE THESIS

"Put it all together and what do you see? That the power shift from Central Canada to the West that everyone speculated about is no longer speculation. It's here." (Ibbitson 2011)

According to some observers, the Laurentian Consensus is all but dead and the platform on which it was built (a robust commercial base in Ontario) is on perilous ground. The reasons cited are fourfold.

First, the introduction of free trade between Canada and the United States and the broader deepening of global trade links has had a profound impact on the political and economic landscape of Canada and Ontario.

As a result of the liberalization of trade, Canada's provinces became less commercially interdependent and more outward looking. Free trade diminished east-west trade and thus became an important rationale for wealth transfers from the core (Ontario) to the periphery.

As noted by David Cameron, "the liberalization of trade effectively reduces the significance of the political border upon which Canada was built and alters the logic of Ontario's geopolitical situation" (1994, 128). Notably, Ontario no longer sees a large economic dividend from its investment in the federation. Furthermore, it is now exposed to the vagaries of global competition for markets, investment, and talent, which requires radical adjustments across a suite of federal and provincial public policies.

Second, the emergence of another economic engine in the West based exclusively on resource extraction has upset the old equilibrium in the economic and political dynamics of the federation. The emergence of a robust resource economy in Western Canada gave rise to an alternative centre of prosperity with a clearly defined set of rival interests and policy preferences that were often at odds, if not anathema, to the Laurentian Consensus. More and more capital and people continue to be drawn to the West, spurring a virtuous circle of prosperity, population growth, and influence.

Third, Ontario's economy and its manufacturing sector in particular, faced steep challenges beginning in the 1990s. Both the diagnosis and the explanation of these challenges are explored in detail elsewhere (Bernard 2009; Macdonald 2008; Wolfe and Gertler 1999). However, Ontario's economy is in the process of restructuring, as is evidenced by a decline in manufacturing sector employment and the relative rise in numbers and duration of unemployment in the province.

National discourse with regard to Ontario now focuses on issues such as whether or not the province is a victim of Dutch Disease, or if it is on the verge of becoming a "rust belt." According to Margaret Wente, a prominent, national columnist, "the mighty engine of Confederation has turned into its rust belt. But nobody in the rest of Canada is feeling particularly sorry for us" (*The Globe and Mail*, 19 June 2012). Such pronouncements are increasingly common.

Fourth, there is growing anxiety about Toronto's position as Canada's corporate headquarters. The Economist magazine recently questioned whether Toronto "has lost its way" and is "being eclipsed" by Calgary. The article notes that, "of the 20 biggest companies in Canada, ten are based in the Toronto area. But six are now in Calgary ... And Calgary has the momentum" (*The Economist*, 18 March 2010).

For proponents of the decline thesis, there are two symbolic nails in the Laurentian coffin. The first was Ontario's qualification for equalization payments in 2009. The emergence of Ontario as a "have not" province confirmed the relative decline of its stature and importance in the federation.

> The transformation of Ontario into a complete waste of time appears to be almost complete ... the province has been reduced to have-not status, the manufacturing base has eroded, Ottawa has been strong-armed into financing a regional development office, unemployment is 8.1% (above the national average and getting worse) and the best solution the government can come up with is a plan to pour money into alternative energy in hopes of jobs (along with about 32 other countries and jurisdictions hoping to do the same thing). (*The National Post*, 22 November 2011)

The second symbolic nail was the election of a majority Conservative government with its political and ideological base located in the West. Traditional Laurentian values, such as the accommodation of Quebec interests, are now largely absent from the federal agenda. In sharp contrast to its prior focus on building Ontario's manufacturing base, Canadian national economic policy is now focused on securing Canada's status as a global energy superpower. The federal Minister of Finance has stated that Alberta is the centre of the Canadian economy today, which in the words of John Ibbitson reads: *"The West isn't just in. It's in charge"* (2011).

A crucial argument here, however, is that the central claims of the decline thesis have been overstated. There is little to suggest that Ontario has been relegated to the economic periphery. Ontario remains Canada's centre for value-added services and manufacturing. For example, Ontario:

- accounted for 37 percent of total Canadian exports, 45 percent of manufacturing sales, and 37 percent of service industries in 2011 (Statistics Canada, CANSIM Tables 228-0034, 304-0014, 379-0025);
- is home to the eleventh largest financial sector in the world (whose employment numbers could soon exceed London, UK) (The Globe and Mail, 4 December 2011);
- attracted $6.1 billion in foreign investment in 2010, second among sub-national jurisdictions in North America (fDi Intelligence 2011);
- is entrenched within a dynamic and highly integrated Great Lakes regional economy representing 30 percent of the US and Canadian population (105 million people) with over $80 billion in exports to the Great Lakes Region in 2011 (Industry Canada 2012).

Ontario has vast amounts of human capital, including:

- half of the country's internationally ranked universities (QS World University Rankings 2011-12);
- post-secondary enrolment of 600,000 students, ten percent of which are international students (Grewal 2010);
- a higher level of post-secondary attainment than any OECD member-state at 63 percent (Commission on the Reform of Ontario's Public Services 2012, chap.7);

- more than 50 percent of Canada's "economic" immigrants (Ontario's Expert Roundtable on Immigration 2012, 9).

All of these assets have the potential to propel Ontario to a place of leadership amongst knowledge-based, advanced economies. A New Ontario is emerging, one that is at the centre of global networks of finance, trade, and commerce, with centres of global leadership in industries as diverse as food processing, asset management, infrastructure financing, business services, and information technology. Two conclusions emerge from this. First, the most important question facing the province is: How will Ontario take advantage of its geographic, human, financial, and natural resource assets? And second, Ontario's relative decline is a story of growing economic vibrancy in other parts of the country, which is good for Canada and liberates Ontario from having to carry a fiscal burden for the country.

CANADA'S NEW POLITICAL ECONOMY AND THE NEW ONTARIO

Although claims that the federal agenda has been permanently captured by the West are hyperbolic, it is clear that the Laurentian elite are indeed no longer in charge. Federal politicians in fact, go out of their way to disassociate themselves from the Consensus.

It is apparently good politics for federal politicians to trash Toronto's "elite." For example, there are only minor repercussions when a federal Minister tells a business audience not to invest in Ontario (CBC 2008). There is barely an outcry when Toronto is snubbed as a potential headquarters for a proposed national securities regulator, despite the security industry being highly concentrated in the city and key to its global competitiveness. Painting your opponent as a "Toronto snob" is considered to be a viable electoral strategy. These actions are symptomatic of a general hostility toward Ontario, equivalent to Trudeau's finger to Alberta.

Canada's fiscal federalism adjusted to Quebec's relative economic decline in the 1970s and 1980s and became more responsive to that province's needs. Equalization became enshrined in the Constitution. The federal government invested billions into Quebec's economic development and transfer payments to Quebec grew significantly. The fiscal arrangements were engineered so that Ontarians would pay the bulk of the bill, which they did willingly.

In contrast, national public policy has *not* adjusted to accommodate the new Ontario and its emerging challenges. On the contrary, there are numerous policy arrangements that are, at worst, discriminatory against Ontario, or at best, benignly negligent. The federal government does not appear to perceive this as a problem.

Historically, Ontario could afford to look the other way. It chose to be a passive player on key national discussions, so long as the framework policies that preserved its prosperity remained in place.

However, the framework conditions are no longer in place. Monetary policy is driven by oil, not manufacturing; tariff barriers are gone; and for the most part (aside from oil and gas pipelines), large scale, national infrastructure development is a relic of the past. Ontario's continued passivity on issues that are now core to its interests and its global ambitionshas the potential to undermine long-term prosperity and competitiveness in the global economy.

THE NEW ONTARIO HAS NEW IMPERATIVES

Neither the federal government nor any federal opposition party have articulated an economic agenda for the future of the province. Federal policy and economic agendas for the other regions are clear, yet federal leaders still fail to think of Ontario as a region with its own distinct interests. This failure can be highlighted by brief reference to some of the most important fiscal, economic, and social issues facing the province: fiscal transfers, labour market policy, and immigration policy.

Federal redistribution of resources away from Ontario through fiscal transfers has not been corrected over the past five years. Despite Ontario's receipt of equalization payments, Ontario still bears a large burden through Canadian fiscal federalism despite its diminished capacity to pay for it.

In 2009-2010, only 34 percent of federal program spending was returned to Ontario. However, Ontario is home to 39 percent of the national population. The result of this disparity was an approximate $12 billion gap (2.1 percent of Ontario's 2009 GDP) in what Ontarians paid into the federation and what they got back (Commission on the Reform of Ontario's Public Services 2012, chap.20).

As the Commission on the Reform of Ontario's Public Services pointed out, "these are resources that would have been available to Ontarians" (2012, chap.20). The federal fiscal transfer system is a significant drain on the province's capacity to invest and continue building the assets necessary to achieve its global ambitions. It is clear that the federal government does not consider this a problem, having offered no proposals to reform Equalization in a manner that would work for Ontario (more detailed discussions on federal fiscal transfers and potential solutions to redress this problem are taken up elsewhere in this book).

Labour market policy is a second important example where federal policies are incompatible with Ontario's interests. Ontario has traditionally been the employment engine of Canada. However, its manufacturing sector and many of its traditional industries were disproportionately impacted by the Great Recession of 2008-9 and growing competition from low labour-cost jurisdictions. As a result, Ontario is experiencing unemployment above the national average, with the duration of unemployment lasting longer in Ontario than elsewhere in Canada.

During the peak of the Great Recession, 38 percent of the unemployed in Ontario were receiving Employment Insurance (EI) benefits from the federal government.

In some other provinces, over 90 percent of the unemployed were receiving benefits (Medow 2011). Although Ontario represented 42 percent of national unemployment in 2009-2010, the province received only 33 percent of the federal training transfer (Mowat Centre Employment Insurance Task Force 2011, 58).

As a result of federal policies, there are huge holes in the safety net for Ontario's workers. More importantly, there is no national human capital strategy in place that responds to Ontario's needs. While other provinces benefit substantially from federal active labour market policies (through EI), Ontario suffers from a significant underinvestment on the part of the federal government. This creates significant challenges for Ontario as it strives to build the skills and human capital needed to compete in the 21st century economy.

Current demographic trends suggest that immigration will account for all net growth in Ontario's working-age population within the next 10 years (Ontario's Expert Roundtable on Immigration 2012, 8). Ontario is expected to face a shortage of almost 2 million skilled workers by 2031 (Miner 2010).

Meanwhile, skilled worker immigration to Ontario has declined by 55 percent since 2001. This decline is due in part, to the exclusion of Ontario from a federal decision to enable some provinces to select skilled immigrants for specific job vacancies in order to meet local labour market needs (Ontario's Expert Roundtable on Immigration 2012).

Unless there are substantial revisions to the federal approach to immigration, the gap between skilled labour need and supply in Ontario will grow, with negative long-term implications for the province's productivity and global competitiveness.

It was once true that when the federal government made big decisions on issues like immigration or labour market policies, Ontario's interests – Laurentian interests – were crucial. This is simply no longer the case. The most important federal policy decisions are no longer made with Ontario's interests in mind.

Although the failure to adjust federal policy in these three key areas is a significant impediment to Ontario's growth and continued prosperity, Ontario has neither articulated significant policy prescriptions aimed at their remedy, nor undertaken a serious campaign to convince Ontario voters of their urgency. In short, voices from the other regions are setting the terms of debate. The voice of the Laurentian system is largely absent.

Admittedly, Ontario Premiers since Bob Rae have challenged the federal government. Mike Harris confronted Ottawa over health transfers. Dalton McGuinty initiated a "fairness campaign" decrying federal treatment of Ontario. In these instances, provincial efforts were tepid and failed to present a coherent and well-articulated vision for national policy that would accommodate Ontario's interests and garner public support. Canada's fiscal arrangements expire after 2013-2014. The federal government is rewriting the rules on Employment Insurance and immigration. We are in a critical period of Ontario's relations with the federal government and Ontario needs to adjust its approach accordingly.

THE NEW ONTARIO NEEDS A NEW NARRATIVE

In the context of multiple competing voices on the national stage, Ontario needs to clearly define, articulate, and defend its interests. This means cultivating support across the general public and building policy capacity to become a policy maker in areas where Ontario has traditionally been a policy taker. Claims of a declining Laurentian Consensus contain elements of truth, but Ontario's relative decline has been aided and abetted by federal policy. Thus far, federal policy makers have demonstrated little interest in supporting Ontario's ambitions through and beyond its current economic transition.

Ontario has not articulated a detailed set of interests with regard to federal transfers, Employment Insurance, and immigration policies, quite possibly because it has not yet defined these interests. The province needs to produce and broadcast evidence-based prescriptions for national policies that are consistent with its new economic realities, its global ambitions, and its evolving place in the federation. By contributing its economic girth and administrative capacity to the national debate, Ontario has the potential to substantially shape the terms of this debate.

Ontarians' perceptions of their province within the federation are shifting. While the rest of Canada expects Ontario to compromise its own interests for the sake of national unity, the Ontario public may no longer be supportive of such a posture, preferring instead a more interest-based approach towards the federation. Ontarians increasingly "resemble other Canadians in believing that there are inequalities in the federation that must be addressed" (Mendelsohn and Matthews 2010). So the question becomes: How can Ontario strategically mobilize this sentiment?

Ontario needs to champion a new narrative centred on the *new* Ontario. Ontario is harnessing its strengths in finance, trade and commerce and is a global leader in these sectors that will define the 21st century economy. The new narrative must present a coherent vision of Ontario's future and the public policies this requires, including the repatriation of Ontario's fiscal resources from the federal government.

To succeed in the era of competing national agendas, Ontario will need to become more confrontational, even if it provokes the ire of commentators who may complain that Ontario is joining a chorus of "whiners." Public servants will need to think more strategically. They will need to predict future intergovernmental challenges and proactively assess the province's interests well in advance of intergovernmental discussions. Most importantly, a growing awareness that Ontario has unique interests will need to be encouraged and cultivated among Ontarians.

Canada's current political economy has displaced the Laurentian Consensus as the prevailing approach to governing. Ontario, however, has been slow to respond to the new, multi-polar dynamic of the Canadian federation. Ontario needs to shake-off the rumours of its decline by exercising its economic and political muscle. It is time for the province to assert its own competing vision, a vision that differs from the traditional Laurentian Thesis, and from the prevailing visions being articulated in other provinces and by the federal government.

REFERENCES

Bernard, A. 2009. *Trends in manufacturing employment*. Ottawa: Statistics Canada Catalogue No. 75-001-X.

The Canadian Press. 2008. "Flaherty calls Ontario 'last place' to invest." *CBC News*, March 1. http://www.cbc.ca/news/canada/toronto/story/2008/03/01/flaherty-budget.html

Cameron, D. 1994. "Post-modern Ontario and the Laurentian Thesis." In *Canada: The State of the Federation 1994*, ed. D.M. Brown and J. Hiebert, 109-134. Kingston: Institute of Intergovernmental Relations.

Commission on the Reform of Ontario's Public Services. 2012. Public Services for Ontarians: a Path to Sustainability and Excellence. Toronto: Government of Ontario.

Grewal, D. 2010. Policy Paper: International Students. Toronto: Ontario Undergraduate Student Alliance. http://www.ousa.ca/research-type/policy-papers/page/3/

Hébert, C. 2007. Ontario Now Taking a Back Seat in the Federation. Toronto Star, 13 July. At http://www.thestar.com/opinion/2007/07/13/ontario_now_taking_a_back_seat_in_the_federation.html.

Homer-Dixon, T. 2012. "All's Not Lost, Ontario. The Future is Green, Not Black." *The Globe and Mail*, April 7. http://www.theglobeandmail.com/commentary/alls-not-lost-ontario-the-future-is-green-not-black/article4098180/.

Ibbitson, J. 2011. "The Collapse of the Laurentian Consensus: On the Westward Shift of Canadian Power and Values." Literary Review of Canada, 5 December 2011. http://review canada.ca/essays/2012/01/01/the-collapse-of-the-laurentian-consensus/ (accessed 15 September 2012).

Ibbitson, J. 2011. "The Common Thread in Ottawa's Moves This Week? They All Point West." *The Globe and Mail*, October 21. http://www.theglobeandmail.com/news/politics/john-ibbitson/the-common-thread-in-ottawas-moves-this-week-they-all-point-west/article2210004/

Industry Canada. 2012. Trade Data Online. http://www.ic.gc.ca/eic/site/tdo-dcd.nsf/eng/Home (accessed 2 October 2012).

Macdonald, R. 2008. Terms of Trade in Central Canada. Ottawa: Statistics Canada Catalogue No. 11-624-M – No. 22.

Marotte, B. 2011. "Toronto's Rise as a Global Finance Centre." *The Globe and Mail*, December 4. http://www.theglobeandmail.com/globe-investor/investment-ideas/torontos-rise-as-a-global-finance-centre/article4236488/.

McParland, K. 2011. "Immigrants Detect the Whiff of Decline in Ontario." *National Post*, November 22. http://fullcomment.nationalpost.com/2011/11/22/immigrants-detect-the-whiff-of-decline-in-ontario/

Medow, J. 2011. Hidden Regional Differentiation: EI and Unequal Federal Support for Low Income Workers. Toronto: Mowat Centre.

Mendelsohn, M. and J.S. Matthews. 2010. The New Ontario: The Shifting Attitudes of Ontarians Toward the Federation. Toronto: Mowat Centre.

Miner, R. 2010. People Without Jobs, Jobs Without People: Ontario's Labour Market Future. Miner and Miner Management Consultants. http://www.collegesontario.org/research/research_reports/people-without-jobs-jobs-without-people-final.pdf

Mowat Centre EI Task Force. 2011. Making It Work: The Final Recommendations of the
　　Mowat Centre EI Task Force. Toronto: Mowat Centre.

Ontario's Expert Roundtable on Immigration. 2012. Expanding Our Routes to Success.
　　Toronto: Government of Ontario.

QS World University Rankings. 2011-12. http://www.topuniversities.com/

Statistics Canada. CANSIM Tables: 228-0034, 304-0014, 379-0025. Ottawa: Statistics
　　Canada

"The Charms of Calgary and the Gloom of Toronto." 2010. The Economist, March 18. http://
　　www.economist.com/node/15726687

Wente, M. 2012. "Go West, Young Canadians." *The Globe and Mail,* June 19. http://www.
　　theglobeandmail.com/commentary/go-west-young-canadians/article544669/

Wolfe, D.A. and M.S. Gertler. 1999. Globalization and Economic Restructuring in Ontario:
　　From Industrial Heartland to Learning Region? Paper prepared for the NECSTS/
　　RICTES-99 Conference on Regional Innovation Systems in Europe. University of Toronto.

5

REGIONALISM IN POLITICAL ATTITUDES, 1993 TO 2010

J. Scott Matthews, Matthew Mendelsohn, and Randy Besco

Le régionalisme a une influence indéniable sur la vie politique canadienne. Notre histoire est marquée de nombreux tournants qui ont révélé ou progressivement établi d'importants clivages politiques. On peut donc s'étonner que les chercheurs se soient si rarement in-téressés aux variations régionales des comportements politiques. Soucieux de combler au moins partiellement cette lacune, les auteurs ont structuré ce chapitre autour de la question implicitement soulevée par l'observation de Gidengil et coll. : *Que signifie le régionalisme en matière de comportement politique ? Et leurs données racontent une histoire en deux volets, à la fois simple et nuancée. Elles montrent d'abord que face à d'importants enjeux politiques, les différences d'attitude entre régions se sont amoindries ces dernières décennies. Mais elles révèlent aussi que notre vie politique reste clairement dominée par le région-alisme, au sens où des écarts grandissants séparent les régions en matière de processus intergouvernementaux et de politiques régionales. Qu'ils soient plus ou moins fondés, ces comportements risquent de compliquer dans les années à venir l'adoption de mesures visant à réduire le déficit, à renouveler les transferts financiers ou à combattre les changements climatiques sans exacerbation des tensions interrégionales.*

INTRODUCTION

The impact of regionalism in Canadian political life is unmistakable. Looking across our history we observe numerous critical turning points that reflected, or came to define, important political cleavages along regional lines – the "conscription crises" of the First and Second World Wars, the collapse of the wheat economy and the rise of the Progressives, the ascent of Social Credit and the CCF-NDP, the Quiet Revolution in Quebec and decades of constitutional turmoil, the National Energy Program, Brian Mulroney's grand coalition and its eventual demise into a pair of manifestly regionalist alternatives – the Bloc Québécois and the Reform Party, and so on. The list is virtually endless.

It is curious, therefore, that regional variation in political attitudes has so rarely been a focus for scholars of Canadian political behaviour. Indeed, notwithstanding formidable literatures on the impact of region in other areas of Canadian political life, students of survey research and political attitudes have had little to say about the nature and psychology of regional differences, especially recently.[1] In introducing one of the rare analyses of regionalism in voting behaviour, Elisabeth Gidengil and colleagues tellingly remark that "[t]he basic facts of regional voting are well known. Much less clear is what they mean" (1999, 247).

This chapter begins to address this gap in our knowledge about Canadian regionalism. Our project is framed by the larger question implicit in Gidengil et al.'s observation above, *what does regionalism in political behaviour mean?* We assume that the "meaning" that matters largely involves the views of Canadians themselves. Therefore, as an operational matter, we ask, what is the nature of regional difference in political attitudes? Regional effects in political attitudes may be great, or they may be small. They may be quite generic in structure – extending across many dimensions of political conflict in a homogeneous fashion – or sharply differentiated by the domain under consideration. Most critically for those interested in Canada's political prospects, regional differences in political attitudes may be stable or they may be in flux – regionalism in political attitudes may grow or shrink over time.

To the task of understanding regionalism in political attitudes we bring a wealth of information from two sources. First, we analyze data across two decades of the Canadian Election Study (CES), covering all elections from 1993 to 2008. Second, we examine the Portraits of Canada surveys and a more recent survey using the same questions conducted by the Mowat Centre.[2] Similar to the CES, The Portraits of Canada-Mowat Centre (PC-MC) series offers longitudinal coverage of political attitudes, although over a slightly shorter interval from 1998 to 2010. Importantly, the CES and PC-MC surveys offer leverage on different attitudinal domains relevant to Canadian regionalism. Whereas the former offers excellent coverage of views on a host of long-standing conflicts over substantive issues of public policy, the latter provides unique indicators of attitudes on the processes of federalism and federal-provincial relations.

---

[1] See Simeon and Elkins (1971); Blake (1972), and Gidengil et al. (1999).

[2] Complete methodological details of the Canadian Election Studies and the Portraits of Canada surveys can be obtained from the Canadian Opinion Research Archive in the School of Policy Studies at Queen's University (www.queensu.ca/cora). Details of the Mowat Centre survey are reported in Mendelsohn and Matthews (2010).

We conclude, among other things, that a proper assessment of regionalism in political attitudes must be attentive to these two domains – of public policy *substance* and federal-provincial *process*. The reason is that regionalism operates quite differently when the object of evaluation shifts from the ends to the means of Canadian federalism. To summarize our findings, regional differences regarding the ends of public policy are small and getting smaller. On the other hand, regional differences over the nature of federal-provincial relations are big and getting bigger. It is also important, and somewhat ironic, that the most significant over-time developments in regionalism are confined to the political attitudes of Ontarians.

WHAT OTHERS HAVE FOUND

The vast geography of Canada has generated a correspondingly vast literature on explaining the significance of regions and regional differences. While some countries have "too much history," Canada, it is said, has too much geography. Although regions are universally considered to be important, there is little consensus on how they affect citizens. Risking oversimplification, we might roughly categorize this literature into four areas – culture, political economy, institutions, and attitudes.

Much of the early literature on regionalism places the emphasis on formative events and the ways these shaped the basic ideals of regional societies. The differing actions and opinions of regions reflect the history and ideas of the past. Perhaps the premier examples are Lipset's account of the American Revolution and Canada's lack of one, (1968, 1990), Bell and Tepperman on the migration of loyalists (1979), and Horowitz's discussion of Canada's "tory touch" (1966), although debates still continue (Ajzenstat and Smith 1997; Wiseman 2007). These authors argue, among other things, that we can attribute differences in opinion among Canadians to historical settlement patterns, and the different ideals that settlers brought with them. Naturally there is disagreement on the details (Forbes 1988; Wiseman 1988), but the key is that we should understand current regional differences in their historical context. The roots of regionalism are not based in economics or institutions, but in contingent – and generally long-past – events. As a result of the long historical time frame emphasized, we expect that regional differences would not change dramatically over a short time period.

Contrary to this focus on the historical development of ideas and political culture, others define regionalism as the product of patterns of economic development and policy responses. Early Canadian political economy (Innis 1930; 1940), focused on the development of "staple" resources as required by imperial and continental relationships. Later elaborations of "hinterland-heartland" scholarship, including Macpherson (1953), Mallory (1954), and others, argued that the hinterland regions were an "internal colony" of Canada, placing the federal government at the heart of economic conflict. For these writers the prime movers are conflicting economic interests between centre and periphery. Important political events, like the emergence of Social Credit, are simply reflections of these economic forces (Mallory 1954, 4). Perhaps the most influential recent author is Janine Brodie, who argued that "regions are political creations that state development strategies cumulatively impose upon the geographic landscape" (1990, 77). It is uneven development that drives regionalism – both the calls for its amelioration and the concentration of economic power. In this literature, southwestern Ontario and the Laurentian region were the economic heartland that treated the rest of the country as an internal colony.

Although political economists recognized the role of the state in shaping economic conflicts, institutional regionalists focus more directly on the role of the state in shaping society. As Donald Smiley notes, our institutions have "a pervasive bias in favor of mobilizing interests which are territorially based and frustrating the political expression of interests and attitudes which are largely non-territorial" (1977, 450). Richard Simeon expressed a similar position, noting that institutions are not simply products of society, but "independent forces" which exert their own influence once established (1975, 504). That institutions matter is relatively non-controversial. The real question is to how much they distort the "inputs" of public desires.

On this issue Alan Cairns had perhaps the most pessimistic view of the effects of institutions. He famously showed how our electoral system favored territorially concentrated parties (1968). Cairns took this argument even farther, arguing that institutions not only distort political outcomes, but dominate and shape the society that they purportedly serve. Governments do not simply strive to follow their constitutional mandates, but are "aggressive actors" (1977) seeking to expand their areas of control. Indeed the literature on province-building makes clear that the process reflected provincial intentions (Black and Cairns 1966; Pratt 1977). While this claim is controversial, there is little doubt that provincial governments often have an interest in exacerbating regional conflicts and reinforcing whatever provincial or regional cultures and identities exist. There can also be little doubt that, until the 1990s, Ontario had been a far less "aggressive actor" than other provinces in the latter half of the twentieth century.

A final area worth review is the work focused on regional differences in the attitudes and values of citizens, both toward policy and toward their governments. One of the earlier students of differences in attitudes and voting behavior was Mildred Schwartz (1974), who argued that Canada was composed of distinct communities and interests, with different regional identities, and that these differences were reflected in voting, party identification and political orientations. Unfortunately, as Smiley (1977) notes, Schwartz did not control for factors such as income, age, or other standard control variables. Blake (1972) examined the effects of region on voting patterns with more sophisticated models, and also suggested that region has a considerable effect on political outcomes, although he moderated this conclusion in later work (1978).

In perhaps the most influential study of regional attitudes, Simeon and Elkins (1980) found small and shrinking differences between provinces on policy issues. These small differences in attitudes were, nonetheless, coupled with a strong sense of "regional feeling" (Clark et al. 1979). Ailsa Henderson has updated Simeon and Elkins' analysis, and questions if what we have been measuring thus far in political culture research is not the existence of provincial sub-cultures, but micro-regional variations. In addition, she argued that since regional clusters perform as effectively as provincial boundaries in accounting for variations in political attitudes and behavior, there is reason to doubt, at the very least, the impact of provincial institutions (Henderson 2004).

In sum, there has been a large literature in Canada on the importance of region and regionalism, with a heavy emphasis on historical analysis of culture, interests and institutions. In more recent decades, empirical studies focused on differences in attitudes or identities have complemented the other approaches. Two general comments should be highlighted as a preface to our chapter. First, the major studies are not recent and do not capture the significant evolution of Canadian regions that has occurred in the past two decades, including increased immigration and the importance of global communication flows. Second, the analysis of regionalism has focused far more intensely on Atlantic Canada, Western Canada and Quebec than on Ontario.

DATA AND ANALYTICAL APPROACH

We use data from the CES for the six elections between 1993 and 2008. The CES in these years was a multi-mode, panel survey, with campaign-period and post-election waves conducted by telephone, and a second post-election wave delivered in the form of a pencil-and-paper mail-back survey. These data contain a very large number of survey items relevant to diverse domains of public policy, and to respondents' general orientations toward the political system, including toward federalism. For two reasons, however, the lion's share of these items is not available to us. To maximize the number of respondents in any given analysis and, equally, to minimize the effects of panel attrition, we confine ourselves to questions asked in the campaign-period and post-election waves of these studies.[3] More

---

[3] Questions from the mailback surveys, therefore, are excluded. These data are highly unlikely to closely represent the general population, as CES response rates tend to fall precipitously between the post-election and mailback waves. The concern is that this relatively self-selected group of respondents are highly interested and engaged in political matters – so much so that they trouble themselves to fill out and return an extended pencil-and-paper survey on political attitudes. This level of cognitive engagement with politics is clearly out of step with the Canadian population as a whole (Fournier 2002).

importantly, we only utilize questions that have been asked in the same – or highly similar – ways over the several surveys. These two constraints sharply reduce the items available for analysis.

Even so, the available items give broad coverage of Canadian political attitudes. Our CES-derived dependant variables are divided into two categories – welfare state attitudes and non-welfare state attitudes. Regarding the former, we have three questions concerning support for spending in various policy areas: welfare, health care, and education. Roughly speaking, the items assess the priority attached to funding in these areas. Notably, the items have proved useful in previous analyses of Canadians' welfare state attitudes (Matthews and Erickson 2005, 2008) and in Canadian and cross-national work on the link between public opinion and policy outcomes (Soroka and Wlezien 2004; 2010). Furthermore, previous research suggests that responses to spending in these areas are differently structured, a reflection of the varying entitlement structures involved (Matthews and Erickson 2008). Building on comparative accounts of welfare state politics (e.g., Korpi 1980; Esping-Anderson 1990), this research suggests that programs that involve means-testing, such as welfare, are more likely to divide Canadians than more "universalistic" programs, such as health care and education, that are in principle accessible by all. This chapter offers an original assessment of this claim with respect to regional divisions.

To these spending items we add a measure concerning the relative roles of government and the private sector in job creation. The measure asks for level of agreement with the proposition "government should leave it entirely to the private sector to create jobs." Previous research reveals that, at least through the 1990s and into 2000, this measure taps something other than value commitments concerning capitalism and the proper role of government in the market. Matthews and Erickson argue that the measure indicates "assessments of the technical capacity of the welfare state – that is, the question at stake is the ability of government to take effective action in the pursuit of its social and economic goals, rather than the nature of those social and economic goals, as such" (2008, 17). Interestingly, the disposition would seem to constitute a rare source of cleavage in Canadian attitudes toward universal social programs (Matthews and Erickson 2008, 14, 17). That said, it is not obvious how – or even if – regional political currents might be reflected in this item.

As regards the non-welfare state items, we have items touching on security and trade, racial diversity, the "national question," and moral issues. Using the same instrumentation as applied in the domain of social spending, we tap the priority Canadians attach to defence spending. In view of the centrality of economic relations with the United States to the history of regional conflict (see, especially, Johnston, Brady, Blais and Crete 1992, Ch. 2), we include a measure of attitudes toward the "closeness" of "Canada's ties" to its southern neighbour. In deference to the political importance and contentiousness of racial and ethnic diversity in contemporary Canada (Banting 2008), we also include a measure of support for "doing more for racial minorities." The place of Quebec in Canada is a regional issue without peer. Accordingly, we tap the domain with an indicator – "how much do you think should be done for Quebec?" – that has proven discriminating in recent work on the spatial foundations of the Canadian party system (Johnston 2008). Finally, regarding questions of morality, we have indicators of support for free access to abortion and for capital punishment. However, as we lack consistent measurement across the full period, we must confine this analysis to 2000 and after. Note that, in the analysis, all CES variables are coded to vary across the (0,1) interval, where 1 indicates "support for" or "agreement with" the object under evaluation.

From the PC-MC data series we extract four variables, each of which addresses a different, albeit related, dimension of federal-provincial relations. Coverage is somewhat inconsistent in temporal terms, as is apparent in the analysis below. Critically, however, for all items we have measurement at both the beginning and end of the analysis period, i.e., in 1998 and 2010, permitting assessments of over-time change.

Our most consistent measure in the PC-MC surveys indicates global evaluations of one's province's treatment at the national level: respondents are asked if their "province [is] treated with the respect it deserves in Canada or not." While rather diffuse in semantic content, on its face, the item would seem to address sentiments in the affectively-charged domain of symbolic recognition – attitudes that have been highly salient in regional conflicts over the years (Taylor 1993; Mendelsohn 2003). To this item we add more narrowly cast indicators of perceptions of one's province's "share" of political influence "on important national decisions in Canada" and perceptions of the dynamics in one's province's political influence. Finally, we have an item focused on the concrete and generally contentious business of federal-provincial fiscal transfers. Respondents are asked if their province receives "more than," "less than," or "about its fair share" in federal spending on "programs and on transfers."

It should be noted that, although we have chosen questions to avoid wording changes as much as possible, a number of the items included in the analysis do contain wording shifts over time. By and large, our sense is that these changes are not of great concern. Moreover, the evolving implications of word choice and social context mean that even identical wording provides no guarantee of conceptual equivalence. At various points, however, where a wording change seems to have produced systematic effects, we are careful to describe the substantive consequences.[4]

---

[4]A related issue concerns the treatment of missing values. Generally, middle values were assigned to those replying "don't know" or refusing to answer, since such responses likely imply attitudinal ambivalence. However, for questions that were potentially controversial, such as those on abortion or racial minorities, we excluded refusals, since those answers may mask answers that are seen to be socially unacceptable.

Our basic analytical approach is simple: we examine regional differences in the attitudes above, and also over-time changes in the magnitude of these differences. We follow standard practice by defining region as a four-category nominal variable, separating Atlantic Canada, the West, and Quebec from Ontario (the reference category in all regression analyses reported). Although Smiley (1987, 164) and others have suggested that British Columbia might properly be treated as its own region, for reasons of scope, we focus on the four-part distinction. Moreover, the small number of observations for British Columbia in any given year makes attention to this finer issue somewhat inadvisable.

In assessing regional differences in policy attitudes, we must attend to the proposition that regions are merely "empty containers" (Simeon and Elkins 1971) and that, consequently, regional political differences are simply "artifacts" of differences in regions' social composition. As Gidengil et al. explain, this view implies,

> that people belonging to similar social categories share the same basic political orientations *regardless* of region of residence. "True" regional differences are present when people belonging to the *same* social categories manifest *different* political preferences from one region of the country to another. (1999, 249) (emphasis in original).

Accordingly, our analysis must attempt to control, as much as possible, for exposure to such structural effects. Rather than reporting simple comparisons of means or frequencies across regions, therefore, we estimate ordinary least-squares regression models of the policy attitudes and report predicted values. These models include measures of the following socio-demographics: income, education, language (French vs. English-speaking), marital status, age, visible minority status, gender, and employment status.[5] Several of these controls reflect explicit claims made in regionalism scholarship. Smiley, for example, suggests that Atlantic Canada's distinctive political views are largely a result of the region's high rate of unemployment (1987, 171). Likewise, levels of income and education may be connected to patterns of regional economic domination (cf. Brodie 1990). Some of the controls we include are not likely to vary from region to region – gender, for example – but help to enhance the precision of our estimates, nonetheless.

For the examination of views on federal-provincial relations, we are able to rely on simpler analytics: we simply report cross-tabulations of the various measures by region. Arguments about compositional effects have not been applied to such attitudes and perceptions, as the link between demographic characteristics (region excepted) and evaluations of the federal system is difficult to imagine.

While our analytical aims are primarily descriptive, it bears noting that significant system-level variation over the analysis period allows suggestive conclusions about the impact of the political context of regionalism. Jointly, our data cover seventeen

---

[5]Precise details of coding for these variables are available from the authors. Note that the mean of income was imputed to those who did not give a valid response on this item.

years of Canada's political history, including six elections, two changes of government and four prime ministers. Moreover, we have data from three party systems.
While we do not observe Canadians prior to 1993, the 1993 election was fought
prior to the implosion of the Progressive Conservatives (PCs). The elections of 1997
and 2000 occurred under quite different conditions. The right was divided between
the PCs and the Reform – later the Canadian Alliance – party, and the separatist
Bloc Québécois competed for official opposition status in the House of Commons.
The 2004 election witnessed another, ultimately pivotal, change – a reunited right
under Stephen Harper and the Conservative Party of Canada.

POLICY ATTITUDES ACROSS THE REGIONS

In line with discussion above, in Figures 1 and 2 we isolate the "pure" effect
of region by plotting predicted values from the regression models.[6] For a given
combination of region and year, we compute the predicted value of the attitude
under consideration for an individual who is otherwise at the national average (in
a given year) on the socio-demographic components of the model. The vertical
distance between the lines, therefore, solely reflects the unique impact of residence
in a given region. Taking the top-left panel of the figure, for instance, we see that
an otherwise average individual living in Atlantic Canada or Quebec in 1993 was
moderately more supportive of welfare spending than her counterpart in either
Ontario or the West.

As it happens, roughly speaking, this pattern of regional difference in welfare
spending attitudes persists over the analysis period. Atlantic Canadians or Quebecers
are most, or second-most, supportive of welfare spending in every year. Conversely,
Ontarians or Westerners are least, or second-least, supportive of such spending in
all years. Overall, regional differences are quite modest on support for welfare
spending, with the scope of regional variation covering little more, and sometimes
a little less, than one-tenth of the range of the survey item. Indeed, from 2000
to 2006 these regional differences are generally not statistically significant. The
exception is 2008, when support for welfare spending spikes across the country,
particularly among Atlantic Canadians. Presumably the pattern reflects the dismal
economic conditions surrounding that election, which was fought amidst a global
financial crisis.

---

[6]Coefficient estimates for the regression models are available from the authors. While
we do not pursue the issue here, it bears noting that the addition of controls to the models
does little to disturb the substance of the results. That is to say, those regional differences
in policy attitudes as exist are largely not a function of compositional differences but are
"true regional differences" in the sense intended by Gidengil et al. 1999.

Figure 1: Welfare State Attitudes by Year by Region, 1993-2008*

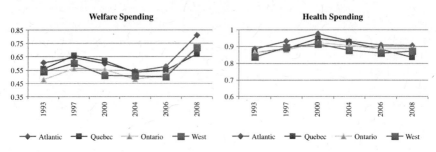

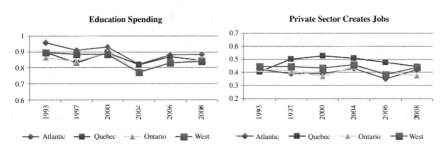

Source: Canadian Election Studies, 1993-2008
*Predicted values, controlling for various socio-demographics

Regional differences in support for health care and education are typically even smaller and less consistent. This comports with the speculation above that these programs, owing to their universalistic entitlement structures, should tend not to divide Canadians. Indeed, looking across the pattern of regional effects on support for health care and education spending, all but nine of the thirty-six coefficient estimates fail to reach statistical significance (at the 0.05 level), and none do so after 2004. Those differences that do reach conventional significance thresholds are tiny – generally covering about one-twentieth of the range of the measure concerned. The largest difference by far is between Ontarians and Atlantic Canadians in 1993 on the priority of education spending. Ontarians are significantly less supportive than those in the Atlantic region in that year, a difference covering about one-tenth of the range of observed opinion. Tellingly, this difference erodes almost completely by 2008.

If the regions are – or have been – divided on the welfare state, then it is largely with respect to the relative roles of government and the market in job creation. The variance is mostly a function of the views of Quebecers. Between 1997 and 2006, respondents in this province are significantly, in both a substantive and sta-tistical sense, more sceptical of government's role in job creation than are other

Canadians. The high point is 2000, when the difference is almost one-sixth of the range of the measure. Differences in views among the other regions are trivial. While we cannot pursue the issue in this paper, the distinctiveness of Quebec after 1993 – and, further, the erosion of this distinctiveness over time – suggests that the pattern reflects, in some degree, the historical rhythms of the unity debate. The sequence of events related to this issue in the 1990s (e.g., the stunning success of the Bloc Québécois in 1993, the Parti Québécois' victory in the province in 1994, the referendum of 1995) no doubt troubled Quebecers' confidence in government's capacity to deliver in diverse areas of public policy, including on job creation. And indeed, there is good evidence that diffuse evaluations of the political system can, in extraordinary circumstances, be affected by short-run political developments.[7]

Turning to non-welfare state attitudes, the pattern of generally modest regional differences continues, with two important exceptions. One exception is attitudes on defence spending, in relation to which we observe significant regional differences in every year. Aside from moderately stronger support for such spending in Atlantic Canada at two points (in 1997 and 2008 the difference is statistically significant), regionalism in regards to defence spending support is entirely a story of Quebec versus the rest. In every year, Quebecers are significantly less supportive of defence spending than all other Canadians. The largest differences are in 1997 and 2000, when the gap between, for example, Ontario and Quebec covers one-fifth of the range of the spending support measure. Perhaps more importantly, in four of the six years in the analysis, the nature of the regional differences is such that Quebec and the rest of Canada are on opposite sides of this issue, with the average Quebecer seeking less spending on defence and the average Canadian outside Quebec seeking more. Of course, this finding reflects a long-standing pattern of division between French-speaking and English-speaking Canada, one that mirrors divisions in the early twentieth century over Canada's "imperial role" (Johnston 2008, 828-9). That said, the pan-regional growth in support for defence spending after 2000 – in the wake of 9/11 and the start of Canada's involvement in the war in Afghanistan – also bears noting. While initial regional divisions were not eroded, all Canadians seem to have responded in similar ways to these events.

The second exception to the general pattern of inter-regional consensus in non-welfare state attitudes is both more dramatic and less surprising. Predictably, Quebecers are far more convinced than other Canadians that "more should be done" for Quebec. At its largest (in 1997), the gap between those in Quebec and elsewhere covers almost one-third of the range of the measure. Less obvious is the pattern of uniformity among the other provinces. Contrary to stereotype, Westerners are quite similar in their views on this issue when compared with Ontarians and Atlantic Canadians. To be sure, those in the West are less supportive than others of Quebec's aspirations, and the difference is statistically significant in most years.

---

[7]See Hetherington 1998 for work on the dynamics of political trust.

Figure 2: Non-welfare State Attitudes by Year by Region, 1993-2008*

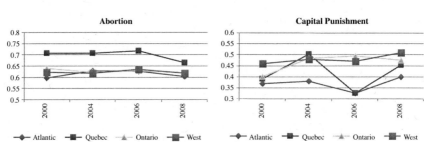

Source: Canadian Election Studies, 1993-2008
*Predicted values, controlling for various socio-demographics

That said, the critical fact is that, even at its largest, this difference covers little more than one-twentieth of the range of observed opinion.

Looking across the remaining attitudes plotted in Figure 2, there are few systematic regional differences. On the issue of ties to the United States, the handful of significant regional effects that emerge are small and inconsistent. For instance, Quebecers are more supportive than Ontarians of close ties in 1993 and 1997, but this modest difference disappears in 2000, and then reverses in 2004. Other variations on this item over time are similar. There is something of a pattern across the regions with regard to "doing more for" racial minorities. Quebecers and Atlantic Canadians consistently give more positive responses than other Canadians, although the size of the differences fluctuates greatly. The typical inter-regional gap is modest – between 0.05 and 0.10 points.[8] The largest regional differences on women's access to abortion are in a similarly small range of magnitude, and always between Quebec and the rest of Canada. Finally, the pattern of regional effects on support for capital punishment is somewhat intriguing. The most consistent result is the gap between Westerners and Atlantic Canadians, with the former more accepting of capital punishment than the latter in every year. The views of Ontarians and Quebecers are more inconsistent. They are sometimes as conservative as Westerners and sometimes as liberal as Atlantic Canadians. Some of this may reflect the issue content and events of election campaigns, particularly the "Boxing Day shooting" prior to the 2006 election. In any event, the larger point is that on this issue, as on almost all other policy matters, regional differences are modest.

Figures 3 and 4 summarize the dynamics of regional differences in policy attitudes. Plotted are "total regional effects," which are equal to the sum of the absolute values of the coefficient estimates on the regional terms in the regression models. As these lines tend toward zero, regionalism can be said to be on the decline; if the lines move away from zero, regional differences are on the rise. Generally speaking, we see no evidence here of an upward trend in regionalism. While a couple of plots indicate recent upticks in regional differences (health spending, private sector creates jobs), all others show flat or downward trends over time. The most striking downward trends are the declines for welfare and education spending, and on "doing more for Quebec."

To summarize our findings so far, the magnitudes of regional differences in policy attitudes are generally small and, to the extent we observe over-time trends, those trends are negative. However, in regards to two matters we observe large regional differences. On the aspirations of Quebec, Canadians are predictably – and greatly – divided. Relatively smaller, yet still notable, are differences between Quebec and the rest of Canada on the issue of defence spending. We discuss the significance of these results in the Conclusion.

---

[8]The sharp increase on this measure in 2000, irrespective of region, seems to reflect an increase in the number of response categories in that year, a wording change that continues across the period. The change permits those who would like to "do more" for racial minorities to express a moderate view ("somewhat more"), whereas prior to that year the only available option for such respondents was "more." Presumably, the binary nature of the earlier question forced some answers into the middle category.

Figure 3: Total Regional Effect on Welfare State Attitudes, 1993-2008*

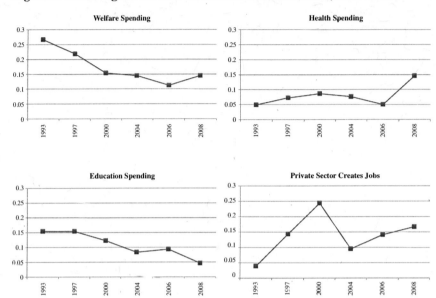

Source: Canadian Election Studies, 1993-2008
*Absolute value of regional coefficients, summed, controlling for various
socio-demographics

REGIONALISM AND VIEWS OF FEDERAL-PROVINCIAL RELATIONS

The image of regional consensus on (most) policy attitudes sharply contrast
with Canadians' views on federalism and federal-provincial relations. Before
turning to specific findings, we must note that, for the remaining measures discussed in this chapter, evidence of regionalism is not to be found in increasing
inter-regional variance in attitudes. Rather, growing regionalism is implied as
the mean of a given attitude increases within a region because the evaluations
themselves, which concern the quality of federal-provincial relations, are direct
measures of regionalist sentiments. That is, as each of these sentiments becomes
more widely held, the magnitude of regionally-focused political grievances would
appear to be on the rise.

Figure 4: Total Regional Effect on Non-welfare State Attitudes*

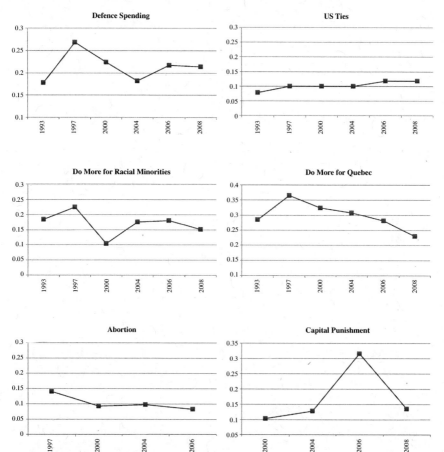

Source: Canadian Election Studies, 1993-2008

*Absolute value of regional coefficients, summed, controlling for various socio-demographics

Figure 5 reports levels of perceived "disrespect" of the respondent's province over time, by region. We have continuous annual coverage on this item from 1998 to 2002, and two further readings in 2004 and 2010. Judged by this item, most Canadians' views on federal-provincial relations have been consistently sour – and are becoming more so. Prior to 2010, outside Ontario, a majority (or, in two cases, virtual majority) of respondents in every region felt that their province was not "treated with the respect it deserves in Canada." Indeed, in most years, roughly 60 percent of respondents outside Ontario have taken this view. In Ontario, by contrast, a minority of less than 30 percent felt the province was "disrespected" in this way. This was until 2010, the first year in which a majority – 51 percent – of Ontarians join other Canadians in feeling their province is not treated with the proper level of respect on the national scene. As the figure reveals, this reflects a massive, nearly 100-percent increase in this sentiment in the province between 2004 and 2010. Elsewhere, over-time change has been modest. Even in Atlantic Canada, which leads the country in feelings of provincial disrespect, temporal variation is modest.

Figure 5: Perceived "Disrespect" Over Time by Region, 1998-2010*

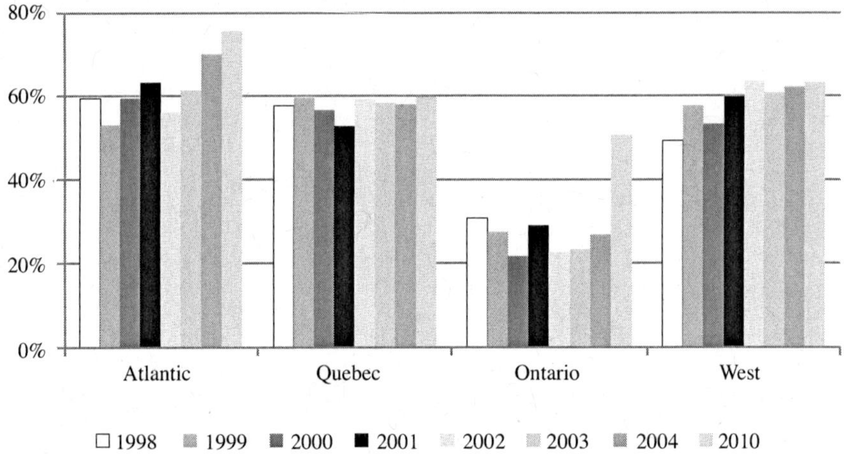

Source: Centre for Research and Information on Canada, *Portraits of Canada Surveys, 1998-2002*; Centre for Research and Information on Canada, *Portraits of Canada Survey, 2004*; Mowat Centre for Policy Innovation, *Survey*, 2010
*Bars indicate (valid) percentage answering "no" when asked: "Is your province treated with the respect it deserves in Canada or not?"

As suggested above, the question of "respect" is likely to elicit fairly affective and symbolic responses. It is interesting to observe, therefore, that significant regional grievances are also evinced on a measure tapping perceptions on the more concrete issue of one's province's "influence" on "important national decisions." Figure 6 reveals that Canadians in Atlantic and Western Canada have consistently concluded that their provinces receive "less than their fair share" of political influence. Indeed, by 2010, this view had become virtually hegemonic in the

Figure 6: Perceived "Influence Deficit" Over Time by Region, 1998-2010*

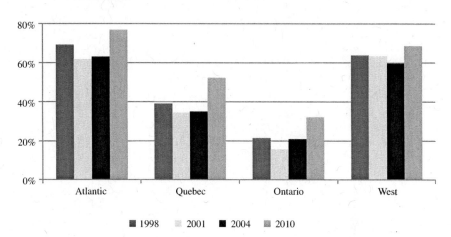

Source: Centre for Research and Information on Canada, *Portraits of Canada Surveys, 1998-2002*; Centre for Research and Information on Canada, *Portraits of Canada Survey, 2004*; Mowat Centre for Policy Innovation, *Survey*, 2010

*Bars indicate (valid) percentage answering "less than its fair share" when asked: "In your opinion, how much influence does your province have on important national decisions in Canada?"

Atlantic provinces. In that year, this evaluation was shared by almost 80 percent of respondents in that region. Quebecers and, particularly, Ontarians have been comparatively sanguine about their level of influence. However, even in Central Canada, the figure indicates that perceptions of an "influence deficit" seem to be increasing. Ontarians' and Quebecers' own perceptions of trends in provincial political influence parallel these findings. When asked in 2010 if their province's "influence on important national decisions" is "increasing, decreasing or staying about the same," almost half of Ontarians – 50 percent – answer "decreasing"; just eight percent of Ontarians think the province's influence is "increasing," a lower figure than in any other region. Likewise, 38 percent of Quebecers think their province's influence is decreasing. Perceptions are comparatively bullish in the West, where more than twice as many as in Ontario – 18 percent – think their province's influence is increasing.

Finally, Figure 7 reveals that the sense of "inter-regional unfairness" extends to views on federal programs and fiscal transfers. On this measure we have just two readings that happily bookend the analysis period. In 1998, only Atlantic Canada contained a majority that felt its region received less than its fair share. In Quebec,

Figure 7: Perceived "Transfer Deficit" Over Time by Region, 1998-2010*

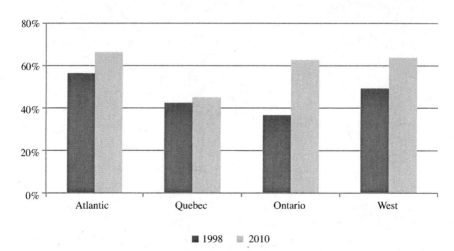

■ 1998   ■ 2010

Source: Centre for Research and Information on Canada, *Portraits of Canada Surveys, 1998-2002*; Mowat Centre for Policy Innovation, *Survey*, 2010
*Bars indicate (valid) percentage answering "less than its fair share" when asked: "Thinking about all the money the federal government spends on different programs and on transfers to the provinces, do you think your province receives... more than its fair share/less than its fair share/about its fair share?"

Ontario and the West, this was a minority view (although narrowly so in the latter region). By 2010, a majority in three regions believed that their province received less than its fair share of federal dollars. The exception to the pattern is Quebec; even there, however, perceptions of a "transfer deficit" have increased over the years. Most remarkable is the growing sense of grievance in Ontario. In this province, discontent over fiscal federalism represents a major break with the past. The last time Canadians were queried on the issue, just 37 percent of Ontarians felt the province received less than it deserved in federal spending, making the province an outlier and remarkably satisfied when compared to other provinces. Today, Ontario's level of dissatisfaction over federal spending is actually above the national average.

Overall, then, in marked contrast to the pattern of growing – or, at least, stable – regional consensus on most policy attitudes, views on federal-provincial relations are contentious and becoming more so. Ironically, what this means is that Canadians' views on *both* public policy and federal-provincial processes are becoming more similar. However, as noted above, a reduction of variance on the former has quite different implications from a reduction of variance on the latter. While Canadians are agreed on what government should be doing, they are also agreed that the way government "does what it does" somehow offends ideals of fair, respectful regional treatment. It is also significant that the growing sense of regionalism is mostly a "made-in-Ontario" story. The largest shifts in perceptions of federalism are occurring in this province-cum-region. The great bulk of Ontario's population means these are developments with potentially profound political implications.

CONCLUSION

The data presented in this chapter tell a simple but nuanced two-part story. First, in recent decades, differences between Canadian regions in political attitudes toward important policy questions have shrunk. Regionalism has always been an important feature in Canadian politics but the data suggest that to the extent that inter-regional conflicts exist, they do not stem from fundamentally opposing political attitudes. Simply put, Alberta is less conservative and Atlantic Canada is less liberal than they were two decades ago. Ideologically, we have today in Canada a more homogenous national political culture.

This has also been coupled with an increase of the Canadian national identity in many regions. Regionalism remains an important element of Canadian political life, but its salience has declined as Canadians have deepened their national identity (Mendelsohn and Matthews 2010, 6).

There are many explanations for this finding, some of which are speculative. They include interprovincial migration, international immigration, and the national and globalized flow of communications. We are particularly interested in the implications of immigration. Newcomers are attracted to Canada and may develop regional attachments, but the national unity debates, historical regional resentments, and provincial claims of injustice are entirely foreign to these newcomers. In fact, one reason many have come to Canada is precisely to avoid these kinds of political disputes. Immigration, we believe, is a source of national unity precisely because immigrants do not know or care about the national unity debates. They have come to Canada in part for national unity, while "National Unity Debates" are simply not part of their DNA.

Second, our political life is still clearly dominated by regionalism. In part, this could be explained by factors not examined in this paper, which include the different political economies of different regions, and the perception that different parties are stronger representatives of particular regions. Conflicts over interests on issues of inter-regional redistribution or the politics of energy, for example, are unlikely to disappear and may intensify. But there is another element which is clearly revealed in these data: there are growing differences between regions about regional politics and intergovernmental processes and outcomes. These attitudes do not find their foundation in, for example, attitudinal differences on the size of the state or value conflicts. They relate to questions of regional status and federal treatment. These attitudes may or may not be well-founded, but they are likely to complicate attempts in upcoming years to deal with questions of deficit reduction, renewal of fiscal transfers, and the costs of climate change in a manner that does not exacerbate inter-regional tensions.

REFERENCES

Ajzenstat, J. and P.J. Smith eds. 1997. *Canada's Origins: Liberal, Tory, or Republican?* Ottawa: Carleton University Press.

Banting, K. 2008. "Canadian as Counter-Narrative: Multiculturalism, Recognition and Redistribution." In *The Comparative Turn in Canadian Policitical Science*, eds. L.White, R. Simeon, R. Vipond, and J. Waller, 59-76. Vancouver: University of British Columbia Press.

Bell, J.D. and L. Tepperman. 1979. *The Roots of Disunity: A Look at Canadian Political Culture*. Toronto: McClelland and Stewart.

Black, E.R. and A. Cairns. 1966. "A Different Perspective on Canadian Federalism." *Canadian Public Administration*, 9(1):27-44

Blake, D. 1978 "Constituency Contexts and Canadian Elections: An Exploratory Study." *Canadian Journal of Political Science* 11(2):279-305.

Blake, D. 1972. "The Measurement of Region in Canadian Voting Patterns." *Canadian Journal of Political Science* 5(1):55-81.

Brodie, J. 1990. *The Political Economy of Canadian Regionalism*. Toronto: Harcourt, Brace, Jovanovich.

Cairns, A. 1977. "The Governments and Societies of Canadian Federalism." *Canadian Journal of Political Science* 10(4):695-725.

Cairns, A. 1968. "The Party System and the Electoral System in Canada, 1921-1965." *Canadian Journal of Political Science* 1(1):55-80.

Esping-Andersen, G. 1990. *The Three Worlds of Welfare Capitalism*. Oxford: Polity Press.

Fournier, P. 2002. "The Uninformed Canadian Voter." In *Citizen Politics: Research and Theory in Canadian Political Behaviour,* eds. J. Everitt and B. O'Neill, 92-109. Don Mills: Oxford University Press.

Gidengil, E., A. Blais, N. Nevitte and R. Nadeau. 1999. "Making Sense of Regional Voting in the 1997 Federal Election: Liberal and Reform Support Outside Quebec." *Canadian Journal of Political Science* 32(2):247-72.

Henderson, Ailsa. 2004. "Regional Political Cultures in Canada." *Canadian Journal of Political Science* 37(3):595-61.

Hetherington, M. J. 1998. "The Political Relevance of Political Trust." *American Political Science Review* 92(4):791-808.

Horowitz, G. 1966. "Conservatism, Liberalism, and Socialism in Canada: An Interpretation." *The Canadian Journal of Economics and Political Science* 32(2):143-171.

Innis, H. 1930 (reprinted in 1970). *The Fur Trade in Canada: An Introduction to Canadian Economic History*. Toronto: University of Toronto Press.

---. 1940 (reprinted 1978). *The Cod Fisheries: The History of an International Economy*. New Haven: Yale University Press.

Johnston, R., H.E. Brady, A. Blais, and J. Crete. 1992. *Letting the People Decide: Dynamics of a Canadian Election*. Montreal: McGill-Queen's University Press.

Johnston, R. 2008. "Polarized Pluralism in the Canadian Party System: Presidential Address to the Canadian Political Science Association, June 5, 2008." *Canadian Journal of Political Science* 41(4):815-34.

Korpi, W. 1980. "Social Policy and Distributional Conflict in the Capitalist Democracies: A Preliminary Comparative Framework." *Western European Politics* 3(3):291-316.

Lipset, S.M. 1968, *Revolution and Counterrevolution: Change and Persistence in Social Structures*. New York: Basic Books.

---. 1990. *Continental Divide: The Values and Institutions of the United States and Canada*. New York: Routledge.

MacPherson, C.B. 1953. *Democracy in Alberta: The Theory and Practice of a Quasi-Party System*. Toronto: University of Toronto Press.

Mallory, J.R. 1954. *Social Credit and the Federal Power in Canada*. Toronto: University of Toronto Press.

Matthews, J.S. and L. Erickson. 2005. "Public Opinion and Social Citizenship in Canada." *Canadian Review of Sociology and Anthropology* 42(4):373-401.

---. 2008. "Welfare State Structures and the Structure of Welfare State Support: Attitudes Towards Social Spending in Canada, 1993-2000." *European Journal of Political Research* 47(4):411-35.

Mendelsohn, M. and J.S. Matthews. 2010. *The New Ontario: The Shifting Attitudes of Ontarians toward the Federation*. Toronto: Mowat Centre for Policy Innovation.

Mendelsohn, M. 2003. "Rational Choice and Socio-Psychological Explanation for Opinion on Quebec Sovereignty." *Canadian Journal of Political Science* 36(3):511-37.

Pratt, L. 1977. "State and Province-Building: Alberta's Development Strategy" In *The Canadian State: Political Economy and Political Power,* ed. L. Panitch, 133-178. Toronto: University of Toronto Press.

Schwartz, M. 1974. *Politics and Territory: The Sociology of Regional Persistence in Canada*. Montreal: McGill-Queen's University Press.

Simeon, R. 1975. "Regionalism and Canadian Political Institutions." Queen's Quarterly 82. Kingston: Quarterly Committee of Queen's University.

Simeon, R. and D. Elkins. 1980. *Small Worlds: Provinces and Parties in Canadian Political Life*. Toronto: Methuen.

---. 1971. "Regional Political Cultures in Canada." *Canadian Journal of Political Science* 8(3):397-437.

Smiley, D. 1987. *The Federal Condition in Canada*. Toronto: McGraw-Hill Ryerson.

---. 1977. "Territorialism and Canadian Political Institutions." *Canadian Public Policy* 3(4):449-457.

Soroka, S. and C. Wlezien. 2004. "Opinion Representation and Policy Feedback: Canada in Comparative Perspective." *Canadian Journal of Political Science* 37(3):531-59.

---. 2010. *Degrees of Democracy: Politics, Public Opinion and Policy*. Cambridge, UK: Cambridge University Press.

Taylor, C. 1993. *Reconciling the Solitudes: Essays on Canadian Federalism and Nationalism*. Montreal and Kingston: McGill-Queen's University Press.

Wiseman, N. 1988. "A Note on "Hartz-Horowitz at Twenty": The Case of French Canada." *Canadian Journal of Political Science* 21(4):795-806

---. 2007. *In Search of Canadian Political Culture*. Vancouver: University of British Columbia Press.

III

Innovation and Economic Development in the New Ontario

6

SMART SPECIALIZATION: A NEW MODEL FOR ECONOMIC DEVELOPMENT

David A. Wolfe

L'Ontario n'est pas seul à devoir repenser son approche du développement économique régional. Un exercice qui place aujourd'hui l'innovation au cœur de politiques de développement « axées sur le milieu », composées de mesures à ancrage territorial dont la structure de gouvernance multiniveaux s'adapte aux réalités de chaque région. Ce chapitre examine comment d'autres territoires, notamment de l'Union européenne et des États-Unis, s'orientent vers des stratégies axées sur le milieu privilégiant la spécialisation intelligente, et comment l'Ontario pourrait s'en inspirer. Une démarche qui nécessite un nouveau type d'approche politique centrée sur des investissements en recherche et innovation dans les domaines les plus prometteurs, dont la mise à profit exige une coordination entre tous les ordres de gouvernement. Or cette approche coordonnée des politiques de développement régional, qui suscite un consensus grandissant, présente un intérêt majeur pour une fédération canadienne confrontée au défi de sa croissance économique.

INTRODUCTION

The impact of the economic recession between 2008 and 2011 has dramatically altered the industrial landscape of Ontario's economy and highlighted the challenges that lie ahead. Manufacturing sectors that have been the mainstay of the provincial economy for much of the postwar period, particularly automotive and related industries, have suffered significant plant closures and job losses. The recovery that has occurred has been concentrated in the service sectors of the economy, including the public sector. Yet, if the Ontario government is to maintain the standard of living and quality of public services that most Ontario inhabitants have come to take for granted, we cannot abandon the future of its industrial economy. While the industries that will predominate in a post-recession economy will undoubtedly be different from those of the past, manufacturing must remain an important part of the overall economic mix. While the fiscal pressures exerted on governments at all levels of the federation make it difficult to think about investing in the industries of the future, many observers in the United States, Europe, and elsewhere maintain that it is now more important than ever to do so, in order to lay a strong foundation for post-recovery growth and expansion. However, the impossibility of funding all the competing demands makes it incumbent for governments to think strategically about how they invest in new areas of growth, and to ensure that future investments in economic development are targeted to maximize their contribution to the economic recovery and future development of the provincial economy.

Ontario is not alone in the need to rethink its overall approach to regional economic development. Not surprisingly, the renewed interest in regional development policy departs from older approaches in fundamental ways. Central to this rethinking is a new focus on innovation as the centre piece of a "placed-based" approach to development policy. Territorially grounded policies that are multilevel in their governance structure and tailored to the specific reality of individual regions are widely seen as the foundation for provincial economic competitiveness and social well-being in an increasingly turbulent global environment. Parallel to this emphasis on innovation and place-based approaches is a solid appreciation of the need to be strategic in the allocation of scarce public funds. Most jurisdictions face the same fiscal limits as Ontario, and this constraint has prompted a rethinking of how economic development policy is focused more strategically on a clear set of priorities. In the European Union this approach has recently been labelled "smart specialization" (Foray, David and Hall 2009).

The goals of such an approach include building institutional capacity, improving accessibility to goods, services, and information in the region, and promoting innovation and entrepreneurship. Policy interventions must be tailored to the prevailing reality of regional contexts and based on the input, experience, and local knowledge of key regional actors. The focus on innovation as the centre piece of such a "place-based" approach to regional development policy arises from a growing body of research that demonstrates that competitiveness in the knowledge-based economy rests on networked relationships and organizational synergies that flow through face-to-face interaction and ongoing dialogue among geographically proximate actors (Barca 2009). Such an approach also requires that policy development and implementation at the regional scale take account of the perspectives of a significant array of other actors at the local level who have significant local interests and are concerned about the economic prospects of the communities where they live and work (Feldman and Martin 2005).

This chapter explores the way in which other jurisdictions, particularly in the European Union and the United States, are moving towards the implementation of "place-based" economic development strategies with an emphasis on smart specialization, and what this means for Ontario. Efforts to sustain the economic performance of regions through periods of disruptive change, such as we have experienced between 2007 and 2011, prompt a radical rethinking of our approaches to economic development policy. The move towards a "place-based" approach at the regional level requires not just a new category of policy approach, but a new style of policy development. Resilient regions are those best able to focus their investments in research and innovation in areas where those investments are likely to have the greatest impact. Capitalizing on these investments requires a coordinated approach across all levels of government. The resources currently allocated to innovation and economic development lack a harmonized vision. Improved coordination to reduce wasteful development spending is crucial given the current environment of government deficits. However, governments alone cannot determine which sectors offer the most potential. Rather, it requires that the governance mechanisms of policy development incorporate exercises to identify and cultivate regional assets, undertake collaborative processes to plan and implement change, and encourage a regional mindset that fosters growth (Wolfe 2010b).

It is important to analyze the ability of regional and local governments to build on specialized regional assets, including public and private research infrastructure, areas of sectoral strength, as well as unique concentrations of occupational and labour market skills. The ability of regional networks to work within and across associational boundaries to support the formulation and refinement of strategic management policies in response to external shocks must also be evaluated. Key lessons will be drawn from this analysis for the changes that Ontario needs to make to implement such an approach.

CHANGING APPROACHES TO REGIONAL ECONOMIC DEVELOPMENT

The role of regional economic development policy has undergone a dramatic change in the past few years across many OECD countries. Despite the vast expenditures on regional development in these countries since the initial burst of enthusiasm in the 1960s, the return on investment has been questioned as evidence has mounted that the programs have failed to reduce inter-regional disparities. The response to this perceived lack of success has prompted a serious rethinking of best-practices in regional development policy, resulting in new approaches diverging in significant ways from historical approaches. A hallmark of the new thinking is the emphasis put on the adoption of a "placed-based" approach to regional development policy. An underlying feature of this policy is the focus on innovation that mobilizes the local assets embedded in a region and taps the economic potential of all places and sectors to attain world class performance (Wolfe 2010a).

Regional development policies designed in the postwar period emphasized top-down redistributive schemes that provided funds for building infrastructure in, or attracting investments to, particular sectors or places in lagging regions. The most traditional approach, which corresponds historically to the Keynesian-era from the 1950s to the 1970s, focused on strategies to attract individual firms to a region or locality, frequently by emphasizing the economic value of cheap factor inputs, and by affording the target firms direct subsidies or tax reductions of an increasingly generous nature. The practice originated in the southern US states that offered low-wage, non-union labour, inexpensive land prices and reduced taxes to attract plants from the industrial North. By the 1970s, most US states and some Canadian provinces, caught in the triple-bind of competition from low-cost jurisdictions, declining productivity levels, and increased international competition, responded with a host of similar policies – including expensive tax abatements, job tax credits, training programs, low interest loans and other government subsidies. In Europe, this approach took the form of building infrastructure and upgrading public infrastructure in order to bring the standards in lagging regions up to those found in more developed areas.

As globalization took hold in the late 1970s and the industrial heartlands of Europe and North America experienced their first wave of deindustrialization, this traditional approach was recognized as inadequate to meet the challenges of the emerging knowledge-intensive economy. In the 1980s, a second phase of economic development strategies took hold that focused on building educational and techno-logical infrastructure to provide the knowledge base for indigenous firms and to attract investment. Numerous policies were introduced by various levels of gov-ernment, including efforts to fill gaps in the capital markets, modernize small- and medium-sized enterprises, accelerate the development and transfer of technology from universities to industry, enhance workers' skills, and provide entrepreneurs with a higher level of management information. These included initiatives like the Edison Centres in Ohio, the Centres of Excellence in New York State and Ontario's own Premier's Council Fund and Centres of Excellence (Wolfe 1994).

By the 1990s, a growing number of provincial and state governments began to perceive the limits to both the first and second "waves" of regional development policy. While the policy target shifted from chasing smoke stacks to building re-search infrastructure and filling market gaps, both approaches relied on the same top-down organizational structures, creating a plethora of new programs admin-istered by discrete branches of individual line departments with little integration of instruments or coordination across programs. Recognition of their institutional and structural limits led to the gradual emergence of a third approach to regional development policy, which has evolved over the 1990s and 2000s. This third ap-proach recognized that regions need to maximize their investments in local assets that cannot be easily replicated or moved to other parts of the globe. Rather than playing in a zero-sum competition for inward investment, the most successful places generate economic knowledge that drives innovation and export success. This new approach acknowledges that regional governments and national agencies cannot continue to layer new programs on existing ones in a disjointed fashion. Instead, regional development strategies must engage in a process of collaboration across different levels of government, and between public and private actors at the local scale, to identify and cultivate assets that are unique to the region and constitute its enduring source of jurisdictional advantage. The resulting emphasis on flexible, associative, and bottom-up participatory approaches to economic development is now understood to be crucial for regional innovation based on economic clustering and industrial agglomeration (Wolfe and Creutzberg 2003).

Despite the challenges faced in implementing these economic development strategies, there is clear evidence that a number of regions are evolving in this direction. As Feldman and Martin (2005) perceptively note, most jurisdictions pursue an economic development strategy which is defined by the collective decisions that actors within that jurisdiction make over time, in coordination or not, and articulated or not. Successful jurisdictional strategies are those that contribute to high and rising wages for workers over time. City-regions are the relevant scale to focus on because the benefits of clustering and agglomeration highlight that compact geographic units are a critical element for industrial performance. Feldman and Martin maintain that jurisdictions can benefit from creating an economic base, with unique and valuable assets that provides a differentiated advantage over other jurisdictions. But they emphasize that "constructing jurisdictional advantage takes the will of all the actors – a consensus vision and vision of uniqueness" (2005, 1245).

The process of constructing jurisdictional advantage often takes the form of "strategic management" at the regional and urban levels. At the core of this approach is "the development and enhancement of factors of production that cannot be transferred across geographic space at low cost" (Audretsch 2002, 174). The formulation of a strategic plan to maximize the economic benefits flowing to a region never starts from a clean slate. Efforts to sustain the economic performance of regions through periods of disruptive change need to commence with building the institutional capacity of those regions to manage their transition. The context in which such strategies are formed is strongly conditioned by regions' industrial structure and institutional underpinnings. The path dependent nature of development in regional economies involves the creation of new paths and the break-down and reconfiguration of existing institutional ensembles. New pathways for economic growth can emerge through various means including: the indigenous creation of new products or processes; the development of new areas of competence or specialization in the context of a regional economy; progression along a value chain to higher value-added activities for existing industries; and the relocation of existing firms and industries into an existing urban economy. However, these emerging pathways are strongly influenced by the existing mix of knowledge assets and labour force skills within the local economy. The key issue is how firms, industries, and institutions in a particular city-region recombine their existing knowledge base and localized capabilities to generate new commercially valuable sources of knowledge in the process of innovation and creativity. "New paths do not emerge in a vacuum, but always in the contexts of existing structures and paths of technology, industry, and institutional arrangements" (Martin and Simmie 2008, 188-89).

The European Union is reframing its regional development policy to integrate it more effectively into its broader goal of creating an Innovation Union by 2020. It has adopted the concept of smart specialization to reflect the idea that regions must build upon their existing industrial base and institutional strengths by using both national and EU programs to create distinctive jurisdictional advantages. This approach starts from the belief that regions need to apply strategic intelligence to identify and support the enhancement of those regional factors of production with the greatest potential to contribute to the region's overall growth and competitiveness. According to Foray et al.:

> The question is whether there is a better alternative to a policy that spreads that investment thinly across several frontier technology research fields ... not making much of an impact in any one area. A more promising strategy appears to be to encourage investment in programs that will complement the [region's] other productive assets to create future domestic capability and interregional comparative advantage. (2009, 1)

The proponents of this approach maintain that it can be pursued both by regions that are already working at the technological and scientific frontier, as well as those that are less advanced in their research and innovation capabilities. The key is to develop complementary research and innovation capabilities that can be linked more effectively across regions. This approach reflects the insight that in a world of increasing technological complexity, the scope for regional specialization and inter-regional cooperation is being enhanced (Arthur 2009; Rycroft and Kash 1999).

Building on this policy rationale, the European Commission has interpreted the adoption of smart specialization strategies in the context of its regional development and cohesion policies to target public funding more closely to enhance distinctive regional capabilities. On a practical basis, it means using available government policies, and economic development funding from an array of sources, to help regions identify and support priority industrial sectors and research institutions where the region already has an established or emerging competitive advantage or recognized capability in research. The process of smart specialization involves business, research institutions, and universities collaborating to pinpoint both the region's important areas of specialization as well as those shortcomings that are impeding its potential to innovate. The implementation of a smart specialization approach involves not only a new set of policy instruments, but a new approach to policy-making that includes mechanisms for reflexive learning through coordinated policy reviews. The goal is to achieve the maximum economic impact from the expenditure of an existing pool of funds, rather than spread them liberally across a wide number of research areas and business sectors. This concentration of resources in recognized or emerging areas of expertise and capability can help differentiate the region's strengths from those of other regions (European Commission 2010b).

THE EVOLUTION TOWARDS PLACE-BASED POLICY-MAKING

The focus on smart specialization follows logically from the concept of "place-based" policy that emerged as the guiding principle of the ongoing review of the European Union's regional development and cohesion policy. The regional development policy has undergone a continuous process of evolution since it was first introduced in 1975. It has become one of the cornerstones of the European Union's programming efforts, and the focus on improving cohesion among member states has taken on even greater significance in the past decade with the accession of ten new members from the less prosperous regions of Europe. During this period, the size and scale of EU cohesion policy (including regional development) has increased significantly. In some of the regions that have benefited most, especially Mediterranean countries such as Spain, and even specific regions in Spain, EU contributions have represented a substantial part of total national and regional budgets.

Over the course of the past three and a half decades, both the overall objectives and the operational design of EU regional development policy have changed. The focus has shifted from an interlinked set of programs and funding mechanisms with a primarily redistributive mechanism tied to the national objectives of individual member states, to a more coordinated approach geared toward EU-wide goals and objectives. While the most recent review of cohesion policy and the role of the structural funds has identified a number of limitations and shortcomings, there is widespread recognition that the goals of regional development and cohesion have been embedded within the broader social and economic objectives of the Union, particularly, the goals and objectives set out in the Lisbon Agenda. In the process, the role of cohesion policy has shifted away from an exercise primarily devoted to redistributing funds from richer member states to poorer ones, towards the channelling of resources across the continent towards a common set of economic development objectives and to improving regional planning and administrative practices in all parts of the Union (Manzella and Mendez 2009, 22).

This redirection of both the overall objectives and program spending of structural funds has involved its own challenges. There continues to be an underlying tension between the Union's goal of promoting the international competitiveness and innovative capabilities of the continent as a whole, and the facilitation of convergence of income levels and employment opportunities in individual member-states, and lagging regions within those states. In starkest terms, this conflict has been portrayed as a choice between concentrating greater resources, particularly under the framework programs devoted to research, development and innovation, in those regions that already enjoy the greatest concentration of research capabilities – sometimes referred to as "islands of innovation" (Hingel 1992) or redistributing funds on a more equitable basis to the lagging regions, at the possible cost of undermining the competitiveness of the most advanced regions.

This trade-off received considerable attention in the recent report on The Future of Cohesion Policy in the European Union prepared as part of the planning process for the design of regional development policy in the post-2013 period. According to the Barca Report, the rationale for cohesion policy in the European Union should no longer be that of financial redistribution from richer regions to lagging ones, or so-called "convergence regions." Rather the rationale should be to foster economic development in all places where economic efficiency exists through the provision of public goods and services. The report labels this alternative notion, a "place-based" development policy. The strategies adopted under a place-based development policy are territorially grounded, multilevel in their governance structure, and innovative and tailored to the specific realities of different regions. The goals of such an approach include building institutional capacity, improving accessibility to goods, services and information in the region, and promoting innovation and entrepreneurship. Policy interventions must be tailored to the prevailing reality of specific regional contexts and based on the input, experience, and "local knowledge" of key regional actors. The report defines place-based development policy in the following terms:

- a long-term development strategy with the objective to reduce persistent *inefficiency* (underutilization of the full potential) and *inequality* (share of people below a given standard of well-being and/or extent of interpersonal disparities) in specific places,
- the production of bundles of *integrated*, place-tailored *public goods and services*, designed and implemented by aggregating *local preferences and knowledge* through *participatory political institutions*, and by establishing linkages with other places; and
- promoted from outside the place by a system of *multilevel governance* where grants subject to *conditionalities* on both objectives and institutions are transferred from higher to lower levels of government (Barca 2009, 4-5).

As the European Union moves towards the implementation of a new cohesion policy for the period after 2013, the place-based approach described above has been recast within the broader framework of its research and innovation goals described as the Innovation Union. The idea of a place-based approach has been refined to focus on the notion of smart specialization described above. This shift reinforces the need to move away from a dichotomous framing of the debate between convergence and competitiveness goals, towards a more holistic set of place-based development goals. It also confirms that this dichotomy, in terms of policy objectives, can be overcome by concentrating on the complementary potential of greater regional specialization and cooperation.

WHY SMART SPECIALIZATION LEADS TO A CLUSTER FOCUS

The shift in regional development thinking from a preoccupation with redistribution and convergence to a focus on the importance of enhancing unique regional assets through smart specialization and the strategic management of non-mobile factors of production has led, not surprisingly, to a renewed interest in the economic contribution of industrial clusters. There is a growing belief in the United States, Europe, and elsewhere that the goal of promoting economic development by means of smart specialization can best be accomplished at the level of the local and regional economy through support for the growth of strategic clusters (as was seen in the recent series of policy measures introduced in the president's budget to Congress in the United States). Clusters can consist of both high-technology firms, which often gravitate towards research-intensive universities or institutes (as in the case of Silicon Valley and its many emulators), or firms based in more traditional sectors, such as the furniture, beer or dairy industries in Denmark. While high technology and industrial clusters have long been a source of fascination for economic policy-makers, their privileged position in the policy toolkit was more an article of faith than the product of solid economic evidence. However, recent research strongly shows that focusing economic resources on emerging or established industry clusters generates considerable economic benefits for regions, provinces, and countries (Porter 2003; Spencer, Vinodrai, Gertler, et al. 2010; Delgado, Porter and Stern 2010).

The growing support for channelling economic development policy through investment in clusters is informed by the substantial contributions that US federal and other government policies have made, often inadvertently, to the emergence and development of regional technology clusters, ranging from Silicon Valley to the Washington-Baltimore corridor (Wolfe and Gertler 2006). The underlying rationale for this emphasis is the distinct advantages that clusters afford to firms, and the communities that house them. First, the cluster acts as a magnet drawing talent; the location of specialized training and educational institutions can supply new skilled-labour to firms in the cluster. Second, membership in the cluster makes it easier for firms to source needed parts and components, thereby enhancing their technological and productive capabilities. A third key benefit of clusters arises from the formation of new firms when larger, anchor firms generate new ideas and research findings that support entrepreneurial spin-offs to take breakthroughs to market. Finally, clusters can provide an important stimulus to public investment in specialized infrastructure, such as communication networks, joint training and research institutions, specialized testing facilities, and the expansion of public laboratories or post-secondary educational institutions. As the depth and value of such investments increase, so do the economic benefits flowing to firms located in the cluster and their surrounding communities. Indeed, the strength of the cluster and its supporting infrastructure of public investments and collaborative institutions create a mutually reinforcing positive feedback loop that benefits the entire region (Wolfe and Gertler 2004).

This is precisely the rationale elaborated in the most recent policy document from the European Commission specifying the various programs and policy mechanisms that can be used to realize the goal of smart specialization. The Commission identifies clusters as a critical component of smart specialization strategies as they provide a convenient means for streamlining the delivery of a range of different policies focused on stimulating innovation in regional economies. Policy initiatives to support cluster development afford policy-makers a lens or focusing device through which they can address a wide range of business needs in a collective fashion. Clusters ensure a cost-effective means of delivering programs to a critical mass of recipients in a manner designed through joint public-private decision-making processes (Landabaso and Rosenfeld 2009). Cluster initiatives are effective as a policy instrument because they can help promote linkages between firms, universities and research institutes, and provide a basis for firms to take better advantage of market opportunities. They also afford the opportunity for small- and medium-sized firms to establish connections with larger partners and multinational firms. There is solid evidence that inward investment from global partners is drawn to regional economies with a strong concentration of research expertise and a dense network of firms with unique local capabilities (Cooke 2005). The European Commission documents ways to implement regional policies for smart growth, in a number of key policy areas, to maximize benefits from existing local and regional clusters. These include support for the internationalization of cluster firms, the commercialization of research results, specialized programs and training institutes for the local labour force, joint branding and marketing programs for cluster firms, and policies to help cluster firms take better advantage of the trend towards open innovation in the research and development (R&D) strategies of large multinationals. Existing cluster organizations can also provide a convenient mechanism for delivering specialized business- and innovation- support programs to cluster firms, and for developing collective strategies to promote the growth of local clusters (European Commission 2010a).

The European Union has not been alone in the recent turn to providing support for clusters as the most effective policy approach for promoting the implementation of its strategies for smart specialization. The election of the Obama administration in the United States increased the centrality afforded by the US government to clusters as a critical instrument of regional development policy. The various lobbying efforts for a more concerted federal strategy to support regional innovation clusters, which had been underway for a number of years, found strong support in the federal budget for FY2011 introduced in February 2010 and updated in the budget one year later. In a series of items that marked the current government as the first US administration to expressly embrace a cluster-focused strategy, the budget introduced several proposals to support the growth of regional innovation clusters through coordinated measures across several different departments. The centrepiece of these measures is the Economic Development Administration's (part of the US Department of Commerce) proposal to establish a $75 million program to support Regional Innovation Clusters with funds for regional planning efforts, and matching grants to support cluster initiatives. The Small Business Administration of the Department of Commerce will also receive $11 million to support the participation of small businesses in regional clusters through the provision of funds for business counselling, training, and mentorship. The Department of Labour will be able to deploy up to $108 million from its new Workforce Innovation Fund to help align workforce development with cluster initiatives by promoting collaboration among training and employment service providers to link worker-training more effectively with emerging job opportunities. The National Science Foundation will receive $12 million to invest in "innovation ecosystems" that support efforts by faculty and students in universities to commercialize research results and stimulate start-up firms. The goal of these budget initiatives is to provide funding across multiple federal agencies, all targeted at supporting the growth of stronger regional clusters (US Office of Management and Budget 2010, 22).

The rationale for the federal government's new approach to regional economic development was spelled out in a speech given by John Fernandez, the former Mayor of Bloomington, Indiana and current Assistant Secretary of Commerce for Economic Development, in January 2010. He noted that dynamic and innovative companies thrive in places where scientists, businessmen, highly-skilled workers and venture capitalists cluster together with similar and interrelated firms, "... place matters. Entrepreneurs and researchers and innovators want to be around each other. They want to feed off the shared creative energy. They want access to a shared talent pool. They want to build relationships." In order to support this process, the federal government was replacing what it referred to as the previous "buckshot approach," with a more focused strategy to support the growth and development of innovative clusters in a multitude of regions across the country. The purpose of the new approach is to provide a framework for local and regional actors to assess their regional strengths, and fashion strategies to bring together the technology, human resources, and financial capital needed to help transform the region's unique assets into the basis for future economic growth and prosperity (Fernandez 2010).

The hallmark of the US government's cluster strategy is the recognition that successful cluster initiatives can be implemented without expending substantial sums of public funds. In most of the measures that have been introduced, public funds represent a small proportion of the total spending to support the growth of the cluster. A recent example of this is the public support for the expansion of the nanotechnology cluster in Albany, New York, where $800 million in public funding has triggered private investment of almost $5 billion. The federal government has wasted little time in rolling out the first round of grants from a range of US agencies under the cluster program announced in the February budget. In September, the Department of Commerce awarded six grants to the winners of the I6 Challenge – a competition held in six different regions of the country for the strongest proposals to accelerate the commercialization of technology and promote new firm formation. In each case, the awards went to cluster groups that were well-organized, had support from broad local coalitions, and had dense networks of firms and support organizations. At the same time, the Small Business Administration provided ten different clusters with awards to support the greater participation of small businesses in cluster activities. The Department of Agriculture also announced the 27 winners of Regional Business Opportunity Grants, which went to well-organized agricultural coalitions each of which has developed a focused innovation strategy. In the largest award made to date, the Department of Energy awarded a grant of $129 million to the Greater Philadelphia Innovation Cluster, a consortium of five industry participants, to support the plan for the Energy Regional Innovation Cluster, designed to create an energy innovation hub in the Philadelphia Navy Yard. There can be little doubt about the longer-term significance for economic development policy of this coordinated approach to stimulating cluster development across the world's largest economy (Sallet 2010).

Thus, both the European Union and the United States have recently recognized that cluster-building dynamics are central to the economics of smart specialization. An underlying principle of smart specialization states that the simple co-location, or concentration of resources in one place, does not necessarily translate into economic innovation. Rather, the key is how such resources are deployed and leveraged into unique jurisdictional assets. The challenge and opportunity for regions is to coordinate and focus the impact of regional development policies in such a way as to exploit the synergies among organizations and industrial sectors. Regions need to blend different kinds of knowledge into high-performing partnerships joining industry and educational institutions, venture capitalists and commercialization incubators, anchor firms and spin-off entrepreneurs, and skills-centres and business associations. The successful cases of the recent round of US cluster awards described above all display these characteristics. Consistent with the policy principle that "no one size fits all," there is tremendous potential for different development projects – reflecting unique territorial assets and economic opportunities across the province – to help transform the Ontario economy. While there has been no concerted policy at the federal or provincial level promoting this approach, a number of valuable and highly instructive projects have emerged at the local level through a bottom-up cluster building strategy including the following example.

Knowledge Economy Corridors

A priority for the southern Ontario economy should be bringing new ideas and products to market through intensive networking among leading researchers and their students, entrepreneurs and venture capitalists, and local or regional economic development agencies. Simply put, southern Ontario needs more globally-oriented business clusters rooted in local communities. An excellent example of such an innovation cluster can be found in south-western Ontario; it links and leverages the knowledge and creativity of Waterloo, Stratford, and London. The cluster finds its origins in the outstanding ability of firms in Waterloo Region to recognize emerging technology trends and mobilize key segments of the local business community, civic associations, and the regional research infrastructure to support new initiatives to capitalize on those trends. The current economic recession has severely impacted the more traditional manufacturing base in the south-western Ontario. In response, the local municipalities have drawn upon existing federal and provincial program initiatives to link the regions' industrial capabilities with the expansion of the its post-secondary institutions into digital media. The Digital Media Corridor brings together the City of Stratford, the University of Waterloo, and the University of Western Ontario, major technology industries, and municipal authorities, for innovation at the intersection of technology, culture, and commerce. The most recent measure involves linking a new branch of the University of Waterloo in Stratford, working on the creation of content for digital media, with a new Digital Media Convergence Centre in downtown Kitchener. With initial support from the CEOs of key local firms, such as Open Text and Christie Digital, and the Communitech Technology Association playing a leadership role, the Digital Media Hub aims to create Canada's largest concentration of digital media research, development, and commercial expertise while developing globally competitive capacity in digital innovation (Wolfe 2010b).

Similar examples of such cluster-based initiatives can be found in other cities and regions in southern Ontario. Hamilton has long been the home to Canada's steel industry and both its university and college have great strengths in traditional and new materials research. The recent launch of the McMaster Innovation Park, the much anticipated relocation of the federal CanMet laboratory to the Innovation Park, and related efforts to expand the local R&D activities of the leading international steel firms in the Hamilton region, represent another critical opportunity to support current and prospective cluster building efforts. Similar opportunities exist in the Windsor and London areas, with their existing concentrations of automotive assembly and parts production, and research expertise in fields ranging from green technologies to tool, die, and mould making. In other Canadian and international regions, national regional development agencies have recognized the transformative potential of such regional clusters of industrial strength and supported them with investments, incentives, and assistance.

Policy Implications and Conclusion

The recent experience of regional development policy in the cases discussed above, those of the European Union and the United States, point in the same direction. There is an emerging consensus on the need to focus public spending, and align resources more effectively across varying levels of government, in support of smart specialization strategies. This reflects the need to focus resources on enhancing regional strengths by concentrating local resources in support of those sectors and clusters with the potential to achieve sustained economic growth. This involves the recognition that regions vary considerably in their growth potential and inno-vative capacity and the most effective development strategies must build on local capabilities to exploit that potential.

There is also a growing consensus on the need for, and value of, collaborative planning processes to engage a broad cross-section of local and regional actors in the formulation and implementation of regional strategies, in other words, what has been referred to elsewhere as the strategic management of cities and regions (Audretsch 2002). The successful adoption of a "strategic management" approach requires not just a new policy approach, but a new style of policy development. Successful regions engage in strategic management exercises that identify and cul-tivate their assets, undertake collaborative processes to plan and implement change, and encourage a regional mindset that fosters growth. These processes can only succeed if the prevailing structures of regional governance provide the necessary support to allow these strategic management exercises to be effective. This involves the recognition that in a complex and interdependent world of policy formation, no level of government holds all the policy levers to implement a successful strategy, and that effective policy design requires some form of multilevel governance.

The other significant shift in the evolution of regional development policy is the growing recognition on both sides of the Atlantic that national and supranational levels of government must work closely with local and regional levels in a new mode of governance that creates a participatory framework for designing and implementing commonly agreed upon regional development goals and objectives. While the organizational mechanisms for implementing this mode of governance vary widely across the different members of the European Union and in the United States, a basic set of common practices includes; integrated multiyear planning, the establishment of partnerships between public and private sector actors, sharing and learning from best-practices across a diverse set of regions and countries, and build-ing common conceptual models and frameworks for regional development policy. The evolution of this new approach to multilevel governance is helping bring about a greater degree of what the OECD refers to as "policy alignment" (OECD 2007).

However, the OECD has also documented the missed opportunities to promote cluster development at the regional scale that result from a lack of alignment and coordination between different policy instruments and across multiple scales of governance. For example, many OECD countries have introduced government funding for research centres or centre of excellence programs in parallel with other innovation support policies. These policies typically develop from a research focus based in ministries of higher education with responsibility for university funding. The centres funded under these initiatives serve to support the development of regional specialization, but without formulating direct linkages to existing regional development policies and strategies, regions cannot capture the full benefits of that research. Similar gaps arise from the lack of integration of science and industrial parks with other programs (OECD 2007). Programs to promote science and industrial parks often originate at the local-level, and are therefore not explicitly aligned with innovation policies and programs originating at the national- or provincial-level. The new focus on smart specialization in the European Union, with a concomitant emphasis on greater coordination of the various policy instruments that fall under both the framework programs to support research and innovation and the structural funds to support cohesion policy, signifies a move towards more effective policy alignment. Similarly, the new coordinated approach to working with regional innovation clusters in the Obama administration, and implementing this approach across a wide range of federal departments and agencies, signifies a similar recognition.

The tension found within the debate over the future direction of European regional development policy is strongly reminiscent of that often found in Canadian debates over the virtue of concentrating greater economic resources in the most dynamic and leading cities and regions of the country, or the goal of distributing regional development funds to the less advanced parts of the country. Echoes of the trade-off between the convergence goals of European Union cohesion policy and the competitiveness and innovation goals of the Lisbon Agenda resonate with Canadian debates over the way in which regional development and redistributive objectives influence a wide array of federal government programs at the expense of the leading research and innovation centres of the country. The gradual evolution of European Union cohesion policy towards a tighter integration of its convergence and competitiveness objectives suggests that Canada has much to learn from the past four decades of regional development policy in the European Union.

One of the key virtues of this approach is the emphasis that it places on involving key actors at the local level in designing effective regional innovation strategies within the framework of existing supranational, national, and regional policies. The relevance of this analysis for regional development policy in Canada highlights the need for a better understanding of the way in which policies at all levels of government affect the innovative capabilities of firms across a wide range of diverse industrial sectors and geographic regions. Considerable resources are expended annually by all levels of government on innovation related programs and economic development initiatives, but they are designed and implemented in a hierarchical and siloed fashion. There is little attempt at policy alignment across different program areas and levels of government.

The emerging consensus around a coordinated approach to regional development policy in Europe and the United States is no longer just an abstract concept of relevance to academic studies of policy-making. It has pressing relevance for the challenge of economic development in the Canadian federation. Many of the existing policies and programs to support regional development have been implemented in a traditional top-down, bureaucratic fashion, administered by individual departments or agencies, with little cross-jurisdictional coordination, and often with little attention paid to the broader implications of the program for cluster development in the local or regional innovation system. One illustration of this dilemma is the Canada Foundation for Innovation, which makes major infrastructural investments in expanding the research capacity of post-secondary institutions and hospitals across Ontario with little regard to the integration of these important new facilities into existing or emerging industrial infrastructure or local clusters in those regions. While these investments must continue to be made on the basis of academic excellence, their potential to support regional- and municipal-level smart specialization represents a classic missed opportunity that we can no longer afford. There is tremendous potential to realize a greater degree of policy alignment, in both federal and provincial spending, on research and innovation programs that support the needs of existing sectoral groups and industry clusters in the dynamic growth regions of Ontario.

REFERENCES

Arthur, W. B. 2009. *The Nature of Technology: What It Is and How It Evolves.* New York: The Free Press.

Audretsch, D. B. 2002. "The Innovative Advantage of US Cities." *European Planning Studies* 10(2):165-76.

Barca, F. 2009. *An Agenda for Reformed Cohesion Policy: A place-based approach to meeting European Union challenges and expectations.* Independent Report prepared at the request of Danuta Hubner, Commissioner for Regional Policy. Brussels: European Commission.

Cooke, P. 2005. "Regional Knowledge Capabilities and Open Innovation: Regional Innovation Systems and Clusters in the Asymmetric Knowledge Economy." In *Clusters, Networks and Innovation*, eds. S. Breschi and F. Malerba, 80-109. Oxford and New York: Oxford University Press.

Delgado, M., M. E. Porter, and S. Stern. 2010. Clusters, Convergence and Economic Performance. Institute for Strategy and Competitiveness, Harvard Business School. At http://www.isc.hbs.edu/econ-clusters.htm (accessed 8 December 2011).

European Commission. 2010a. Document Accompanying the Commission Communication on Regional Policy Contributing to Smart Growth in Europe 2020. COM (2010) 553 Final. Commission Staff Working Document. Brussels: European Commission.

---. 2010b. Regional policy contributing to smart growth in Europe 2020. COM (2010) 553 Final. Communication from the Commission to the European Parliament, the Council, the European Economic and Social Committee and the Committee of the Regions. Brussels: European Commission.

Feldman, M., and R. Martin. 2005. "Constructing jurisdictional advantage." *Research Policy* 34(8), October:1235-49.

Fernandez, J. 2010. *Remarks prepared for delivery to the Chicago Rail Summit.* Chicago, Illinois: Economic Development Administration, US Department of Commerce.

Foray, D., P. A. David, and B. Hall. 2009. Smart Specialisation – The Concept.
Knowledge Economists Policy Brief no. 9. Brussels: European Union. Hingel, A. J. 1992.
Science, Technology and Community Cohesion: Research Results and RTD Policy
Recommendations. Monitor-FAST Programme, Prospective Dossier No. 1. Brussels:
Commission of the European Communities.

Landabaso, M., and S. Rosenfeld. 2009. "Public Policies for Industrial Districts and Clusters."
In *A Handbook of Industrial Districts*, eds. G. Becattini, M. Bellandi, and L. De Propris.
Nottingham: Edward Elgar.

Manzella, G. P., and C. Mendez. 2009. *The turning points of EU Cohesion Policy*. Background
Working Paper prepared for the Report on An Agenda for a Reformed Cohesion Policy
(Barca Report). Brussels: European Commission.

Martin, R., and J. Simmie. 2008. "Path Dependence and Local Innovation Systems in City-
Regions." *Innovation: Management, Policy& Practice* 10(2-3):183-96.

OECD. 2007. Competitive regional clusters: National policy approaches. OECD Reviews of
Regional Innovation. Paris: Organisation for Economic Co-operation and Development.

Porter, M. E. 2003. "The Economic Performance of Regions." *Regional Studies* 37(6&7):549-78.

Rycroft, R., and D. Kash. 1999. "Innovation Policy for Complex Technologies." *Issues in
Science and Technology*.

Sallet, J. 2010. Innovation Policy in Tough Times on Tight Budgets. Keynote address.
American Chamber of Commerce's EU Innovation Conference. Brussels. At http://www.
scienceprogress.org/2010/10/innovation-policy-tight-budgets-and-tough-times/ (accessed
8 December 2011).

Spencer, G., T. Vinodrai, M. S. Gertler, and D. A. Wolfe. 2010. "Do Clusters Make a
Difference? Defining and Assessing their Economic Performance." *Regional Studies* 44(6),
July:697-715.

US Office of Management and Budget. 2010. *Budget of the US Government, Fiscal Year
2011*. Washington, D.C.

Wolfe, D. A. 1994. *The wealth of regions: Rethinking industrial policy*. Working Paper
No. 10, Canadian Institute for Advanced Research, Program in Law and the Determinants
of Social Ordering. Toronto: Canadian Institute for Advanced Research.

---. 2010a. *From Entanglement to Alignment: A Review of International Practice in Regional
Economic Development*. Mowat Centre for Policy Innovation Paper. Toronto: Mowat
Centre for Policy Innovation.

---. 2010b. "The Strategic Management of Core Cities: Path Dependence and Economic
Adjustment in Resilient Regions." *Cambridge Journal of Regions, Economy and
Society* 3(1):139-152.

Wolfe, D. A., and T. Creutzberg. 2003. *Community Participation and Multilevel Governance
in Economic Development Policy*. Background Report prepared for the Ontario
Government Panel on the Role of Government. Toronto.

Wolfe, D. A., and M. S. Gertler. 2004. "Clusters from the Inside and Out: Local Dynamics
and Global Linkages." *Urban Studies* 41(5-6), 1071-1093.

---. 2006. Local Antecedents and Trigger Events: Policy Implications of Path Dependence for Cluster Formation. In *Cluster Genesis: Technology-Based Industrial Development*, eds. P. Braunerheim and M. Feldman, 243-63. Oxford: Oxford University Press.

7

CANADA'S INNOVATION UNDERPERFORMANCE: WHOSE POLICY PROBLEM IS IT?

Tijs Creutzberg

Face à la persistance du faible rendement du Canada en matière d'innovation, ce chapitre puise à trois corpus de recherche pour faire valoir la nécessité d'une refonte des mesures de soutien à l'innovation. L'auteur y met en relation de récentes études sur ces mesures de soutien, qui préconisent une démarche stratégique plus équilibrée que celle du Canada, et d'autres recherches sur les villes innovantes soulignant les dimensions régionales du rendement de l'innovation, le tout mis en perspective par un troisième corpus sur la subsidiarité qui indique comment les différents ordres de gouvernement devraient soutenir l'innovation. Il en conclut à la nécessité d'un effort fédéral-provincial conjoint pour reformuler notre politique de soutien à l'innovation en entreprise, mais aussi pour adopter une approche plus directe du développement des capacités industrielles dans les secteurs émergents. Il propose enfin de mieux répartir les responsabilités politiques pour renforcer l'efficacité administrative et optimiser les résultats. Ottawa devrait ainsi maintenir un soutien indirect et générique aux processus d'innovation, tandis que les provinces devraient privilégier les investissements stratégiques.

It is one of the most consistently underperforming attributes of Canada's economy. So reliably underwhelming is Canada's innovation performance that new studies decrying this fact are anything but surprising. Whether it be the latest benchmarking report from Canada's Science, Technology and Innovation Council (STIC 2011), another "D" grade on the Conference Board of Canada's periodic report cards (2008, 2010), or the assessment by the Council of Canadian Academies (CCA) scrutinizing the root causes of Canada's innovation performance (CCA 2009), the basic message has differed little from their predecessors decades prior (Britton and Gilmour 1978; Science Council of Canada 1979; Ontario. Premier's Council 1989).

Such poor performance is not for want of policy attention. Innovation has been on the forefront of policy discussions for over twenty years now, and has resulted in a myriad of new initiatives and strategies from various governments, and departments – yet Canadian firms continue to underperform in innovation when benchmarked against rivals. All the more remarkable is the fact that Canada has one of the most generous tax incentive programs for Research and Development (R&D) among OECD countries and a sound research system of universities and public research organizations; neither of which appear to have brought Canada a comparative advantage in innovation.

So what is the problem? Research has identified a number of reasons for this underperformance and ultimately highlights that there are many factors at play. As summarized by the CCA, these include having: a relatively low number of innovative Canadian-based multinationals; more firms upstream in North American value chains specializing in primary and intermediate goods; business culture factors including comparatively low customer focus; and small and geographically fragmented markets which are less effective in driving innovation than larger and more competitive markets (CCA 2009).

There has, however, only been limited debate as to whether Canada's policy approach to supporting innovation is part of the problem. Canada, more so than its OECD peers, relies heavily upon the federal government's incentives to encourage business R&D, a policy that has been enhanced in recent years by a programmatic push to get more innovation results from investments in public research capacity.[1] Direct forms of support such as targeted R&D grants and subsidies have been sporadic at best, or limited to a few sectors such as aerospace.

Given our track record and national aspirations to do better, clearly now is a good time to fundamentally rethink the way in which not just the federal, but also the provincial governments collectively support innovation. Indeed, there is now sufficient support from various strains of research – and from Ontario's experiences – to suggest that Canada's primarily federal and indirect approach may be part of the problem. Evidence questioning whether tax credits are, on their own, sufficient to foster strong innovation outcomes, along with recognition of the importance of the local and regional dynamics of innovation performance, both challenge the current policy approach. Another factor is the decentralized manner of Canada's innovation programming, which has resulted in considerable duplication and overlap in a number of innovation support areas, and which has introduced confusion among

---

[1] Canada's 2007 Science and Technology Strategy is the most recent articulation of the latter approach, framing research investments in terms of establishing an entrepreneurial, knowledge and people advantage for Canada (Canada. Industry Canada 2007).

the very companies these policies are intended to support. Moreover, such duplication and overlap gives rise to important questions about the cost-effectiveness of Canada's collective effort.

All of this calls for, at the very least, a debate on how the federal and provincial governments are supporting innovation. To its credit, the federal government is currently re-examining how it is supporting R&D, under the direction of a Research and Development Review Panel, which is due to report this fall. This paper is a further contribution to this debate in the hope that some serious discussion can transpire that will inspire action for policy change.

To this end, this paper argues that a joint federal-provincial effort is required to reformulate Canada's innovation policy support so that it is not only more balanced in terms of the types of financial support for business innovation but that it also re-embraces a more direct approach to developing industrial capacity in emerging sectors. This paper also calls for a clearer division of policy roles to ensure maximum administrative and outcome effectiveness. Accordingly, it is argued that the federal government should focus on the indirect and generic support for the innovation process, while the provincial governments should concern themselves primarily with strategic investments.

INNOVATION SUPPORT IN CANADA

To describe Canada's approach to innovation as indirect and mostly federal is in one sense, misleading, given the considerable breadth of policies from both federal and provincial levels of government that shape the country's innovation system. Though there has been no national innovation policy per se, over the years both federal and provincial governments have developed, in a largely uncoordinated manner, a broad mix of policies administered through an equally broad range of departments and agencies targeting directly or indirectly, one of the many facets of the innovation process. These departments and agencies range from those with direct mandates for innovation, such as Industry Canada and the Ontario Ministry of Research and Innovation, to those with no obvious responsibilities for innovation such as the federal Public Works and Government Services, whose Office of Small and Medium Sized Enterprise entered the innovation space in 2010 with the launch of a small procurement program for innovation.[2] The result is a myriad of policies and programs supporting: Canada's research capacity; university-industry partnerships; international collaboration support; entrepreneurship training; commercialization; innovation skills development; venture capital financing; innovation networks; and not least tax credits for firm expenditures on R&D. All of these

---

[2] See Canadian Innovation Commercialization Program, https://buyandsell.gc.ca/initiatives-and-programs/canadian-innovation-commercialization-program.

policies and programs, to varying degrees, enhance the capabilities of, and incentives for, individual firms to bring new products, services, or processes to market. An example of this breadth of support for innovation can be seen in the agricultural sector in Ontario, where one study identified seven federal and provincial departments administering 45 policies and programs that impact either value-added agriculture directly or innovation more generally (HAL Corporation 2009). This count does not include the additional and significant support for innovation that comes from the research system consisting of universities, colleges and government research organizations. Nor does it include the over 50 Ontario-based support organizations, such as business incubators, regional technology associations, or sector innovation organizations that offer more generic advisory support and related resources for companies on matters of innovation. Taken together, these policies, programs, and organizations point to a complex system of institutional infrastructure supporting innovation within the province.

Given this complexity, it is useful to categorize the breadth of policies and programs by the aspect of innovation that they target, be it directly or indirectly. Table 1 breaks innovation supports into one of three groups: those that support innovation indirectly through framework conditions; those that directly support the innovation process generically; and those that directly support specific sectors and clusters with strategic investments.

- **Indirect support, framework conditions:** the specific regulatory and tax policies that shape the incentives for firms to invest in product and service development and support for research (given the role of the research system in supplying new knowledge and skilled labour). Examples include the Scientific Research and Experimental Development (SR&ED) Tax Incentive Program, the single largest R&D program in Canada.
- **Direct support for innovation process:** Largely sector and technology neutral, this type of support can be directed at cluster networking, technology startups, collaboration, or at technology transfer from postsecondary institutions to industry. Examples include Ontario's Ministry of Research and Innovation's Ontario Network of Excellence Program, which funds regional innovation centers, and FedDev's Technology Development Program, which has recently launched a program to support collaborative innovation projects between public and private actors.
- **Direct support specific to sector or cluster:** This support is targeted and often in the form of subsidies to firms in selected sectors or regions. Though such strategic investments are in some instance discretionary and ad hoc, as in the case of the 2008 bailout of the auto sector, they are typically administered through programs. The Strategic Aerospace and Defence Initiative (SADI) from Industry Canada and the Agricultural Flexibility Fund from Agriculture and Agri-Food Canada (AAFC) are examples of direct strategic support for sectors.

Table 1: Taxonomy of Innovation Support

INDIRECT	*DIRECT*	
Framework Conditions	*Innovation Process*	*Sector or Cluster Specific*
• Regulations – product and environmental	• Cluster networking support	• Targeted R&D grants and procurement programs
• R&D tax incentives	• Technology transfer programs	• Specialized infrastructure
• Research support	• Mentoring services for start-up companies	• Locational subsidies

Source: Author's compilation

EMPHASIS OF CANADIAN INNOVATION SUPPORT

Of these three categories, however, Canada's innovation system is heavily weighted toward the first, largely as a result of the Scientific Research and Experimental Development (SR&ED) Tax Incentive Program, the single largest R&D program in Canada. Administered by Finance Canada, this program is designed to lower the real costs and risks of conducting R&D, and supports over 20,000 companies each year at a cost of some C$ 4.7 billion in foregone revenue (McKenna 2011).[3] To put this in perspective, if treated as a federal Science and Technology (S&T) expenditure, this is equivalent to a quarter of the government's commitment to supporting R&D, and is three times the amount of direct support provided by the federal government to businesses (Figure 1).[4]

Finance Canada has now evaluated the SR&ED program on two occasions, once in 1997 and again in 2007, both of which found a positive impact. In 1997, drawing on data from the early 1990s, Finance Canada and Revenue Canada found that when assessed on the basis of the tax incentives' incremental impact on R&D spending, the program resulted in an additional R&D expenditure of 32 per cent. In

---

[3] This is an increase in foregone revenue of 57 percent from 2006 levels of C$3 billion cited in *Mobilizing Science and Technology to Canada's Advantage* (Canada. Industry Canada 2007).

[4] These figures exclude R&D performed in by government departments and agencies. Total federal S&T expenditures for 2005-06 amounted to C$9.3 billion, including 5 billion for in-house S&T, and C$2.7 billion for higher education.

Figure 1: Federal Government Support for Science and Technology, 2007

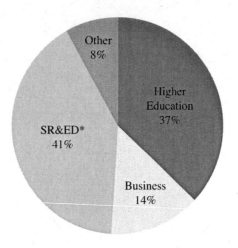

Source: Canada. Industry Canada 2007
*Excludes S&T performed by government departments and agencies.

terms of cost-effectiveness, the program amounted to C$ 1.38 of additional R&D spending for every dollar of foregone federal tax revenue. In updating the econometric model to include R&D spillovers as well as additional costs, Parsons and Phillips, in their 2007 evaluation, found the net benefit to be C$ 0.11 of additional R&D spending per dollar of foregone revenue. In both cases, these findings are consistent with other studies, many of which using US data, that show positive net benefits (Parsons and Phillips 2007; OECD 2007).

Research and Development tax incentives, compared to more direct forms of support such as grants and subsidies, also have the advantage of being non-discriminatory toward sector, technology, or region, and are more cost effective to administer (Canada. Finance Canada and Revenue Canada 1997). Moreover, they are consistent with the dominant view in Canada, as articulated in the original 1983 policy principles for SR&ED, that "the private sector is in the best position to determine the amount and type of industrial research and development that it should undertake" (Canada. Finance Canada and Revenue Canada 1997, 42). Indeed, this policy preference for neutrality is an important part of the rationale for Canada's current reliance on tax incentives (Madore 2006).

Given Canada's poor innovation performance, however, an important question is whether this emphasis on the indirect R&D tax incentives is in fact appropriate. Quite apart from recent claims that the SR&ED program is being abused by false claims,[5] the fact remains that Canada has not sufficiently improved its business R&D performance over the nearly three decades that the federal government has maintained the SR&ED. All the more remarkable is that, in its current form, the SR&ED is the second most generous R&D tax incentive among OECD countries, after Spain (Warda 2005).

This fact is particularly notable in work by Jaumotte and Pain (2005) which shows Canada as an outlier in international comparisons of its mix of indirect R&D tax and more direct subsidization policies (Figure 2). Compared to Sweden and Germany, for example, both of which are low tax and high subsidy countries – and even the US, which maintains high tax incentives and high subsidies – Canada's high tax incentive, low subsidies approach coincides with below average business R&D intensities.[6,7]

THE CASE FOR DIRECT SUPPORT

A recent study, which uses Canadian innovation survey data to look at innovation outputs (i.e., new products and services) as opposed to just inputs (i.e., business expenditures on R&D), warrants attention. In their examination of Canadian firms using the results of the 2005 Survey of Innovation, Bérubé and Mohnen (2009) compare the performance of those Canadian-based firms receiving tax credits but no R&D grants, with those that received both tax incentives and grants, thereby controlling for differences in national innovation systems. The authors found that firms that benefited from both policies were more innovative than firms that made use of only tax incentives. Moreover, not only were they more innovative, but Canadian firms using both types of programs also made more world-first innovations and were more successful in commercializing their innovations.[8]

---

[5] According to one estimate, one third of the SR&ED cost is being wasted by misuse (McKenna 2011).

[6] Business R&D intensity is defined as the ratio of Business Expenditures on R&D (BERD) to a country's Gross Expenditures on R&D (GERD).

[7] This debate is unlikely to be settled anytime soon, not least because in comparative research, the impact of R&D incentives cannot readily be isolated from the broader innovation system of a given country (OECD 2007). Jaumotte and Pain (2005) put forth a similar finding, concluding that both tax incentives and direct subsidies are linked to higher innovation levels, but that the degree of impact of degree to which subsidies have an impact is more influenced by particular national conditions.

[8] Specifically, they note that that 25 percent of firms using tax incentives and R&D grants reported world first innovations compared to 17 percent that used only tax incentives and that 81 percent of the former reported having introduced at least one innovation in the past three years, compared to 72 percent of the latter. And finally, some 61 percent of those making use

Figure 2: The State of Tax and Subsidization Policies, 1996-2000, Average Per Annum

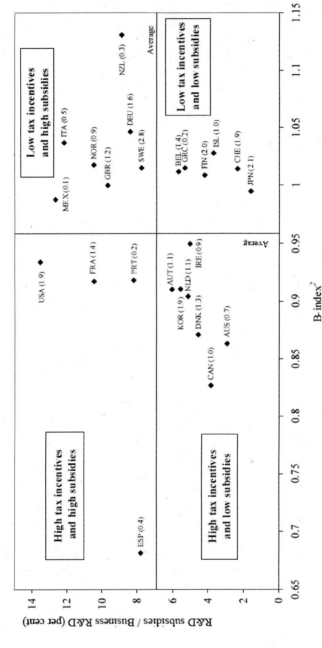

1) The numbers in parentheses are the average business R&D intensities in 1996-2000.
2) The B-index is defined as one minus the rate of tax subsidy for R&D.
Source: OECD Main Science and Technology Indicators database for data on R&D subsidies; OECD, STI/EAS Division for data on the B-index.

Source: Jaumotte and Pain 2005; reproduced with author permission.

In addressing the question of why direct support for R&D may yield different outcomes than tax incentives, David, Hall and Toole (2000) note that tax incentives are likely to favor projects that will generate greater profits in the short-run, as firms look to expand their R&D activities in response to tax offsets against earnings. The result is that longer-term R&D, which has the potential for higher social rates of return and spillover benefits, will be less favored by this policy instrument. In contrast, direct subsidies, which raise the rate of return for individual R&D projects (i.e., the private marginal rate of return (MRR)), are often targeted by governments towards projects that are considered to offer higher social rates of return on investments in knowledge. Thus along with raising the private MRR, direct subsidies can lead to greater spillover benefits. Czarnitzki and Toole (2007) also show how direct support can be beneficial, finding that R&D subsidies are particularly good in helping mitigate uncertainty in the product market, a factor that is related to under-investing in R&D. As the authors note, "while subsidies themselves do not reduce uncertainties, they can offset the incentive to delay investment in times of product market uncertainty by increasing the expected return to the firms' R&D investment" (Czarnitzki and Toole 2007, 179).

In short, this research suggests that Canada should re-evaluate its policy mix for supporting innovation and consider resourcing more direct forms of support than those currently provided. From a policy standpoint, direct forms of support have the advantage of being more strategic in supporting the development of innovation capacity, especially in emerging sectors and developing regions (Czarnitzki and Licht 2006). When strategic public investments are aligned with market forces and technology trends, they have been shown to have a significant impact in developing industrial and innovation capacity in new sectors. China, Taiwan, and Singapore are all testaments to such aggressive strategic investing; they have reshaped the global geography of innovation in desirable knowledge intensive sectors such as semiconductors (Howell 2003; Leachman and Leachman 2004). Direct forms of support can also be better targeted towards creatively addressing innovation weaknesses specific to Canada as identified, for example, in the 2009 CCA report.

This more direct manner of investment is often disparaged as either "corporate welfare" (Taylor 2008) or as a distortion of markets. However, such investments were pivotal in building capabilities in what became leading sectors in Ontario. While in essence it requires "picking winners," it is about picking sectors and not technologies. This is an important distinction and one that is often lost amidst the confusion surrounding the term's use in ideological debates over industrial policy. Indeed, "picking winners" was a term originally used in a paper by Nelson and Langlois (1983) in reference to the practice of government officials picking specific technologies to commercialize, a practice that was found to be the least

---

of both types of programs reported having earned revenue from their innovations compared to only 53 percent of those that made use only of tax incentives (Bérubé and Mohnen 2009).

successful form of government support identified in their research. As Rycroft and Kash (1992) point out, since then the term has been inaccurately used to disparage any direct government role in economic development, irrespective of the fact that governments have long played a critical role which, while not without failure, has also brought about major successes. In Ontario, examples include the development of a post-war petrochemical sector in Sarnia (Cobban 2008) and the emergence of a microchip industry in the Toronto region (Creutzberg, Wolfe, and Nelles 2006).

THE IMPORTANCE OF REGIONS

Strategic investments can play a catalytic role in establishing new industries and developing a highly skilled labour pool. While these strategies are not necessarily repeatable in the current economy and political environment, the importance of strategic action remains undiminished. Today, however, the locus for strategic initiatives comes less from the federal level and more often from the regional or local level, if at all. One example of the role that regional governments can play was Quebec's successful strategic efforts to build an entertainment software industry with a generous multimedia labour tax credit in 1996. With that incentive in place, together with strategic recruiting efforts by the government, Quebec attracted one of the world's largest gaming companies to Montreal, UbiSoft, which has since grown its facility there into its largest studio with approximately 1700 employees. Along with having attracted talent from the US and Europe, UbiSoft has helped train a pool of talent with the latest skills in video game design, some of whom have moved on to create their own companies (HAL Corporation 2009). Here the dynamic is similar to previous eras of strategic intervention, whereby the initial strategic investment helps build and secure a critical mass of capabilities in people who often carry these skills with them to other companies within the region, in a process well documented in cluster literature (Saxenian 1994; Bramwell and Wolfe 2008).

A second illustrative local example is Sarnia. Subject to a number of external shocks including globalization of production, emerging petrochemical capacity in Asia Pacific and the Middle East, and an increasingly cost-competitive environment, Sarnia has witnessed plant closings and significant layoffs from companies such as Dow Chemical and Nova Chemicals. Another prominent challenge for the region's petrochemical firms is the accelerating global economic transformation driven by companies and consumers shifting to greener, cleaner and healthier products and services. With the promise of reducing both dependency on declining petroleum-based energy sources, and the ability to meet the challenges of a carbon-constrained economy, this transformation has significant potential to impact Sarnia's economy. To address these concerns, Sarnia companies including LANXESS AG, which bought the original Polymer Corp facility, are being engaged by local leadership to take strategic action towards re-establishing their competiveness to address the above challenges (Lee and Associates 2010). A key focal point for this local effort is to foster the development of a "hybrid" cluster that responds to new market opportunities in areas of non-petroleum alternatives such as bioplastics and biopolyols but which makes use of existing industrial processes.

The pivotal role of regions is now increasingly well understood in the large body of research that has examined the successes of such places as the Raleigh-Durham region of North Carolina, Waterloo, Ontario, and Cambridge, UK. This research, as summarized by Bradford (2010), highlights several ways in which particular attributes of a region can influence firm-level innovation, three of which are particularly relevant here.[9]

The first is the local and regional geography itself, which has been described as "fundamental and not incidental, to the innovation process" (Asheim and Gertler 2005). It is fundamental to: the learning processes among innovation actors; the sharing of knowledge (Lam 2000); social assets that allow local / regional firms to take advantage of specialized capabilities (Maskell and Malmberg 1999); the concentration of specialized skills (Wolfe and Lucas 2005); and access to supplier networks (Czarnitzki and Hottenrott 2009). In other words, geography, or rather proximity, facilitates access to key input factors that are important to a company's ability to innovate. Ultimately geography helps explain why firms seek to cluster in specific regions.

The second is place-based policy. Place-based policy emphasizes the need for governments to allow for and recognize the importance of geography in policy and programs related to regional development; especially innovation. As Bradford notes, "public policy is crucial in creating places with the appropriate innovative milieu" (2010, 7). Indeed, many policy decisions from upper levels of government have a local or regional impacts whether it is recognized or not. Policy decisions often manifest themselves with a physical presence, be it in the form of a commercialization facility or a special research program. These investments, for example, will often preferentially benefit particular research institutions that are either closest to it or which have the necessary expertise to meet a research program's objectives. As a result, though federally-funded research organizations may not have a local mandate per se, they nonetheless have an economic impact and potential role in strengthening the local innovation economy particularly in the context of cluster development.

Important dimensions of placed-based policies are local or regional innovation strategies. They are often developed by a coalition of local actors that look to mobilize resources and stakeholders, and coordinate investments towards transforming

---

[9] Bradford (2010) identifies five themes of new regionalism: clusters and regional innovation systems; place based policy; socially sustainable development; multilevel governance; and policy learning and knowledge transfer.

and adapting local industry to the competitive reality of global markets. Ensuring that governments align their interventions in support of these strategies is another aspect of place-based policies, a practice that is important for provincial and federal levels to recognize.

A third factor is how all three levels of government can make the collective decisions ultimately necessary if government policies are to be effective in supporting local innovation priorities and strategies. Given the complexity of the innovation system as a whole, with its national and regional aspects and multitude of departments and institutions, no one level of government has the necessary capacity to effectively support innovative regions. The decision-making process must therefore include whoever's authority, expertise or resources are needed to resolve a particular public problem related to cluster development. This is ultimately a process that includes more than one level of government and which can address cluster development issues that are both economic and social in nature. (Rosenfeld 2002; Bradford 2010). Making improvements to the vitality of the downtown core and to the transportation system can, for example, be essential to successfully drawing highly skilled people and innovative firms to the region.

In summary, the research analyzed above all points to a need for a more regionally and locally focused innovation policy approach than currently exists in Canada. There are examples of federal programs with some sensitivity to regional and local innovation dynamics but these are few in number.[10]

AN ENTANGLED INNOVATION POLICY MIX

Thus far, this paper has discussed two reasons why Canada should re-examine the manner in which it supports innovation. The final one is that the current approach of decentralized policy development related to innovation, which can span not just two but three levels of government, gives rise to the potential for policy and program duplication. Such overlap that can lead not only to inefficiencies, but also to confusion for the companies that policies are intended to serve. Much of the problematic overlap exists not so much in the support for framework conditions but in the generic and strategic support for innovation. As an example, consider again Canada's efforts to support value-added agriculture through innovation. These efforts are led by AAFC at the federal level and the Ontario Ministry of Agriculture, Food and Rural Affairs (OMAFRA) at the provincial level, both of which both provide a range of programming directed toward the agricultural sector from research funding

---

[10] Agriculture and Agri-Food Canada's innovation programming under the federal-provincial and territorial agreement, Growing Forward, and the Industry Canada's Community Futures program are two such programs. The former aligns investments with provincial innovation priorities, and the latter supports local innovation among rural firms.

to commercialization and networking to business start up support. Though these programs may be successes, they do overlap with more generic innovation support offered by all three levels of government. Take the case of Guelph, Ontario, which has recently committed itself to the development of the Guelph Agri-Innovation Cluster to build on existing strengths in the region's food, wellness, and agribusiness sectors. Companies in Guelph can benefit from eight commercialization support organizations, some of which are funded by the city, others by the province or federal government, or by both (HAL Corporation 2010). Of these eight, five are targeted at agriculture and three are more generic in their focus. Companies in the Guelph region also fall within the remit of Industry Canada's Community Futures Program, whose local Community Futures Development Corporations (CFDC) offer loans and related support to companies. Canada Business, a Canada-wide program also from Industry Canada also has local offices that offer advisory and intelligence services in all manner of business, not least innovation. For companies on the ground, the policy landscape can be confusing, as was noted by a number of companies interviewed for various innovation related studies conducted by the author. It also raises the question of whether such jurisdictional overlap is impeding cost-effectiveness in the innovation space. As Mendelsohn, Hjartarson, and Pearce (2010) argue in a call for a more efficient and effective Canadian federation, a number of policy areas, innovation included, could yield not only considerable savings but also improved policy outcomes if rationalized.

There are, of course, a number of reasonable explanations for this duplication. Foremost is that, owing to the prominence of innovation on political agendas at both the federal and provincial level, there are a wide range of departments that now endeavor to support innovation without much horizontal and multilevel co-ordination. Related to this is the fact that innovation is a multifaceted process that can be influenced by a broad mix of policies. The policy domains of training and education, research, industry, along with sector portfolios, such as natural resources, agriculture and environment, can all influence the many facets of innovation, such as knowledge generation and transfer, commercialization, partnerships and collaboration, and business strategy advice. This adds to the number of government organizations engaged in the innovation space.

A SUBSIDIARITY APPROACH FOR INNOVATION POLICY

Is there a better way? Given the complexity of the innovation policy environment, this question is not easily answered. Yet, given Canada's performance to date, it is certainly not an unreasonable one to ask. To return to each of the critiques put forth thus far, the recommendations for Canada's innovation policy are as follows: to rebalance the policy emphasis toward more direct forms of innovation support; to align and support innovation policies and programs with place-based policies; and to rationalize programming efforts to mitigate overlap and inefficiencies.

And while these policy paths are at one level distinct and disparate, the principle of subsidiarity offers a mechanism to bring them together in a coherent manner. Subsidiarity is an organizing principle at the core of federal systems that holds that matters of governance ought to be handled by the smallest, lowest or least centralized competent authority (Halberstam 2008). Stated in another way, under subsidiarity, the central authority should play a subsidiary role, performing only those tasks which cannot be performed effectively at a more immediate or local level.

While now a common principle in European Union treaties, and one that has been directly relevant to the European Commission's Competiveness and Innovation framework program (Lejour, Koskenlinna and Sluismans 2008), subsidiarity has had no such traction in Canada despite its potential as an organizing principle for innovation policy. The relevant question then is how much of Canada's innovation policy should be centralized?

Falk, Hölzl, and Leo (2008) identify four criteria for determining the degree of policy centralization. The first is variation across regional preferences, whereby the greater the regional diversity, the stronger the case for decentralization. For larger jurisdictions, the case is stronger than for smaller ones. The second criterion is the extent to which economies of scale can be realized; the greater such economies, the stronger the rationale for centralizing a given policy especially if it can lead to creating critical mass.

Third is the degree to which policy externalities, or rather, unintended consequences, are created as a result of administering a policy at one level over another. Centralization of policy can be justified if it results in benefits to all regions, as is the case with research funding, or if it minimizes negative impacts, such as wasteful competition that could arise from location specific policies. The last criterion is that of policy learning, which is promoted through decentralization, as when different regions experiment with different policies their experiences can then be shared.

In applying these four criteria to the three categories of innovation support presented earlier in this paper (Table 2), one can begin to rationalize a new approach for supporting innovation that clarifies roles and addresses the critiques presented in this paper. To begin with the framework conditions, the federal level is undoubtedly the appropriate level for administering R&D tax policy and to support research given the administrative economies of scale achieved in both the positive policy externalities associated with research. For the provinces, the implication would be that they stop offering additional R&D tax credits to firms under the SR&ED program.[11] This change would deter the one-upmanship competition in R&D tax incentives that has happened in sectors such as digital media across Canadian provinces.[12]

---

[11] Ontario administers three such tax incentives: the Innovation Tax Credit, the R&D Super Allowance and the Business-Research Institute Tax Credit.

[12] Seven of Canada's provinces now offer some form of additional R&D tax incentive support for digital media firms, most targeting labour costs, with refundable tax credits reaching 40 percent of eligible labour expenditures (HAL Corporation 2008, 20).

Table 2: Subsidiarity in an Innovation Policy Context

Criteria Category	CENTRALIZE		DECENTRALIZE		POLICY LOCUS
	Economies of Scale	Policy Externalities	Policy Learning	Diversity	
Indirect-Framework Conditions	Administrative	Maximizes positive spillovers	Minimal benefit	No benefit	Federal
Direct Innovation Process	Administrative	Minimizes overlap/ duplication	Minimal benefit	Some benefit: cluster networking	Federal
Direct-Sector/ Cluster Specific	Some administrative: for smaller regions	Minimizes interregional competition	Strong benefit	Strong benefit: place based policy	Provincial

Source: Author's compilation

Support for the innovation process includes policies and programs that target different facets of the innovation, would also benefit from centralization. In addition to achieving administrative economies of scale, primarily federal administration would help minimize duplication of, and overlap with, similar provincial policies and programs, which, as has been noted, can be significant. It could also help achieve greater consistency in innovation support across regions and help ensure that services are of a high quality.

For the third category, that of strategic support, the importance of local and regional differences and sector specialization, as previously discussed, validates a primary role for the provinces. The provinces, given their closer relationship with public and private innovation actors, and a closer understanding of industry capabilities, are better positioned to align strategic investments with both provincial and local strategies and build on existing strengths. In doing so, there is also an opportunity for policy learning, as provinces can share their experiences with different programs and policies.

Moreover, giving the provinces jurisdiction over strategic support would help address the long-standing federal-provincial tension around dealing with regional development at the national scale in a country with notable regional disparities in wealth (Simeon 1979). At the root of this tension are opposing logics. From an economic standpoint, regional development requires that investments be concentrated in regions with the greatest potential to realize their benefits. This logic has only grown stronger in the global economy where knowledge, capabilities, and wealth consistently clusters in innovative milieus, and in the Canadian policy context where the federal Regional Development Areas (RDAs) themselves are now looking to innovation programming to support their broader economic development objectives (Bradford 2010). This economic reality is however at tension with the political logic through which regional development is viewed as a means of addressing regional disparities in wealth, equality and fairness. "Provinces," writes Savoie (1986), "have come to expect Ottawa to work toward a fair distribution of economic activity throughout the country, with some smaller provincial governments claiming that this is in fact the federal government's main responsibility." But when fairness determines investment decisions, the result is a dilution of critical mass which ultimately translates into lower investment impacts.

Shifting the policy locus of strategic support to the provincial level would not be without negative consequences. It could exacerbate uneven industrial capacity across the federation and, indeed, may stoke wasteful interprovincial competition as provinces vie to attract inward investment in the same emerging sectors. Yet both such consequences also manifest under the current policy approach. The inherent geographic clustering of knowledge economies, together with historical development patterns of industrialization in Canada, are realities that make regional asymmetries in capacity an unavoidable feature of Canadian federalism.

On balance, the benefits of having the provinces responsible for strategic investments are too important to ignore. With greater strategic resources at their disposal, the provinces would be better positioned to rapidly respond to emerging opportunities, to fund technology grant programs in keeping with strategic priorities and strengths, and to support local strategic initiatives that look to upper levels of government for resources to build specialized research infrastructure or enhance local cluster capabilities.

For strategic support to be a viable element of Canada's innovation policy, therefore, more R&D grant programs and strategic investment funds need to be established at the provincial level as part of a long-term commitment to a new approach for supporting innovation. While this could involve new funding, the alterative would be to reallocate resources from existing federal programs to provincially administered strategic funds. Reducing the SR&ED tax incentive program to levels that are comparable to other countries could make more funds available for strategic support, as could the transfer of all relevant direct innovation funding currently administered at the federal level, including innovation support activities from the Regional Development Agencies.

Short of a new cash transfer to the provinces, which is unlikely to garner much federal support in the current climate, there are proven policy models that can offer the needed flexibility to allocate federal funds to meet provincial strategic objectives. Recent federal-provincial-territorial agreements established for agriculture, for example, provide a possible template. In negotiating the current agreement, Growing Forward, which is a five year, C$ 1.3 billion cost-shared program, each province was given the flexibility to determine how best to allocate the funding set aside for innovation in agriculture in the context of provincial needs and priorities. Ontario, for its part, used its funding to support the development of two science clusters and to strengthen its support for agri-tech innovation and commercialization organizations. Such a model gives primacy to provincial strategies while avoiding having the federal government acting directly as a regional player, which would only compound the overlap and duplication problem.

CONCLUSION

In their 2009 report, the Canadian Council of Academies wrote that "[i]n broad terms, and over time, Canada has provided a progressively more encouraging environment for business innovation, at least in respect of those factors over which public policy has direct influence ñ for example, prudent fiscal and monetary policies, a trend of lower tax rates and support for university research" (2009, 9). By most measures of Canada's innovation performance, however, this indirect and mostly federaal framework approach has under-delivered. And unless Canada engages in some innovative thinking and action on this issue innovation performance from last three decades suggest that the country will continue on this underwhelming trajectory.

This paper provides an initial step toward rethinking Canada's approach by arguing that the country needs to shift toward offering more direct forms of support that are better designed to address the fundamental weaknesses in Canada's innovation performance. Increased direct forms of support, in concert with competitive framework conditions, would provide a more balanced policy environment that is more in tune with the strengths, weaknesses, and differences across Canadian industries.

Any commitment toward such a shift, should, however, coincide with a rationalization of innovation policy across federal and provincial levels so that "who does what" reflects the principle of subsidiarity. By doing so, policies and related programming would be able to accommodate the place-based dimension of innovation, and strengthen the strategic focus of support that is essential to innovation-based economic development. The resulting potential for improved innovation performance could also coincide with improved cost effectiveness associated with a federally and provincially rationalized innovation policy that minimizes overlap and duplication. Only then will Canada be able to claim to have a viable national innovation policy.

REFERENCES

Asheim T., and M. Gertler. 2007. "The Geography of Innovation" in *The Oxford Handbook of Innovation*, eds. J. Fagerberg, D.Mowery, and R. Nelson,291-317. Oxford: Oxford University Press.

Bérubé, C., and P. Mohnen. 2009. "Are Firms that Receive R&D Subsidies More Innovative?" *Canadian Journal of Economics* 42 (1):206-225.

Bradford, N. 2010. *Regional Economic Development Agencies in Canada: Lessons for Southern Ontario*. Mowat Centre for Policy Innovation.

Bramwell, A., and D. A. Wolfe. 2008. "Universities and Regional Economic Development: The Entrepreneurial University of Waterloo." *Research Policy* 37 (8):1175-87.

Britton, J., and J. Gilmour. 1978. *The Weakest Link: A Technological Perspective on Canadian Industrial Underdevelopment*. Ottawa: Science Council of Canada.

Canada. Finance Canada and Revenue Canada. 1997. *The Federal System of Income Tax Incentives for Scientific Research and Experimental Development: Evaluation Report*. Ottawa: Department of Finance Canada and Revenue Canada.

Canada. Industry Canada. 2007. *Mobilizing Science and Technology to Canada's Advantage*. Ottawa: Industry Canada.

Canada. 2011. Imagination to Innovation: Building Canadian Paths to Prosperity. State of the Nation 2010. Ottawa: Science, Technology and Innovation Council Secretariat.

Cobban, T. 2008. "The Role of Municipalities in Stimulating Economic Growth: Evidence from the Petroleum Manufacturing Industry in Southern Ontario." PhD diss., University of Western Ontario, London.

Council of Canadian Academies (CCA). 2009. *Innovation and Business Strategy: Why Canada Falls Short*. Ottawa: Council of Canadian Academies.

Conference Board of Canada. 2008. *How Canada Performs: A Report Card on Canada*, November.

Conference Board of Canada. 2010. *How Canada Performs: A Report Card on Canada*, February.

Creutzberg T., D. Wolfe, and J. Nelles. 2006. "At the Crossroads: Strengthening the Toronto Region's Research and Innovation Economy." Toronto Region Research Alliance.

Czarnitzki, D., and A. Toole. 2007. "Business R&D and the Interplay of R&D Subsidies and Product Market Uncertainty." *Review of Industrial Organization* 31:169-181.

Czarnitzki, D., and G. Licht. 2006. "Additionality of Public R&D Grants in a Transition Economy: The Case of Eastern Germany." *The Economics of Transition* 14 (1):101-131.

Czarnitzki, D., and H. Hottenrott. 2009. "Are Local Milieus the Key to Innovation Performance." *Journal of Regional Science* 49 (1):81-112.

David, P., B., Hall and A. Toole. 2000. "Is Public R&D a Complement or Substitute for Private R&D? A Review of the Econometric Evidence." *Research Policy* 29:497-529.

Falk, R., W. Hölzl and H. Leo. 2008. "On the Roles and Rationales of European STI-Policies." In *Subsidiarity and Economic Reform in Europe*, eds. Gelauff, G., I. Grilo and A. Lejour, 129-142. DEU: Springer Berlin Heidelberg.

Halberstam, D. 2009. "Subsidiarity in a Comparative Perspective." in *Global Perspectives on Comparative Constitutional Law*, eds. V. Amar and T. Tushnet, 34-47. Oxford: Oxford University Press.

Hickling Arthurs Low (HAL) Corporation. 2009. Canada's Entertainment Software Industry: The Opportunities and Challenges of a Growing Industry. Research Paper 2009. Entertainment Software Association of Canada.

Hickling Arthurs Low (HAL) Corporation. 2010. Strategic Plan for the Guelph Agri-Innovation Cluster. Research Paper HAL Reference 7838. Guelph: HAL Corporation.

Howell, T. 2003. "Competing Programs: Government Support for Microelectronics." In *Securing the Future: Regional and National Programs to Support the Semiconductor Industry*, ed. C. Wessner, 189-253. Ottawa: National Research Council.

Jaumotte, F., and N. Pain. 2005. "Innovation in the Business Sector." Working Paper No. 459, OECD Economics Department. Paris: OECD Publishing.

Jenkins, T. "A Simple Solution to Canada's Innovation Problem." *Policy Options*. September 2011.

Lam, A. 2000. "Tacit Knowledge, Organizational Learning, Societal Institutions: an Integrated Framework," *Organizational Studies* 21-3: 487-513.

Leachman, R., and C. H. Leachman. 2004. "Globalization of Semiconductors: Do Real Men Have Fabs, or Virtual Fabs?" In *Locating Global Advantage: Industry Dynamics in the International Economy,* eds. M. Kenney and R. Florida, 203-231, Palo Alto, Calif.: Stanford University Press.

Lee, J. and Associates. "Sarnia Lambton petrochemical Industry Study." Presentation to Sarnia Lambton Economic Partnership Annual General Meeting. 23 June 2010.

Lejour, A., M. Koskenlinna and R. Sluismans. 2008. Subsidiarity and EU Support for Innovation. Inno Learning Platform.

Madore, O. 2006. *Scientific Research and Experimental Development: Tax Policy.* Parliamentary Information and Research Service. Ottawa: Library of Parliament.

Maskell, P., and A. Malmberg. 1999. "Localized Learning and Industrial Competitiveness." *Cambridge Journal of Economics* 23:167-86.

McKenna, B. 2011. Flawed R&D Scheme Costs Taxpayers Billions. *Globe and Mail*, 11 March.

Mendelsohn, M., J. Hjartarson, and J. Pearce. 2010. *Saving Dollars and Making Sense: An Agenda for a More Efficient, Effective and Accountable Federation.* Toronto: Mowat Centre for Policy Innovation.

Nelson R. and R. Langlois. 1983. "Industrial Innovation Policy: Lessons from American History." *Science* 219:814-18.

OECD. 2007. R&D Tax Treatment in OECD Countries: Comparisons and Evaluations. Workshop Report. Working Party on Innovation and Technology Policy (TIP).

Ontario. Premier's Council. 1989. *Competing in the New Global Economy: Report of the Premier's Council, Volume 1.* Toronto: Queen's Printer.

Parsons M., and N. Phillips. 2007. An Evaluation of the Federal Tax Credit for Scientific Research and Experimental Development. Working Paper 2007-2008, Finance Canada.

Rosenfeld, S. 2002. *Just Clusters: Economic Development Strategies that Reach More People and Places*. North Carolina: Regional Technology Strategies, Inc. Carroboro.

Rycroft R. and D. Kash. 1992. "Technology Policy Requires Picking Winners." *Economic Development Quarterly* 6 (3):227-240.

Savoie, D. 1986. *Regional Economic Development: Canada's Search for Solutions*. Toronto: Toronto University Press.

Saxenian, A. 1994. *Regional Advantage: Culture and Competition in Silicon Valley and Route 128*. Cambridge: Harvard University Press.

Science Council of Canada. 1979. *Forging the Links: A Technology Policy for Canada*. Report 29. Ottawa: Supply and Services Canada.

Simeon, R. 1979. "Federalism and the Politics of a National Strategy." In *The Politics of an Industrial Strategy: A Seminar*. Ottawa: Ministry of Supply and Services.

Taylor, A. 2008. Minister Prentice, it's Time to Stop Corporate Welfare for Profitable Companies. *National Post*, 28 March.

Warda, J. 2005. Measuring the Value of R&D Tax Provisions: A Primer on the B-Index Model for Analysis and Comparisons. Brussels: OMC Working Group.

Wolfe, D. A., and M. Lucas 2005. *Global Networks and Local Linkages*. Montreal: McGill-Queens University Press.

IV

Social Policy in the New Ontario

8

ONTARIO AND SOCIAL POLICY REFORM: FROM OFFSIDE TO OFFENSIVE?

Peter Graefe and Rachel Laforest

Tout est affaire de synchronisme et de positionnement en matière de relations intergouverne-mentales, une bonne stratégie de négociation permettant de concilier les avis, intérêts et aspirations d'acteurs voisins. Ce chapitre examine les schémas ontariens de participation intergouvernementale du dernier quart de siècle, et notamment la façon dont l'Ontario a géré ses liens avec le gouvernement fédéral. L'analyse porte sur quatre domaines de poli-tique sociale : aide sociale, politique d'immigration et d'établissement, garde d'enfants et réduction de la pauvreté. Elle examine aussi comment l'Ontario pourrait dynamiser les réformes dans ces domaines pour se hisser au rang de chef de file. La province pourrait en effet imposer son leadership si cette démarche produisait une série de politiques publiques adaptées aux nouveaux risques sociaux.

INTRODUCTION

In the realm of intergovernmental relations, timing and placement are everything. A good strategy negotiates the positions, interests, and desires of neighbouring players. For Ontario, the federal government has long been the "playmaker" – the player who can make the killer pass and who sees the field of intergovernmental relations like no one else. As a result, Ontario's tactics have usually relied on collaboration with the federal government and Ontario's interests have found expression within national projects. Yet, since the late 1980s, Ontario's participation in intergovern-mental social policy reform processes has increasingly been "offside" with Ottawa (Courchene and Telmer 1998; Cameron and Simeon 1997). This pattern has been observable not only in negotiations surrounding economic and budgetary policies, but also those regarding social assistance reform, immigrant settlement, early childhood policy, and the social union framework. Indeed, Ontario has repeatedly staked out positions that differed substantially from those of the federal government and that failed to rally a strong interprovincial consensus. With a few exceptions, Ontario has either stymied or blunted federal reforms, or it has been left waiting for the federal partner to participate in reforms that it has proposed.

This pattern of participation in intergovernmental relations is problematic as it has limited Ontario's ability to develop public policies to respond to the new social risks identified in international social policy discourses and in the government's own 2002-2004 Role of Government Panel (Ontario 2004). In order to address the demands of the new social policy agenda, the Ontario government will have to rethink its strategy and relationships to players on the field if it is to play a leadership role. Given that the growing risk aversion of post-2004 minority federal governments, coupled with the ideological leanings of its governing Conservative party since 2006, have largely taken the federal government out of the game, it is worthwhile to consider how Ontario could go on the offensive with a more provincialist social policy strategy in order to address emerging social policy challenges. This chapter examines Ontario's patterns of intergovernmental participation over the past quarter century focusing on the following four social policy fields; social assistance, immigration and settlement policy, childcare, and poverty reduction. It analyzes the interactions between Ontario, its provincial counterparts, and the community sector, as well as Ontario's interaction with the federal government. Based on this analysis, this chapter explores how Ontario could crank its reform energies up a notch or two in both these areas into a real position of leadership in the intergovernmental realm.

A PAGE IN ONTARIO'S PLAYBOOK

Since the early 1970s, Ontario's approach to intergovernmental relations has shifted significantly. In the 1970s and the 1980s Ontario was depicted as working in concert with the federal government. Not only did Ontario Premier Bill Davis provide support to the federal government in certain endeavors such as constitutional patriation, the Foreign Investment Review Agency (FIRA), and the National Energy Program, but Ontario also received support from Ottawa in the wake of the 1970s and 1980s recessions. Nevertheless, after the victory of Peterson's Liberals in 1985, Ontario increasingly adopted a critical pose toward the federal government, most notably in regard to the Canada-U.S. Free Trade Agreement. This critical approach continued under McGuinty's leadership in 2005 when a campaign was launched to narrow the $23 billion gap between Ontario's contribution to the federal government and the benefits it receives in return. Then dynamics changed again during McGuinty's second term in office in 2007 when Ontario took on a somewhat effaced "federalism-taker" role.

The perceived shift in Ontario's goals and strategies in intergovernmental relations over the past three decades requires an explanation, yet most explanations are now a decade old and date from Harris's early years in office. These interpretations stress that Ontario was increasingly "offside" with the federal government after being a trusted ally, but this may simply be historical revisionism. In the mid-1970s, a review of Ontario's place in federal-provincial relations could convincingly paint a picture of ongoing (if muted) conflict that increased from the late-1960s, and centred on the division of taxing and spending responsibilities (Martin 1974; McDougall and Westmacott 1975, 199-204).[1] The stance of Premier McGuinty on "fairness for Ontario," a reprise of stands taken by the Harris Conservative government, or indeed of Rae's "fair-shares federalism," correlates with Simeon's view that questions of finance have always been of central importance for Ontario and that "Ontario has emphasized the need for fiscal autonomy – for a smaller federal tax burden which would allow the province room to expand its own taxes" (Simeon 1980, 189).[2] Similarly, those wishing to stress continuity over change might cite Woolstencroft's observations from the early 1980s. He noted that Ontario's intergovernmental specialists were opposed to program entanglement because it "threatens the constitutional integrity of both orders of government and blurs the lines of responsibility and accountability" (Woolstencroft 1982, 56).

Notwithstanding the echoes of these past patterns in the present, the overwhelming interest of recent contributions is to explore and explain seeming patterns of change. The boldest contemporary interpretation of the shift in Ontario's federal-provincial relations continues to be Courchene's region-state hypothesis, which mirrors some elements of the more cautious work of Wolfe and Cameron (Courchene and Telmer 1998; Cameron and Simeon 1997; Cameron 1994; Wolfe 1997). For Courchene, the last twenty years of the twentieth century were marked by tectonic changes in economic geography that upset the political strategies and alliances of the past. The impact of this situation on federal-provincial relations is clear-cut. Courchene and Telmer baldly state that "the pervasiveness of economic forces necessarily means devolving greater autonomy to the regions so that they can pursue their distinctive economic futures" (1998, 295). These same forces also make it Ontario's interest to assume powers needed to nurture the region-state, and to be far more active in interprovincial redistribution and economic union

---

[1] In an interesting echo, the authors note that "the federal government has attempted to avoid this conflict by using its superior revenue-creating power to construct and deliver programs directly to the public," with confusing effects at the community level (McDougall and Westmacott 1975, 207).

[2] Joe Martin likewise argued that "to Ontario the key aspect of federal-provincial relations is finance" (1974, 2)

issues. Indeed, if Canadian federalism is to be driven more by intergovernmental processes than by constitutional structures, Ontario will want to assure itself a say in limiting redistribution to the equalization program, and ensuring that equalization does not impede the functioning of internal trade and mobility (Courchene and Telmer 1998, 300-4).

Similar economic forces also recur in the accounts of Noel, as well as Cameron and Simeon. Noel, for instance, draws on his work on Ontario's political culture to argue that Ontario has historically sought to be the pre-eminent player within Confederation, and that Ontarians have consistently pursued the imperative of economic success. With the shift to a north-south economy, old political forms no longer nurture this economic success. The post-Charlottetown period thus corresponds to a re-evaluation of Ontario's core interests. This period has given rise to calls for rebalancing to meet Ontario's competitiveness needs, as well as demands for more say in the pan-Canadian social programs its residents subsidize (Noel 1998, 272, 275, 279, 282-4). Cameron and Simeon (1997) provide a broader range of factors driving the "New Ontario," including increased ethnic diversity, deficit shifting, and ideological divergence. Nevertheless, Ontario's changed geo-economic situation figures prominently, as does the decline of pan-Canadian sentiment among Ontario's Confederation partners (which cannot be disassociated from economic factors). In Cameron and Simeon's view, the shift to a north-south economy does not erode Ontario's attachment to the federation, but does result in reduced confidence in Ottawa's leadership ability, and attempts to find new means of protecting the economic and social union (1997, 169-78).

While structural change may logically presuppose a more aggressive role for Ontario as it seeks to cement its predominance in an evolving federal system, there is no necessary reason why it has followed its course from backing Meech, to being a Social Charter activist, to defining Social Union talks around the vision of province-led policy coordination of Courchene's (1996) ACCESS model, to most recently being a "federalism taker," engaging on a case-by-case basis with the federal government. Ontario could indeed have adopted a number of different strategies to increase its capacity to define its regional competitiveness. While the pursuit of interprovincial and federal-provincial framework agreements is one approach, it could have also chosen to follow Quebec's example in pre-empting the federal government by taking the lead in policy development.[3]

---

[3] For instance, Quebec's success in expanding control of labour force development activities owes something to its activism in creating the SQDM. See Haddow and Sharpe 1997, 150-51.

PLAYING ON THE SOCIAL POLICY FIELD

The work tying intergovernmental relations strategies to these large shifts in economic structures is important. Ontario has unequivocally found itself facing new conditions with mounting economic pressures. Nevertheless, it is quite some distance to travel from the abstraction of structural changes and big picture inter-governmental relations strategies, where actors are absent, to specific negotiations and policy choices. Certain dimensions of intergovernmental relations are more closely linked to economic and structural adjustments, while others may be more political (Lecours and Béland 2010). Ontario's new conditions in the federation have given rise to contentions between Ontario and the federal government as they kick around ideas about the future. These conflicts, seemingly tied to a greater extent to partisan ideological dynamics and shifting political forces than to large-scale economic determinants, have been most visible in the field of social policy. Ontario has not followed Quebec in investing in intergovernmental relations machinery to the extent of imposing a clear and coherent strategy across policy fields, instead it continues to define its strategy in practice.

While a social policy focus gives a useful smaller picture, we are cognizant that it comes at a cost. In areas such as infrastructure or economic development, relationships may follow a different dynamic: witness the close and productive relationships in restructuring the automotive sector or in infrastructural investments during the recent recession, even as there was some tension around the future of the Canada-Ontario Immigration Agreement. That said, it should be noted here that our interest is not the usual questions of qualifying the degree of conflict or cooperation in federal-provincial relations or of assessing "whose ox got gored." This chapter instead asks the question of how Ontario has tried to realize key social policy goals, and assesses how the intergovernmental realm has assisted or impeded their realization.

Ontario has traditionally been a strong supporter of the national project in Canada, embracing a vision of citizenship that emphasizes equality and access to the same level of services for all citizens in Canada regardless of place. Yet, its provincial interests have increasingly become out of sync with this representation of the national project. In the late 1980s, as Ontario embarked on its "Quiet Revolution," the Ministry of Intergovernmental Affairs' recognized that Ontario's activist plans for long-term social and economic renewal diverged not only from the other provinces (that were seen as preoccupied with short-term economic problems), but also from the federal government's emphasis on budgetary restraint, regional disparities, and free trade.[4] This presented a difficult strategic context of trying to engage an unsympathetic federal government, without necessarily having much of a free hand

---

[4] Ministry of Intergovernmental Affairs, *Federalism Forecast 1987-88*, Internal Document, September 1987, 2, 7.

to organize a provincial position. These new conditions led to frustration in several social policy fields, although this frustration manifested itself differently in each.

Social Assistance Reforms

In social assistance, the Ontario government tried to maintain a degree of freedom of action in the implementation and administration of its programs relative to the federal government (Boychuk 1998; Graefe 2006). In the late 1980s, welfare rates and expenditures were on the rise. The Ontario Liberal Premier, David Peterson, appointed a Social Assistance Review Committee to assess the situation and examine the province's social assistance programs. The committee's report, entitled *Transitions*, was released in 1988 and called for an extension of benefits and programs to cover the basic needs of welfare recipients. Social assistance was conceptualized as primarily an income support system that nevertheless could enable recipients to become self-reliant and to fully participate in society. The structure of benefits and programs were not to be tied to labour market participation. This vision of social assistance differed from that of workfare proposals at the time, which made benefits conditional on participation in job placement schemes, and with which many provinces were experimenting. Nevertheless, the Ontario government had signaled a willingness to proceed with the recommendations of the Social Assistance Review Committee's *Transitions* report, which included both the enhancement of benefits, and the development of "opportunity planning" services to enable recipients to have access to developmental opportunities, including those aiding transitions into paid work.

While the federal government encouraged provinces to move in this direction of emphasizing the employability of social assistance recipients, for instance through the *Employability Enhancement Accords* and a lax interpretation of the Canada Assistance Plan in the case of proto-workfare programs in British Columbia, Quebec, and Saskatchewan, it was not prepared to support just any vision of employability. The Ontario plan of promoting employability, while also improving the social rights of social assistance recipients, was controversial to a deficit-conscious federal Conservative government. This was especially the case when the limited provincial capacity to provide high-end employability programs meant that early reforms were heavily tilted towards benefit enhancements rather than new training initiatives.

This conflict was settled to Ontario's disadvantage by the unilateral imposition of a cap on Canada Assistance Plan (CAP) payments to non-equalization receiving provinces by the federal government (effectively Alberta, British Columbia, and Ontario).These provinces would be fully responsible for paying for all increases in social assistance costs beyond five percent. In other words, the federal government would only cost-share the first five percent annual increase in social assistance costs. Considered in terms of a "steady-state" social assistance system, this decision had significant ramifications for the cost of any benefit improvements, or for investments in the system to increase procedural fairness. However, Ontario was not in a steady-state in the early 1990s as labour market changes drove up the social assistance caseload. In this instance, simply maintaining the existing system became increasingly costly, as the cyclical pressures of a recessionary economy were compounded by having to pay the full marginal cost of caseload increases once the 5 percent threshold was crossed. The *Transitions* reform was effectively derailed.

It is generally argued that the cap on CAP was put in place largely to protect the federal treasury from rapidly increasing social assistance resulting from the Ontario Liberal government's 1989 reforms to social assistance. The popular press often plays up the contribution of the NDP government's purportedly extravagant benefit increases, but even a largely unsympathetic critic like Courchene points out that the main driver of social assistance costs in Ontario was a ballooning caseload resulting from the early 1990s recession. Had Ontario kept its existing social assistance system and not started implementing some of the SARC's recommendations, it likely would have qualified for at least C$300 million more per year in CAP funds than it did under the cap on CAP, and likely significantly more (Courchene and Telmer 1998, 146-7).

It is worth noting that the cap on CAP did not solely constrain increased benefits, but it also to narrowed the range of possible employability programs, an area where Ontario might have innovated post-*Transitions*. While the SARC's recommendations on benefits certainly required higher spending, other expenses were generated by the generous vision of "opportunity planning" where training and employment programs involved meaningful investments in skills and were surrounded with increased rights to housing, transportation, child care, and other supports. The cap on CAP not only served to close the door to higher benefits, but also to employability programs that would privilege skills and personal development over immediate labour force attachment. As the Rae government regrouped and tried to push a smaller and less generous package of social assistance reforms based on a child benefit and work integration programs (set out in the *Turning Point* initiative), it again had to pull back due to the lack of federal buy-in and the continued constraint on federal cost sharing. The federal government effectively thwarted Ontario's social assistance reform agenda by constraining its options.

The election of a Conservative government committed to a "work-first" vision of workfare narrowed the gap between the governments, while the rolling up of the Canada Assistance Plan and its conditions (in addition to the prevention of residency requirements) in the 1995 budget also reduced the amount of overlap. Indeed, social assistance *per se* dropped off the federal-provincial agenda. Breaking down the purported "welfare wall" that motivated the employability focus however lived on as an objective in the National Child Benefit negotiations. Here again Ontario was largely in line, albeit also in league with other "tough on welfare" provinces like Alberta, in seeking to keep the level at which children were deemed to be "off welfare" quite low (Boychuk 2002). While these initiatives kept peace with the federal government, they did little to deal with the social risks of poverty, or to foster experimentation with best-practices in welfare-to-work that occurred in the United States and the United Kingdom at the same time (Herd 2006).

Immigrant Settlement Services

Fiscal pressures and retrenchment also hugely impacted Ontario's immigrant settlement policy agenda in the 1990s. Immigration has long been a policy area of shared jurisdiction between the federal and provincial governments. Federal legislation prevails over Canada's immigration program and provinces and territories are mainly responsible for integration and settlement services. In the context of growing fiscal constraint, all parties share an interest in reducing the costs of the services they are providing while maximizing the economic and social benefits of immigration.

In the early 1990s, the Chrétien Liberal government made a number of changes to entrance requirements in an effort to decrease the costs of settlement and integration services for both the federal and provincial governments. The federal government began to privilege "economic class" immigrants, professionals and skilled workers, over others. To enter Canada immigrants also had to pay a landing fee and meet language requirements. Immigrants that met these criteria were deemed to be more "self-sufficient" and to be able to integrate more quickly into Canadian society, thereby reducing the financial burden on the system (Abu-Laban 2006).

The federal government also began to reassess its role in settlement services. Already in 1976, the *Immigration Act* had established the legislative authority for the federal government to consult with the provinces on immigration. This had enabled the federal government to sign agreements with individual provinces over the management and coordination of immigration and settlement services. As part of its 1994 Program Review, the federal government determined that delegating service delivery to voluntary organizations would be a more effective way to cut costs in the settlement area while maintaining the same level of services. Shortly thereafter, it launched the "settlement renewal initiative" to withdraw from settlement services and devolve the administration of these programs to provincial governments (Abu-Laban and Gabriel 2002, 68-9).

Over the next couple of years, the federal government signed agreements with all of the provinces for settlement renewal, with the exception of Ontario.[5] In order to support economic and social development priorities, the federal government developed the Provincial Nominee Program to enable provinces or territories to set criteria for nominees to meet specific regional needs. While Manitoba,

---

[5] Quebec had signed an immigration agreement covering settlement with the federal government in 1991.

Saskatchewan and the Atlantic provinces quickly developed plans to use this program, Ontario was not interested in negotiating the devolution of the federal government's responsibilities: negotiations stalled. Ontario continued to look to the federal government to be the playmaker, just as the federal government was inching its way off the field.

It is estimated that over this period Citizenship and Immigration Canada's settlement budget decreased from 46 percent of CIC's total budget in 1997-98 to 37 percent in 2001 (Bloemraad 2006, 121). Provincial governments, much like the federal government, were aiming to reduce the size of the state and their immigrant settlement budgets also declined over this period of time. Ontario was no exception, and in 1995 the newly elected progressive conservative government cut back close to 50 percent of its budget on direct service provision in the area of immigrant settlement (Frisken and Wallace 2003; Shields 2004; Mwarigha 1998). The combined effect of provincial cuts and the lack of an agreement between the federal government and Ontario placed enormous pressure on the settlement services sector, and particularly voluntary organizations (Richmond and Shields 2004).

The Canada-Quebec Accord on Immigration, signed in 1991, had become a particular irritant to the Ontario government. This agreement guaranteed a minimum of C$90 million per year to Quebec for settlement and training services. Quebec was therefore receiving a third of the federal funding available for immigrant settlement, yet it received only 18 percent of the immigrants. Without any settlement agreement between Ontario and the federal government, Ontario was receiving the lowest per capita allocation in the country.[6] Yet, it had the largest immigrant intake in Canada at the time, receiving 59.3 percent of all immigrant arrivals to Canada in 2001.[7] Waiting for the federal government to take on a leadership role in settlement and immigration meant that Ontario gradually found itself out of sync with both the federal government and its provincial counterparts.

The dynamic changed following the election of Dalton McGuinty's Liberal government in October 2003. In its quest to obtain its "fair share," Ontario identified federal funding for immigrant settlement services as an area that had contributed to the C$23 billion gap that had developed. While British Columbia and Manitoba had successfully negotiated greater control over settlement policy, Ontario continued to look to the federal government to play a stewardship role in the area as part of its nation-building role (Seidle 2010). In 2005, the Canada-Ontario Immigration Agreement (COIA) was signed and the federal government continued to exercise complete administrative control over settlement services in the province. This agreement reduced the gap between Ontario and the other provinces significantly although by 2009, Ontario had only received C$407 million of the C$600 that had been promised in the COIA.

---

[6] It is estimated that each immigrant in Ontario received $800 in support services from the federal government, while those in Quebec received $3800 (Ontario government budget).

[7] Visit ontarioimmigration.ca.

While the federal government honored its commitments, an effective Ontario policy and program response to settlement was still hamstrung by the federal approach. Indeed, since the election of a conservative federal government in 2006, a number of incremental policy changes have been adopted in the immigration area which taken together amount to nothing less that a major reconsideration of the role of the federal government in the immigration system. Over the years, the federal government has enabled newcomers to take multiple routes to immigrate to Canada by promoting programs such the temporary foreign workers, the Canadian Experience Class, and removing caps on the Provincial Nominee Program. However, upon arrival these newcomers do not enter the country with the same rights and protections as permanent residents as they are not eligible for language and settlement services. Yet these services are vital to successful social, economic, and cultural integration and as the number of newcomers entering Canada under these three categories expands, more immigrants will find themselves in vulnerable positions and having difficulty integrating into Canadian society. For Ontario, the province that receives the largest proportion of immigrants, this poses some significant challenges to the effectiveness of its settlement services. The growth of these programs has prompted many advocates in Ontario to lobby for the federal government to redress these issues by taking on a more proactive role and recognizing immigration as critical to nation-building (Alboim 2009; Goldring 2010; Canadian Council for Refugees 2010).

Childcare and Early Learning

The clearest example of the frustration related to a strategy of collaborative engagement with the federal government comes from the field of childcare and early learning, where two attempts to innovate failed as a loss of interest at the federal level left the province hanging. Mahon provides the fullest account of these two episodes (Mahon 2010). In the first, the Peterson governments of 1985-90 elaborated a plan to reclassify public childcare from the area of welfare policy to a core support for working parents in a modern knowledge economy. This included measures to increase the number of available spaces in public and non-profit care, as well as to increase quality through greater support for wages and closer integration with the school system. The plan nevertheless was contingent on the Conservative federal government following through on their announced childcare plan. When this plan was delayed due to significant criticisms of its shortcomings, and then shelved following the 1988 election, the province proceeded with a far more modest set of changes. Attempts by the NDP to revive and expand the Peterson plan, either as a big package, or more quietly through targeted responses to the recession, likewise did not take flight. They were hamstrung on the one side by the cap on CAP, and on the other by the unwillingness of the Chrétien Liberals, elected in 1993, to either rescind the cap on CAP or follow through on their childcare election promises.

This situation replayed itself in a more compressed time frame between 2003 and 2006. Here again, the newly elected provincial government ramped up its strategy of extending full-day kindergarten to four year-olds, thereby freeing up resources to step up early childhood education for two and a half to four year-olds. This time, the government met a willing federal partner that shared a similar policy commitment to developing this area, as well as a similar fiscal conservativism in terms of rolling out changes in small increments. Ontario was among the first provinces to sign a bilateral childcare agreement in November 2005. The change in federal government in 2006 scuttled this agreement. Rather than continuing to roll-out its planned policy, Ontario instead drew down its monies from these agreements slowly to fund the first batch of new spaces. While it has continued to support these spaces with its own funds, its own early childhood strategy has been delayed and largely limited to the full-day kindergarten initiative. Once again, the difficulty of coordinating provincial reform with federal initiatives left Ontario, and its social policy ambitions, with no one to play with.

As this chapter details, the Ontario experience with intergovernmental relations in social policy has not been particularly successful over the past quarter century. Whereas Ontario was relatively content with strategies that stressed the pursuit of Ontario's interest within those of the broader nation, the last decade has seriously challenged its approach. Using old tactics has left Ontario offside on the social policy field. From the torpedo-ing of the *Transitions* project, to the tension between punitive workfare and national child benefits, the Ontario and federal governments have been working at cross-purposes. As Ontario has not been able to mobilize a broader interprovincial consensus in its battles with the federal government. The result has been to stymie changes in social assistance. In immigrant settlement and childcare and early learning, the pattern has been slightly different. The province developed plans that depended on federal participation and commitment that never arrived, or came as too little, too late.

THE NEW SOCIAL POLICY AGENDA: A FAMILIAR FIELD?

This might not be overly concerning if the social policy challenges facing Ontario were relatively minor ones. However, consistent with the new social risk profiles facing western post-industrial states, including Canada, Ontario is facing a number of important challenges if it wishes to avoid social and economic decline.[8] Recognition of the necessity of retooling social policy as an economic strategy in

---

[8] On the "new social risk" perspective, see Esping-Andersen, G., D. Gallie, J. Myles and A. Hemerjick, 2002, and Jenson, J., 2004.

knowledge-based economies reaches back to at least the strategic thinking of the Rae New Democrats, and can even be seen in elements of the *Transitions* report in the late 1980s (Mahon 2010). The alarm bell was rung again in 2002-2003 by the Panel on the Role of Government, where research contributions underlined that the social risks around poverty, early learning, and the socioeconomic integration of new Canadians were not being met with robust and coherent policy initiatives (Maxwell 2003). This is not solely a concern of social democrats and left liberals, but has indeed spurred a strengthened "corporate reform" voice, as seen in the Toronto City Summit Alliance (recently renamed CivicAction) and its income support working group, or in the diagnoses of the TD Bank.

In this light, the McGuinty government elected in 2003 has taken a number of steps to address these social risks, including, the extension of junior kindergarten, supporting the federal childcare initiative in the dying days of the Martin government, developing the Ontario Child Benefit, and targeting small initiatives in the education system for the "at risk," (the latter two being rolled into a broader Poverty Reduction Strategy). However, ignoring the high politics of the government's "fairness" campaign during its first mandate, it has otherwise been a "federalism-taker."

The trouble with this strategy is that there is not much "federalism" to take at the moment. The compound effects of a string of risk-averse minority governments in Ottawa coupled with a Conservative government that does not have a substantial program of social welfare policy expansion or renewal (beyond some gimmicky tax credit schemes), means that there is not a lot to engage with. Across a number of policy fields, the provinces are in a holding pattern, waiting for a sign of federal intention. In disability policy, for instance, the 2003 Labour Market Agreement for Persons with Disabilities, has been rolled over annually since 2006, despite strong provincial views that it needs to be revisited. This revisiting might be part of a larger deal involving the movement of the income and social services aspects of disability policy, along the lines of the National Child Benefit. The federal government could assume more of an income support role and provinces would be able to claw money out of their social assistance budgets and apply it to employment and other supports for persons with disabilities. Along similar lines, Ontario and several other provinces appear ready to look favourably on a childcare program along the lines of the bilateral agreements signed in the dying days of the Martin government, but looking to Ottawa as the engine to bring such a program into existence is akin to announcing a lack of interest in the file.

In immigrant settlement, the federal government also appears to have withdrawn itself. With multiple streams of entry and new players taking the lead in defining criteria for entrance, national control of immigration is likely to diminish. The paths to citizenship in Canada are now more diverse, and multiple players have come to share significant influence over the composition of immigration to Canada. Many observers have warned that this may undermine the country's ability to use the immigration system as an instrument of nation-building. Naomi Alboim, for example, notes that "the federal government has devolved to others much of its role in selecting the future citizens of this country.... Such bodies do not have the national interest as their primary mandate or objective in selecting people who ultimately become permanent residents or citizens" (2009, 11). Similarly, Tom Kent has argued that "the federal government's response to the problems has been to shuffle much of the responsibility to provincial governments and to employers for ostensibly temporary work. In the resulting confusion, the national purpose for immigration is lost" (Kent 2010, 1). Until the COIA is renegotiated, and Ontario gains the control over settlement that it has requested, it is stuck in a holding pattern.

Poverty reduction provides another interesting example. Social assistance largely fell off the policy radar in the 1990s but concern for developing policies to deal with poverty reemerged in the early 2000s. Almost all the provinces have recently worked on developing poverty reduction strategies, or are taking new steps to alleviate poverty through existing health and social services infrastructure. In all cases, the strategies look up to the federal government to assist in meeting their poverty reduction goals. Predictably, long-standing federal responsibilities around employment insurance and aboriginal peoples are identified, as are calls for action on early learning and affordable housing (Ontario 2008, ch. 7). However, if the Ontario case is at all representative, success in meeting reduction targets is also calculated on the basis of increased federal effort around child and working income tax benefits. It is felt that these can move a sufficient number of low-wage workers (and by extension their children) from just under to just over the poverty line, thereby helping to meet poverty reduction targets.

This tendency to wait on the federal government is reminiscent of the Ontario pattern on childcare and immigration, be it under Peterson, Rae, or McGuinty. The difference is that in those cases, there was every reason to believe that the federal government would bring something forward as it was working on its own consultations and reflections on the file. In the current case, the federal government is mostly inactive, making the strategy even less likely to bear fruit. This may be a handy form of blame avoidance, but not a terribly effective strategy of retooling social policy for a new era.

Two objections might be raised to this analysis.[9] First, it could be asked whether we overstate the weight of Conservative partisan disinterest in social policy, confusing that with the risk aversion of the minority government situation. A Conservative majority government, in that view, might return to the field with a stronger agenda, particularly in the 2014 renegotiation of the Health and Social transfers and equalization. This is certainly quite possible, but in many ways provides more incentive to Ontario to "go it alone." This would ensure that Ontario's longer-term social policy goals are more fully integrated into any larger plan of rebalancing "who does what," or alternatively to head off further attempts to deliver "social policy" directly to Canadians through boutique tax credits. Second, a reviewer asked if the

---

[9] We thank our anonymous reviewer for his/her useful comments.

idea that the federal government should be "in the game" is built into the DNA of Ontario voters and, by extension, Ontario governments. While Ontarians have long supported a strong federal role (though see our comments in the conclusion), it is not thereby clear that they see unilateral provincial initiatives as somehow illegitimate. To our knowledge, such a critique has not had traction around recent largely unilateral initiatives such as the extension of full-day learning to four year-olds, the development of a poverty reduction strategy, or the extension of basic dental benefits to children of parents with low incomes. It may be that Ontarians have far more instrumental than organic conceptions of federalism than many academic observers of federalism would like to believe.[10]

ONTARIO, PLAY BALL: TAKING THE OFFENSIVE?

In the context of the early 2000s, and the reflections of the Ontario Role of Government Panel, the one commissioned report on federalism saw Ontario as placed between collaborating with the federal government in specific areas or joining Quebec in resisting all federal involvement. The report, by the economist Paul Boothe, came down clearly on the side of collaboration using a "separate but complementary" approach. This supported a strategy of pushing for increased transfers instead of more tax room, recognizing that while tax room was better for Ontario, it was not politically feasible to obtain this from Ottawa, especially if the point was to be collaborative (Boothe 2003).

This sort of collaborative approach remains congenial to a number of thinkers. To return to poverty policy, recent reflections on the "adult benefits" system propose a separate but complementary approach whereby income support is largely uploaded to the federal government, and the social assistance money this frees up is invested in more substantial and effective training systems as well as other supportive social services (Stapleton 2004; Battle 2006) The Eggleton/Segal Senate report on poverty provided a somewhat less Cartesian division (Standing Senate Committee on Social Affairs, Science and Technology 2009). The Mowat Centre's paper in this volume on a next great intergovernmental conversation takes a similar line, albeit remaining agnostic on the particular case of income security. The general line could be extended elsewhere such as policies for people with disabilities, as alluded to above or as set out more controversially in Rick August's report for the Caledon Institute (August 2009).

However, the change in dynamic caused by the reluctance of the federal government to propose policies to deal with new social risks should lead us to revisit Boothe's conclusions. The choices seem to be less between resisting Ottawa or

---

[10] For a discussion of citizens' instrumental and organic conceptions of federalism, see Fafard, Rocher and Côté 2009.

channeling Ottawa into efficient collaborations, than about taking the offensive or of waiting for Ottawa to eventually develop a renewed sense of social purpose. The latter course seems particularly risky for several reasons. These include, the indeterminate wait for that social purpose to arise, as well as the time involved in achieving some grand new bargain, provided such a bargain is in fact attainable and politically saleable. There is also the possibility that Ottawa's social purpose will fit imperfectly with provincial priorities, or will subjugate provincial performance for federal credit-taking. For instance, given the current state of labour markets, it is not impossible to imagine a situation where a federal guaranteed income delivered through a negative income tax proves effective, while provincial training programs fail to do much for clients with numerous barriers to employment. Nor is it impossible to think of blame-shifting games where an inadequate annual income pushes the meeting of basic needs and associated costs on provincially delivered services, including housing.

The Quebec alternative in the current period, then, is less one of resisting intrusion, than of taking the lead so as to limit and shape future federal involvement (Noël 2000). Given the interdependence characterizing contemporary governance, it is not as if the federal government can be pushed out of the game. Nevertheless, the capacity of Quebec to carve out a distinctive family policy, and to receive compensation without losing policy control when the federal government moved into the field (albeit with some loss to Quebecers in their ability to fully make use of the childcare expense deduction) is instructive. Ontario obviously lacks the credible national project that gave Quebec additional bargaining leverage, for instance in the case of parental leaves. It also lacks the set of organized social actors to support it in conflict with the federal government. However it would still be difficult for the federal government to implement a program that directly contradicted or undermined key aspects of a well-entrenched Ontario innovation. And it is also true that provincial innovations based on dialogue with organized interests would begin to develop an "Ontario consensus" to back the government.

It would in fact be more difficult to overturn such innovations in cases where Ontario had worked with other provinces to define and debate policy alternatives. Indeed, taking the lead could also take the form of developing the policy role of the Council of the Federation. Rather than having the Council serve largely as an anvil for hammering out provincial common fronts in disputes with the federal government, there might be a point in investing it as a place for provinces to more systematically share their social policy planning and practices. This would locate a space of social policy learning outside the sphere of the federal government and allow for an aligning of provincial policy horizons separate from federal agendas. This would differ from some proposed forms of interprovincialism from the 1990s, such as the ACCESS proposal, as the idea of national standards would not be in play. The point would not be to set and police a national minimum, but instead to develop some shared ideas about policy objectives and of consequential steps to achieving them regardless of federal involvement. Indeed, this strategy might even appeal to those in favour of engaging the federal government, as such discussions might prod the latter into action for predictable reasons of statecraft and citizenship (Banting 2006; Béland and Lecours 2008). In the case of poverty reduction, for instance, thought could be given to defining a set of successful provincial interventions that could at the same time serve to limit the range of possible federal interventions when and if the latter came to the table.

In the case of immigration policy, Ontario has asked for more control over immigrant settlement services. This would enable the province to adopt more successful integration policies and work more collaboratively with its municipal and voluntary sector partners. Already, programs like Local Immigration Partnership Initiatives, have proven very effective by fostering more localized services and activities, tailored to the needs of newcomers and communities. There are opportunities to be seized by Ontario in the field of immigrant settlement to pursue its own agenda. The disengagement of the federal government from social policy stewardship has altered the balance of political forces in the area. New actors, such as municipalities and voluntary sector organizations are now more central to the process of governance. These collaborations could prove very useful in order to support Ontario if it goes on the offensive. What is more, issues of civic participation, engagement, and inclusion in political and social life are now dealt with at these local and regional scales. Not surprisingly, access to the political arena for many newcomers is increasingly more regionalized or locally based, and detached from the federal government. This means that loyalties and forms of belonging will be increasingly local and could be mobilized to serve the provincial interest if Ontario is so inclined.

Taking the lead would in turn force a reconsideration of the trade-off between transfers and tax points as a means of funding such social policy innovation. In either case, one could imagine that the debate with the federal government would not be gentle, and might take the form of the earlier debate over fiscal imbalance, albeit now in a context where there are no longer predictions of indefinite surpluses. The trade-off between transfers and tax points would instead need to be determined on the basis of the preferences of potential provincial allies, and of their capacities to undertake path-shaping reforms under one formula or another.

The changes that we have observed in social policy have altered the constraints and opportunities facing Ontario. They have opened up a space to make claims and representations in the name of those provincial interests. Ontario has long been wedded to the idea that the federal government was the playmaker, stewarding a vision of pan-Canadian citizenship. Those days are gone. With a deficit estimated at C$21.3 billion (March 2010 budget) and a long road to recovery ahead, Ontario needs to get in the game.

Whether Ontario citizens will mobilize around this identity remains to be seen. Ontarians have a long attachment to the Canadian nation. However, there are signs that this attachment is dwindling, or at least shifting (Matthews and Mendelsohn

2010). Recent work on this attachment has remained too focused on Ontarians as customers, and their impressions of getting a "fair share" or being well-treated by different orders of government. But identities are also forged through an active politics of representation. Political representation is a vital pillar of democratic engagement and serves as a training ground for citizenship. The federal government has become increasingly detached from citizens, has cut off many routes to political representation and cut funding to advocacy organizations. Leading based on dialogue with organized interests in Ontario might be surprisingly generative of the necessary supportive provincial identities. Provincial identities could become particularly strong if the result of these dialogues is a set of effective public policies designed for our modern social risks.

REFERENCES

Abu-Laban, Y. 2006. "Jean Chrétien's Immigration Legacy: Continuity and Transformation." In *The Chrétien Legacy: Politics and Public Policy in Canada,* eds. L. Harder and S. Patten, pp. 142-159. Montreal and Kingston: McGill-Queen's University Press.

Abu-Laban, Y. and C. Gabriel. 2002. *Selling Diversity: Immigration, Multiculturalism, Employment Equity and Globalization.* Peterborough: Broadview Press; University of Toronto Press.

Alboim, N. 2009. *Adjusting the Balance: Fixing Canada's Economic Immigration Policies, Immigration Policies.* Toronto: Maytree Foundation.

August, R. 2009. *Paved with Good Intentions: The Failure of Passive Disability Policy in Canada.* Ottawa: Caledon Institute of Social Policy.

Banting, K. 2006 "Social Citizenship and Federalism: Is a Federal Welfare State a Contradiction in Terms?" In *Territory, Democracy and Justice: Regionalism and Federalism in Western,* ed. S. L. Greer, 44-66. New York: Palgrave MacMillan.

Battle, K., S. Torjman and M. Mendelson. 2006. *Towards a New Architecture for Canada's Adult Benefits.* Ottawa: Caledon Institute of Social Policy.

Béland D. and A. Lecours. 2008. *Nationalism and Social Policy: The Politics of Territorial Solidarity.* New York: Oxford University Press.

Bloemraad, I. 2006. *Becoming a Citizen: Incorporating Immigrants and Refugees in the United States and Canada.* Berkeley: University of California Press.

Boothe, P. 2003. Renewal in the Centre: Working with Ontario's Federation Partners. Paper prepared for the Panel on the Role of Government, September 2003. Ottawa: Canadian Policy Research Networks.

Boychuk, G. 1998. *Patchworks of Purpose: The Development of Social Assistance Regimes in Canada.* Kingston and Montreal: McGill-Queen's University Press.

Cameron, D. and R. Simeon. 19978. "Ontario in Confederation: The Not-So-Friendly Giant." In *The Government and Politics of Ontario,* ed. G. White, 158-85. Toronto: University of Toronto Press.

Cameron, D. R. 1994. "Post-Modern Ontario and the Laurentian Thesis." In *Canada: The State of the Federation 1994*, eds. D. M. Brown and J. Hiebert, 109-34. Kingston: Institute of Intergovernmental Relations.

Canadian Council for Refugees. 2010. "Immigration Policy Shifts: From Nation Building to Temporary Migration." *Canadian Issues*, Metropolis, Spring: 90-3.

Courchene, T. 1996. *ACCESS: A Convention on the Canadian Economic and Social Systems*. Paper for the Ontario Ministry of Intergovernmental Affairs. Toronto: Ontario Ministry of Intergovernmental Affairs.

Courchene, T. and C. Telmer. 1998. *From Heartland to North American Region State: The Social, Fiscal and Federal Evolution of Ontario*. Toronto: University of Toronto Centre for Public Management.

Esping-Andersen, G., D. Gallie, J. Myles and A. Hemerjick. 2002. *Why We Need a New Welfare State*. New York: Oxford University Press.

Fafard, P., F. Rocher and C. Côté. 2009. "Clients, citizens and federalism: A critical appraisal of integrated service delivery in Canada." *Canadian Public Administration* 52(4): 549-58.

Frisken F. and M. Wallace. 2003. "Governing the Multicultural City-Region." *Canadian Public Administration* 46(2): 153-77.

Gerard Boychuk. "Social Union, Social Assistance: An Early Assessment." In *Building the Social Union: Perspectives and Directions*, ed. T. McIntosh, 51-67. Regina: Canadian Plains Research Center.

Goldring, L. 2010. "Temporary Worker Programs as Precarious Status: Implications for Citizenship, Inclusion and Nation Building in Canada." *Canadian Issues*, Metropolis, Spring: PAGE RANGE.

Graefe, P. 2006. "State Restructuring, Social Assistance and Canadian Intergovernmental Relations: Same Scales, New Tune," *Studies in Political Economy*, 2006, 78, 93-117.

Haddow , R. and A. Sharpe. 1997. "La Société québécoise de développement de la main-d'oeuvre: A Postscript." In *Social Partnerships for Training: Canada's Experiment with Labour Force Development Boards* eds. A. Sharpe and R. Haddow, 147-54. Kingston: School of Policy Studies.

Herd, D. 2006. *What Next in Welfare Reform: A Preliminary Review of Promising Programs and Practices*. Paper for the City of Toronto Department of Social Services. Toronto: City of Toronto Social Services.

Jenson, J. 2004. *Canada's New Social Risks: Directions for a New Social Architecture*. Ottawa: Canadian Policy Research Networks.

Kent, T. 2010. *Immigration: For Young Citizens*. Caledon Institute.

Lecours, A. and D. Béland. 2010. "Federalism and Fiscal Policy: The Politics of Equalization in Canada." *Publius: The Journal of Federalism* 40(4): 569-96.

Mahon, R. 2010. Childcare, New Social Risks and the New Politics of Redistribution in Ontario. Paper presented at the Workshop on the New Politics of Redistribution, Toronto, University of Toronto, May 2010.

Martin, J. 1974. *The Role and Place of Ontario in the Canadian Confederation*. Toronto: Ontario Economic Council.

Matthews S. and M. Mendelsohn. 2010. *The New Ontario: The Shifting Attitudes of Ontarians toward the Federation*. Toronto: Mowat Centre for Policy Innovation.

Maxwell, J. 2003. The Great Social Transformation: Implications for the Social Role of Government in Ontario. Paper for the Panel on the Role of Government. Ottawa: Canadian Policy Research Networks.

McDougall, A.K. and M.W. Westmacott. 1975. "Ontario in Canadian Federation." In *Government and Politics of Ontario,* ed. D.C. MacDonald, 199-204. Toronto: MacMillan of Canada.

Mwarigha, M.S. 1998. "Issues and Prospects: The Funding and Delivery of Immigrant Services in the Context of Cutbacks, Devolution, and Amalgamation." In *Who's Listening: The Impact of Immigration and Refugee Settlement on Toronto,* ed. P. G. Hunter, 90-6. Toronto: The Advisory Committee on Immigration and Refugee Issues of Toronto.

Noël, A. 2000. "General Study of the Framework Agreement," In *The Canadian Social Union Without Quebec: 8 critical analyses* eds. A.G. Gagnon and H. Segal, 9-35. Montreal: Institute for Research on Public Policy.

Noel, S. 1998. "Ontario and the Federation at the End of the Twentieth Century." In *Canada: The State of the Federation 1997 – Non-Constitutional Renewal,* ed. H. Lazar, 270-93. Kingston: Institute of Intergovernmental Relations.

Ontario. 2004. *Investing in People: Creating a Human Capital Society for Ontario.* Toronto: Panel on the Role of Government.

Ontario. Ministry of Child and Family Services. 2008. *Breaking the Cycle: Ontario's Poverty Reduction Strategy.* Toronto: Ministry of Child and Family Services.

Pearce, J., J. Hjartarson and M. Mendelsohn. 2010. *Saving Dollars and Making Sense: An Agenda for a More Efficient, Effective and Accountable Federation.* Toronto: Mowat Centre for Policy Innovation.

Richmond, T., and J. Shields. 2004. "NGO Restructuring: Constraints and Consequences." *Canadian Review of Social Policy* 53 (Spring/Summer): 53-67.

Seidle, L. 2010. *The Canada-Ontario Immigration Agreement: Assessment and Options for Renewal.* Toronto: Mowat Centre for Policy Innovation.

Shields, J. 2004. "No Safe Haven: Markets, Welfare and Migrants." In *Immigrants, Welfare Reform and the Poverty of Policy,* eds. P. Kretsendemas and A. Aparacio, 35-60. New York: Praeger.

Simeon, R. 1980. "Ontario in Confederation." In *The Government and Politics of Ontario,* 2nd ed., ed. D.C. MacDonald . 158-85. Toronto: Van Nostrand Reinhold.

Standing Senate Committee on Social Affairs, Science and Technology, Subcommittee on Cities. 2009. In *From the Margins: A Call for Action on Poverty, Housing and Homelessness.* Ottawa: Senate of Canada.

Stapleton, J. 2004. *Transitions Revisited: Implementing the Vision.* Ottawa: Caledon Institute of Social Policy.

Wolfe, D. A. 1997. "The Emergence of the Region State." In *The Nation State in a Global/ Information Era: Policy Challenges,* ed. J. Courchene, 205-40. Kingston: John Deutsch Institute.

Woolstencroft, T. B. 1982. *Organizing Intergovernmental Relations.* Discussion Paper No. 12. Kingston: Institute of Intergovernmental Relations.

9

POLICY FRAMEWORKS IN THE CANADIAN FEDERATION

Jennifer Wallner

La classe politique des États fédéraux est depuis longtemps confrontée à cette épineuse question : comment concilier une logique de diversité inscrite dans le principe fédéral avec des mesures et des programmes raisonnablement uniformes entre les territoires constitutifs de la fédération ? Les décideurs y parviennent en recourant à des cadres stratégiques, soutient l'auteure. Mais si l'on tient pour acquis qu'Ottawa doit participer à l'élaboration de ces cadres, comme il l'a d'ailleurs souvent fait, il a réduit ces dernières années le rôle qu'il jouait dans leur élaboration, au grand dam de nombreux observateurs. S'appuyant sur l'exemple de l'enseignement primaire et secondaire, l'auteure démontre que les provinces et territoires peuvent eux-mêmes concevoir des cadres stratégiques efficaces sans intervention directe d'Ottawa. Mais pour assurer la collaboration indispensable à cet exercice, ils doivent maintenir de solides organismes intergouvernementaux et disposer de ressources financières comparables.

INTRODUCTION

Politicians and policy-makers in federal states have long wrestled with a fundamentally vexing question: how should the logic of diversity, embedded in the federal principle, be reconciled with the need for policies and programs that are reasonably consistent across the individual jurisdictions that constitute a federation? The division of powers may allow pluralist communities to reconcile differences and foster policy creativity and innovation, while simultaneously enabling local governments to be more responsive to and reflective of particular needs and interest (Elazar 1982; Burgess 2006; Rocher and Gilbert 2010; Tiebout 1956), but these valuable opportunities are accompanied by a number of challenges. By constitutionally dividing jurisdictional responsibilities and policy competencies between (at least) two orders of government, federations often experience greater challenges than their unitary counterparts when building an integrated economy, establishing comprehensive and consistent programs, and meeting the needs of citizens in an efficient, effective, and equitable fashion (Laski 1939; Pierson 1995; Banting 2005). Policy-making in federations thus often involves finding the balance point on a teeter-totter. Tilt too much in favour of policy consistency, and run the risk of smothering the federal principle of diversity. Tilt too much towards diversity, however, and the integrity of the state itself could be compromised. Some balance must therefore be struck between these two poles – a challenge that Canadian decision-makers have become particularly acquainted with.

To help find this balance, decision-makers across the orders of government in Canada often formulate policy frameworks to install a particular type of logic that manages the various policy systems and sectors of the country. These frameworks can establish a foundational scaffolding to guide decision-makers and filter their activities and initiatives in various policy areas. As such, frameworks may be used to overcome some of the challenges that beset policy-making in federal systems by fostering a certain degree of interjurisdictional consistency while simultaneously permitting the necessary latitude to nurture self-rule, innovation, and policy diversity. The Canada Health Act, for example, sets out the primary objectives of Canadian health policy and establishes certain criteria and conditions that the provinces and territories must fulfill to receive federal funding. It thus constitutes a policy framework that tries to encapsulate the core principles of Canadian health care to help ensure some substantive similarity across the provinces and territories, despite substate autonomy in the field.

Rather than focusing on the details of the frameworks themselves, this chapter considers a different set of questions. How are overarching policy frameworks created in Canada? What are some of the enduring challenges to framework development in the country? What are the intergovernmental processes and mechanisms that have been commonly deployed? And what trends are appearing on the horizon? While Ontario takes centre stage in this volume, here I pull back the lens to assess the dynamics at play across the country as a whole. However, to narrow the scope of this inquiry, I focus in on the patterns and trends in social policy. Social policy sectors offer a remarkable opportunity to explore the alternative routes to framework formulation, as virtually all advancements required intergovernmental interactions to build the scaffolding that has evolved into the Canadian social safety net.

Conventional wisdom in some Canadian corners suggests that Ottawa needs to be involved in the development and installation of policy frameworks, particularly in areas of social policy. The federal government is often seen as the necessary actor in framework formulation capable of bringing all the jurisdictions together around a common table engaging them through vertical negotiations and speaking on behalf of Canadians as a whole. Indeed, Ottawa frequently figured prominently throughout the history of social policy development, hammering out the terms and parameters of a number of programs to weave together the threads for the social safety net in the country. Deploying the federal spending power and the federal government's considerable policy capacity, Ottawa intervened in a variety of areas of provincial competency with conditional grants to ensure a modicum of social citizenship for Canadians across the country.

Over the past two decades, however, Ottawa has scaled back its role in social policy. Ottawa's gradual reduction in framework formulation, I suggest, is simultaneously a reflection of enduring structural realities and a result of contemporary economic, political, and ideational considerations. Pan-Canadian policy frameworks have never come easily, in part due to the deep economic and social diversities that characterize Canada. Having managed to overcome these enduring challenges, ballooning federal deficits forced Ottawa to first unilaterally cap, and subsequently cut, provincial and territorial funding in areas of social programming exposing substate officials to major uncertainty. These actions frayed intergovernmental relations driving a considerable wedge between federal, provincial, and territorial decision-makers. Many of the recent developments in social policy have centred on addressing these problems, that peeked in the 1990s, to rebuild trust among the orders of government, including attempts to limit the federal spending power, foster greater fiscal stability, and delineate clearer boundaries on the respective responsibilities of the orders of government. In the meantime, most provinces have augmented their own policy capacity, further eroding the need to rely on federal expertise. As such, we seem to be entering a new period of policy-making where the provinces and territories may increasingly take the lead.

For some, the diminution of the federal government is a cause for concern. Without federal interventions, some observers suggest that the provinces and territories are unlikely to work together. As Steven Kennett opines, "the development and enforcement of national principles or standards through interprovincial or federal-provincial mechanisms represents a significant collective action problem, particularly if the threat of unilateral federal action is withdrawn" (1997, 4). In this chapter, however, I argue that vertical interactions are only one pathway to framework formulation. Using the case of elementary and secondary education as an example, we can see that substate governments can achieve de facto policy frameworks via horizontal interactions mobilized through learning and cooperation. Provinces (and now increasingly the territories) can work together and achieve a remarkable degree of policy consistency and find a balance between the two poles of diversity and uniformity without the direct intervention of the federal government.

This chapter proceeds in four parts. It opens with a discussion of policy frameworks in federal systems, outlining the potential positive and negative results that can emerge in their wake, and highlighting the enduring structural challenges particular to Canada that decision-makers must circumnavigate. I then move to review the ways in which Ottawa has acted as a steward of framework formulation and consider the contemporary factors encouraging a reconfiguration of the federal role. The third section demonstrates that – contrary to conventional wisdom – substate governments can formulate policy frameworks without the direct intervention of the federal government. This does not, however, mean that Ottawa has no role to play. Rather than taking the helm, the federal government should reorient its efforts away from developing substantive policy proposals in favour of supporting provincial and territorial interactions through Canada's fiscal arrangements and sustaining effective intergovernmental organizations. I then conclude with a brief discussion of the rising challenges coming into view on the horizon.

POLICY FRAMEWORKS AND FEDERATIONS

The term "policy frameworks" is becoming increasingly ubiquitous, used by governments and political parties, interest groups and think-tanks, commentators and academics alike. A quick search on Google, for example, immediately leads one to the Government of Canada's "Gateway and Corridor Approach," which recently established a national policy framework designed to oversee marine, road, rail, and air transportation infrastructure.[1] In 2009, the Mental Health Commission of Canada set out its vision for an integrated mental health strategy with seven broad goals that call for the transformation of mental health systems across the country.[2] And, most recently, a growing chorus of voices is rallying for the establishment of a national securities regulator to oversee the operation of Canada's financial markets. What, then, are the defining features of these frameworks?

Policy frameworks are the scaffolding that can guide the actions and choices of decision-makers. They are made up of principles, supporting concepts, long-term goals, and processes. They establish a foundation for policy activity within a particular sector, thereby affording certain degrees of direction for decision-makers to orient planning and development to, while simultaneously permitting degrees of freedom to tailor strategies to local needs and priorities. While frameworks vary in terms of the level of details contained within them, hallmarks include: defined objectives and goals, stipulations of programs, specification of instruments and methods of administration, and monitoring and enforcement mechanisms to track whether or not the framework is being respected. Frameworks thus structure activity by installing a particular logic for policy-makers from different jurisdictions to

---

[1] Government of Canada, *Canada's Gateways: National Policy Framework*. http://www.canadasgateways.gc.ca/NationalPolicyFramework/nationalpolicy4.html

[2] Mental Health Commission of Canada, *Toward Recovery and Well-Being: A Framework for a Mental Health Strategy for Canada*. (Ottawa: Mental Health Commission of Canada, 2009) http://www.mentalhealthcommission.ca/SiteCollectionDocuments/boarddocs/15507_MHCC_EN_final.pdf

use as a marker, informing choices as they develop and deploy individual practices within a broader sector of their respective territory.

In principle, frameworks can provide four benefits that address in turn the ideas of equality, efficiency, effectiveness, and accountability. By establishing a baseline, frameworks can help ensure that all constituent governments adhere to a standard modicum of practice, so that all citizens may equally enjoy the benefits of the country, regardless of their place of residence, which translates into the achievement of universal social citizenship within a federation (Marshall 1950). Invoking this notion of social citizenship, Keith Banting offers the following poignant example, "a sick baby should be entitled to public health care on the same terms and conditions wherever he or she lives" (Simeon 2006, 32). Frameworks can also help avoid such situations as one recently revealed in British Columbia. Due to changes introduced by that province in 2004, British Columbia has some of the most permissive child labour laws in the world, allowing children the age of 12 to work in virtually any job – save for mines, taverns, bars and loungers – at any time of day or night, except during mandatory school hours (Bakan 2011). If Canada had an explicit framework on child labour, so an argument favouring frameworks would assert, the potential for such internal discrepancies would be diminished. By encouraging substate decision-makers to invest at comparable levels, establish similar entitlements, and introduce common regulations on various activities, policy frameworks can contribute to the realization of interjurisdictional equality within a federation fostering a common citizenship for all.

Secondly, frameworks contribute to efficiency by sharing policy-making tasks across multiple jurisdictions, potentially elevating the capacity of the various governments to act in their respective spheres of competency. Federal, provincial, and territorial governments cannot consistently maintain strong policy shops across every single policy sector. Collective framework formulation thus offers the opportunity to pool resources, build policy capacity, share expertise, and generate collective responses to common problems. What is more, frameworks may simultaneously smooth out interjurisdictional inconsistencies disrupting public activity. An overarching scaffolding thus helps ensure that the quality of products – be it the regulation of goods and services or the execution of public programs – is reasonably consonant across the constituent jurisdictions, ideally promoting economic growth and reducing internal transaction costs.

Building from efficiency, frameworks carry implications for policy effectiveness in a federation. If the actions and activities of the constituent governments are not somewhat coordinated, or if major discrepancies exist across regions, policy outcomes as a whole may suffer. Policing provides a poignant example. If the various municipal, provincial, and national forces lack a protocol for information exchanges, public security and safety will be compromised. Similarly, if certain jurisdictions install radically different regimes for food safety regulations or vaccinations, the overall health and wellbeing of the population as a whole may suffer.

Finally, frameworks involve identifying such things as goals, standards, and policy instruments. The articulation of these elements can contribute to the achievement of accountability both within and across the orders of government. By advertising benchmarks and targets that various governments are expected to meet on a regular basis, frameworks can enhance government-to-citizen accountability in pertinent policy areas. Citizens can use the frameworks as a touchstone to evaluate the effectiveness of their elected representatives, particularly during election campaigns. The effects of these frameworks for government-to-citizen accountability, however, are not always positive as governmental activities that transcend constitutional boundaries require citizens to assess the degree of responsibility each government bears for a particular policy outcome (Cutler 2004). A complicated exercise in its own right, governments are prone to further confounding the situation by buckpassing or stealing credit, using overarching standards and priorities as a way to either avoid blame or gain recognition. "Under these conditions voters who see something amiss may find it difficult to translate that judgment into an effective voting decision" (Cutler 2004, 19).

Frameworks can also – albeit more controversially – be used to foster government-to-government accountability. "Respect for the federal principle," writes Phillips (2003, 94), "makes it difficult for governments to hold each other directly accountable for spending or for public policy." Frameworks can be crafted in such a way to include provisions requiring governments to answer for certain actions (or inactions), use funds in a specified manner, and include monitoring practices to ensure effective compliance with the terms of particular agreements. If the conditions are not met, either in the form of failing to provide funds or meet particular standards, penalties or sanctions may be imposed on the offending jurisdiction. What is more, this issue of accountability gains new meaning in federations marked by significant gaps between fiscal capacity and the allocation of jurisdictional responsibilities between the orders of government.

The "vertical fiscal balance" refers to the match (or mismatch) between the central and substate governments in the allocation of policy responsibilities and access to fiscal resources. In Canada's case, the federal government has access to significant fiscal resources, while the provinces and territories have primacy over most social policy competencies, subsequently complicating the development and maintenance of policy frameworks. Consequently, in exchange for federal funds to support substate initiatives, Ottawa attaches conditions (admittedly in fewer cases currently) in an effort to see the monies used to realize specified objectives, as federal politicians remain accountable to the national legislature for its budget. The flip side of this coin, however, is that if the priorities of the federal government shift and a decision is made to cut funding for a particular program upon which citizens have come to rely, the provinces and territories are left to fill the fiscal gap.

It is crucial to acknowledge that frameworks neither require *uniformity* of programs and practices nor *unanimity* of all the players. To be sure, frameworks seem to privilege one aspect of the federal principle – namely shared-rule – while sacrificing the principle of self-rule to standardize practices, achieve coordination, and realize certain degrees of interjurisdictional coherence. However, the construction of frameworks does not mean that all the governments in the Canadian federations will mirror one another precisely and abandon the federal principle of diversity. Rather, frameworks can be designed in such a way as to tolerate considerable degrees of inconsistency and incoherence, leaving the room for various jurisdictions to strike out on their own and pursue individualized policy pathways guided by the general scaffolding that is collectively agreed upon. In fact, perhaps somewhat counter-intuitively, one could argue that tolerance for inconsistency, diversity, and asymmetry is a crucial ingredient for the long-term viability and success of a policy framework.

It is here that certain caveats need to be made. Not all frameworks are equally beneficial and there are a number of negative consequences that can accompany their development and installation. To start, the benefits that may be derived from frameworks are heavily dependent on the suitability of their design and execution. If they are overly broad, frameworks may be too vague to provide meaningful guidance to the decision-makers who desire it; overly specific, however, and frameworks then run the risk of being unsuitable for the varying conditions within each constituent jurisdiction, increasing the likelihood that decision-makers will simply abandon them. Furthermore, policy frameworks may distort governmental priorities if the objectives of one authority supersede the goals and priorities of the others. Finally, intense sanctions or coercive instruments – particularly if applied by the central government onto the constituent units in their areas of jurisdictional authority – have the potential to breed considerable resentment among the respective parties. Consequently, navigating these waters is not an easy task.

Before delving into the ways in which the federal government has acted as a steward for policy frameworks, it is important to acknowledge the embedded challenges to pan-Canadian frameworks. Geographic, economic, and societal factors argue against robust federal stewardship in social policy. The physical environment makes the imposition of strict standards practically impossible. As Prime Minister Mackenzie King once famously lamented before the House of Commons, Canada has "too much geography." Furthermore, there are objective differences in economic conditions from one province to the next. These differences, writes Kennett "constrain policy integration or harmonization aimed at strengthening the economic and social union" (1997, 7). Even variations in the relative size of the constituent units influence the politics of framework formulation. Economically strong governments, for example, "quite regularly find it more beneficial to 'fend for themselves' and strive for special deals" (Bolleyer 2009, 9). In the meantime, there is no doubt that the smaller, economically weaker provinces have tended to view federal engagement in areas of provincial competency more positively. A strong federal government with the power to redistribute wealth and intervene in a variety of policy areas is regarded as essential to their well-being, a sentiment that persists today. In 1996, for example, Nova Scotia Premier John Savage issued the following strong statement, "[f]or the first time Nova Scotia and the five other have-not provinces voiced a resounding and harmonious 'no' to an option that obviously had some appeal to Canada's rich provinces . . . we still see a role for the federal government in developing national standards, provided they are achieved in consensus with the provinces" (Courchene 1997, 60). Consequently, the entrenched variations between the larger and smaller Canadian provinces and territories inject further tensions into the politics and processes of framework formulation, a theme that will be revisited in the conclusion of this chapter.

Without a doubt, though, the social composition of the Canadian polity presents the greatest obstacle for policy frameworks developed and installed primarily by the federal government. James Alexander Corry succinctly made this point in 1978 when he described Canada as an "incorrigibly federal country ... any constitution that gives parliament the power necessary to safeguard the interest of the whole will be open to the overriding preferences of Quebec on particular points" (Smiley 1987, 31). As Claude Ryan put it, "I doubt that, in the areas directly linked to its distinct character, Quebec will be willing to cede to an outside authority its constitutional jurisdiction" (2000, 209). Quebec has always consistently opposed federal interventions into its jurisdictional competencies, pioneering the opt-out (or as Courchene recasts – a right to opt-in) option from various federal initiatives, encouraging formal asymmetry in Canada Assistance Plan funding, de facto asymmetry in immigration policy, while simultaneously implementing its own unique package of social programs that differentiates the province considerably from virtually all of North America.

Despite these enduring challenges, over the years, Canadian decision-makers have managed to install policy frameworks through intergovernmental interactions. The subsequent section addresses a story that is familiar to many Canadians – Ottawa as steward and architect of pan-Canadian social programs.

FEDERAL STEWARDSHIP

Ottawa has a formidable history as an interlocutor in social policy frameworks, formulating pan-Canadian programs, standards, and policy frameworks often by intervening in areas of provincial jurisdictions.[3] Programs such as old age pensions

---

[3] Amendments to the constitution during the 20th century gave the federal government jurisdiction over key areas of social policy. One in 1940 gave full authority for unemployment insurance, leading to the installation of the national Unemployment Insurance program. Using its authority in unemployment insurance, the federal government introduced a swath of programs including extended benefits in regions with high levels of unemployment, sickness and temporary disability pay, and maternity (now parental) leave. Four years later, the federal government created a universal, flat rate Family Allowances program. Another

(1927), social assistance (1927, 1937, 1951, 1954 and the Canada Assistance Plan), hospital insurance (1957), and Medicare (1966), in many ways owe their existence to federal initiatives as decision-makers in Ottawa used a series of levers at their disposal to create these policy frameworks. Analysts of social policy development in Canada attribute this expanding federal role to four factors.

During the early years of Canadian history, the federal government demonstrated considerable disinterest in most areas of social policy, choosing instead to direct its attention to areas of economic development and infrastructure. The trauma of the Great Depression, however, revealed critical failures within the Canadian state and contributed to the emergence of a broad public consensus resting upon the principles of Keynesian economics, which favoured a major expansion of governmental activity in areas of social policy (Simeon and Robinson 1990, 47). Secondly, as Keith Banting (2005, 98) notes, both federal and provincial leaders were concerned about the implications of labour and capital mobility in a federal state. In the words of Prime Minister Mackenzie King, "insurance against unemployment, sickness and invalidity can never be successful if each province has a different system or if one province has a system and another does not" (Banting 2005, 98). Someone, therefore, needed to make sure that comparable programs were effectively installed and that "someone" increasingly came to be seen as the federal government. Thirdly, due to the strength of the federal public service, Ottawa enjoyed considerably greater policy capacity than the vast majority of its provincial counterparts throughout the 1950s. The federal government could thus draw on these resources to develop proposals and design policies that could conceivably reach the identified objectives. Finally, and perhaps most crucially, the federal government has markedly greater fiscal resources at its disposal and could use its financial clout to encourage the provinces to cooperate with federal initiatives that would otherwise have exceeded their fiscal capacities.

These four factors allowed the federal government to intervene in a variety of areas of provincial jurisdiction to construct the frameworks for social policy. How did these interventions unfold and what were the ensuing results? In some situations, federal engagement came at the provinces' request. The funding of hospital insurance unveiled at the federal-provincial conference in 1955, for example, came at the urging of provincials officials. In others, the federal government chose to encourage the dissemination of models developed provincially, as famously evidenced by the diffusion of Saskatchewan's medical insurance regime. At the federal-provincial

---

constitutional amendment, this time in 1951, later allowed the federal government the opportunity to provide pensions directly to citizens enabling the Old Age Security program, subsequently extended in 1966 with the Guaranteed Income Supplement. All of these programs had major implications for areas of provincial competency; however, Ottawa acted with scant consultation with the provinces. For more on the historical development of these programs see: Banting 1987.

conference in 1965, Prime Minister Lester Pearson announced a new shared-cost program whereby the federal government would cover half the costs of provincial medical insurance plans. According to Maioni, to "ensure a measure of uniformity, the Medical Care Insurance Act stipulated that provincial programs would have to be comprehensive, universal, portable, and publicly administered" (2002, 90). These stipulations thus paved the way for the future framework that continues to define the parametres of provincial action for health care in Canada to this day.

The federal government extended its initiatives beyond health care in areas of provincial jurisdiction through the Canada Assistance Plan (CAP). Emerging from a number of federal-provincial Ministerial Conferences between May 1964 and January 1966, the CAP had two primary objectives: to assist the provinces in providing welfare services and social assistance in appropriate facilities; and to foster the creation of services that would prevent or lessen the causes and effects of poverty, dependence on public assistance, and child neglect. It operated as a shared-cost program where the federal government refunded approximately 50 percent of the eligible costs incurred by the provinces. For nine of the ten provinces, CAP involved cash transfers only. Quebec, however, secured a different agreement that saw the province receive a five-point tax abatement on personal income tax solidifying a legacy of asymmetry in the program. In return for the funds and tax abatements, the federal government set certain conditions including forbidding provincial residency requirements for individuals to receive social assistance and exclusions based on provincially-defined notions of need.

Ottawa's initiatives in health care and welfare neatly encapsulate the vertical routes to framework formulation that are likely quite familiar to many Canadians. Due to the combined efforts of federal and provincial decision-makers, core components of Canadian social policy we mapped out throughout the 1950s and 1960s where in exchange for federal funds, the provinces agreed to institute certain programs subjected to particular specifications. What is more, federal and provincial acceptance of asymmetry appears to have been integrated right from the outset, as evidenced by the alternative funding arrangement provided to Quebec. Consequently, through vertical interactions, the basic blueprints for Canadian social programs were realized, which installed a certain degree of regularity and predictability, while simultaneously allocating space for flexibility to strike some balance between the principles of shared-rule and self-rule.

So far, however, this snapshot seems to suggest that all members of the Canadian federation welcomed Ottawa's interventions and that these negotiations were bloodless. But intergovernmental policy-making spearheaded by the federal government was far from conflict free. The notion of Ottawa encouraging or imposing requirements in areas of substate jurisdiction has never resonated universally across all the provinces. Medical insurance, for example, faced stiff opposition from provincial leaders in Alberta and Ontario. "The Social Credit government in Alberta . . . preferred its 'Manningcare' model of voluntary insurance plus public subsidies for the poor; Conservative premier John Robarts in Ontario referred to the federal policy as 'political fraud'" according to Maioni (2008, 166). In fact, Ontario and several other provinces waged "a campaign against the federal medicare programme, which was seen as a costly and unwarranted federal involvement in provincial priorities" (Simeon 1972, 86). It seemed that provincial officials were already attuned to the fact that overarching frameworks could distort their own priorities while forcing them to adhere to federally-desired agendas, principles, and practices, which included the stipulations for public administration and non-residency requirements to nurture social citizenship.

After two decades of progressive expansion, Ottawa's activity in social policy began to wane in the 1970s. This gradual retrenchment can be attributed to a series of changing circumstances. Faced with rising deficits and stagnating economic growth, Ottawa entered a period of chronic deficits that would not end until 1998 (Brown 2008, 73). Furthermore, under the terms of the initial shared-cost agreements to fund hospital insurance, medical care, post-secondary education, and the Canada Assistance Plan, the federal government had exposed itself to uninhibited provincial expenditure growth, which was an intolerable situation. Economic contractions also dislodged the political consensus on the Keynesian paradigm, such that by the early 1980s federal-provincial fiscal arrangements had lost their shared sense of purpose that had emerged in the post-Second World War period (Lazar 2000,4).

In addition, as Stilborn asserts, the provinces "were increasingly dissatisfied with the inflexible requirements of the hospital insurance agreements, and with the federal audit that determined shared costs" (1997). During the 1950s and 1960s, Ottawa could lead the policy agenda in part because the provinces had limited organizational capacities and the federal government had greater policy expertise. Since the 1960s, many provinces have made great strides, building up their internal bureaucracies to manage an increasingly wider array of policy portfolios that now rival federal levels of expertise (Leone and Carroll 2010, 402). Having invested in this capacity, it is unlikely that all the provinces will allow it to decay, meaning that the possibility of a return to highly interventionist federal leadership in social policy is increasingly remote.

On a somewhat related note, certain pathologies can accompany federal initiatives in social policy that stem from discrepancies in the nature of federal and provincial policy expertise. As Courchene affirms, "apart from providing certain social services to First Nations, Ottawa is not really a player in the social policy design and delivery game" (1997, 81). This signals that there is a considerable gap in the type of knowledge and expertise that the respective officials bring to the table. The federal Homelessness Initiative unilaterally introduced in 1999 neatly encapsulates this problem.

According to Ian Peach, the initiative was "a new national program that was, essentially fully formed in Ottawa and had not been the subject of intergovernmental discussion prior to its launch" (2010, 47). For Saskatchewan the problem was simple. Officials in Ottawa designed the program for people living on the streets; in Saskatchewan, however, homelessness manifests itself as "couch surfing," which meant that it was not recognized under the terms of the initial agreement. Only after significant lobbying by senior Saskatchewan officials was the federal program revised to accommodate this alternative form of homelessness experienced in the province. "If the design of a response to homelessness had begun at the level of local or provincial/territorial governments" writes Peach "the resources expended by the federal government in designing a program that subsequently had to be re-designed . . . could have been expended, instead, on actually addressing the needs of the homeless." (2010, 52). This program is but one example that confirms the importance of local knowledge in understanding particular policy problems, recognizing how they can manifest in particular ways depending on local circumstances, and the need for a different type of expertise to craft a solution that effectively responds to the problem at hand.

Federal disengagement incrementally advanced through a series of often unilateral decisions on the transfer payments for social programs. This began in 1977 with Established Programs Financing (EPF) that was accompanied by the transfer of federal tax points to the provinces, accelerated in 1990 with the "cap-on-CAP," and culminated in 1995 with the introduction of the Canada Health and Social Transfer (CHST), later divided into the Canada Health Transfer and the Canada Social Transfer. The transfer of tax points to the provinces signaled the beginning of a long era of selective federal engagement in social policy. Cuts to the transfer payments were instituted unilaterally, driving a significant wedge between federal and provincial politicians and decision-makers. Moreover, despite the fact that provinces were now responsible for the rising costs of social policy, they were still obliged to meet certain criteria laid out in federal legislation, including the Canada Health Act (CHA) of 1984 (Maioni 2002).

Since 1995, the federal government has attempted to redefine its role in social policy and rebuild frayed intergovernmental relations through a series of landmark agreements including the Social Union Framework Agreement (SUFA) in 1999 and the health accords of the 2000s. When SUFA was signed, some greeted it as a stepping stone to a new era in Canadian federalism, capable of bringing in "an unprecedented level of cooperation, formality and civility to intergovernmental relations" (Gibbins 2003, 31). The agreement stemmed from provincial and territorial desires to establish some formal constraints on federal spending power that, left unchecked, carried major risks because the federal government could unilaterally withdraw support for programs on which citizens had come to depend and that federal decision-makers had largely inspired. Unfortunately however, for reasons that go far beyond this chapter, the SUFA has largely failed to live up to expectations, and is widely regarded as a dead agreement.

Where the SUFA failed, the health accords of 2003 and 2004 managed to achieve predictable and stable funding provided by Ottawa to the provinces and territories over a ten-year period. Additionally, the accords included requirements for the establishment of comparable health indicators to reflect particular themes such as access to health services, quality of care, and health status and wellbeing.

Furthermore, the accords included stipulations for a series of extra initiatives including wait-time reductions, additional investments in primary health care, home care, and catastrophic drug coverage bundled together under the Health Reform Fund. According to the fund agreement, the federal government recognized "that provinces and territories are at differing stages of reforms in these areas." As such, "the Fund will provide the provinces and territories the necessary flexibility to achieve the objectives ... Premiers and Territorial Leaders agree to use the Health Reform Fund to achieve these objectives. Therefore, these funds to be transferred to the provinces and territories will be available for any of the programs described in the Health Reform Fund, at their discretion."[4] Consequently, the federal government remains somewhat engaged in social policy frameworks while the provinces and territories appreciate the flexibility over program control and design. However, the health accords nevertheless confirm the expectation of federal fiscal support and once again re-expose provincial and territorial policy-makers to the priorities and preferences of federal decision-makers and the federal budgetary situation.

The scaling back of the federal government in social policy has gained new meaning under the leadership of Prime Minister Stephen Harper whose commitment to "open federalism" includes a stated preference for "disentanglement" and calling for Ottawa to "do what the federal government is supposed to do," instead of "sticking its nose into provincial and local matters" (Jeffrey 2010, 110). As Peter Graefe and Rachel Laforest suggest in their contribution to this volume, "disengagement of the federal government from social policy stewardship has altered the balance of political forces in the area." Tom Courchene has similarly argued that, "the provinces have to be brought more fully and more formally into the key societal goal of preserving and promoting social Canada" (1997, 78). Given the winnowing of federal intervention and the need to integrate the other orders of government, it seems prudent to explore the plausibility of substate stewardship in policy frameworks – and the case of elementary and secondary education is particularly illuminating.

SUBSTATE STEWARDSHIP

Canada is one of the few countries in the world without a national department of education or formal national standards for public schooling. Through horizontal learning and cooperative policy-making, the provinces have established a highly coherent system of elementary and secondary education that is entirely managed and operated under ten separate structures. The provinces make comparable investments in education, record similar results on international tests, and deploy policies that are

---

[4] 2003 First Ministers' Accord on Health Care Renewal. http://www.hc-sc.gc.ca/hcs-sss/delivery-prestation/fptcollab/2003accord/index-eng.php

highly akin to one another (Wallner 2010). This is not to suggest that differences do not exist. In fact, many do. For example, Quebec's unique bridge between secondary and post-secondary schooling colloquially known as "CEGEP," variations in the internal applications and implications of assessment regimes, and the myriad of regulations governing teacher preparation and certification, all confirm the fact that provinces maintain distinct strategies. However, in the main, all Canadians can access reasonably similar elementary and secondary education programs that are guided by shared principles of universality, administrated by public authorities, and financed through public funds. And all this emerged without direct interventions from Ottawa. How did the provinces accomplish this seemingly Herculean task?

The emergence of an interprovincial policy framework in education began with organizations. While vested with the constitutional authority to act independently, provincial decision-makers recognized early on that they could not develop education policies and practices completely autonomously. In 1891, government and non-government educationists gathered in Montreal and established the first interprovincial organization dedicated to the field, known then as the Dominion Education Association (DEA) that later evolved into the Canadian Education Association (CEA). Engagement in the organization was voluntary and initiatives could advance without universal support such that if some jurisdictions identified a common area of interest, they could pursue the initiative without unanimous consent. Under the auspices of the CEA, provinces sporadically tracked the policy developments in other jurisdictions, formulated student-transfer guides to contend with students moving between the jurisdictions, and gradually built up a connective network of educators and officials from coast to coast.

In 1967, the CEA was eclipsed by the creation of the Council of Ministers of Education, Canada (CMEC). The organizational transformation had a number of implications that were particularly salient for learning and cooperation across the provinces. Reflecting the principles of executive federalism, the new Council isolated the political realm from non-governmental stakeholders by making it the exclusive domain of government officials. All of the individuals around the table now exercised similar types of authority, were empowered by comparable political structures, and thus responsible to parallel bodies. This type of arrangement seems to have inculcated a greater sense of cohesion among the participants, securing stronger trust ties, elevating the potential for cooperation and collaborative policy-making above the level previously possible under the auspices of the DEA. In recent years, these effects have been felt as robust interprovincial collaborations have occurred with the provinces creating a pan-Canadian assessment program, and ratifying common learning outcomes in science. It seems that an agreement to ease interprovincial teacher mobility is also on the horizon.

The council includes a permanent secretariat, which provides an institutional memory for the provincial political and bureaucratic education officials. Given that the average shelf-life of a provincial minister of education ranges from 18 to 24 months, the council secretariat offers crucial support to the constantly changing political leaders reminding them of initiatives, keeping them abreast of developments, fostering consensus, and shepherding policy development. The council also regularizes meetings among the officials, meaning that inter-provincial/territorial interactions are a predictable occurrence. Finally, following the legacy of the CEA, the CMEC preserves the principle of substate autonomy as agreements are non-binding and initiatives can advance without unanimity. This decision-making framework serves to abate any fears of unilateral incursions by certain jurisdictions to either impose preferences or stymie initiatives that are desired by others.

Despite its strengths, the CMEC has a number of pertinent weaknesses. The council is often an unwieldy body that at times can act simply as a soapbox for individual ministers who have little interest in learning from others at the table. Furthermore, some officials have noted that pan-Canadian programs can be watered down by the compromises that are required to integrate the multitude of voices. The science learning outcomes provide a telling example. They are so expansive that they offer little guidance for curriculum designers across jurisdictions when they revise science education. Working through the full council, moreover, can be quite time consuming as evidenced by the protracted negotiations surrounding teaching certification. Since the ratification of the Agreement on Internal Trade in 1995, the provincial and territorial ministers of education have been trying to achieve an agreement on teacher mobility under the auspices of the CMEC. These lengthy negotiations are a testimony of the challenges of reaching an agreement that encompasses all of the jurisdictions.

To counteract these deficiencies and advance more targeted projects, some provinces have opted to pursue regional initiatives. The Western Protocol on Curriculum, for example, brings together curriculum developers from the western provinces and territories and maps out a common set of learning outcomes across a variety of subject areas. More concretely, under the terms of the New West Partnership, British Columbia, Alberta, and Saskatchewan have achieved an agreement securing teacher mobility. Meanwhile, on the opposite side of the country, Newfoundland, Prince Edward Island, Nova Scotia, and New Brunswick joined together under the auspices of the Council of Atlantic Ministers of Education and Training (CAMET). The collaborative accomplishments of the CAMET are formidable, including the complete harmonization of elementary and secondary curriculum across the four provinces. Interestingly, these regional initiatives on the two sides of the country have not translated into greater variations between areas of the country, which is a testament to the durability of the broader pan-Canadian education framework.

Looking beyond the organizational features and the decision-making practices of the education sector, citizens themselves have a role to play in the creation and maintenance of policy frameworks. As Richard Simeon cogently argues, "even if policy-making and delivery are highly decentralized to provincial governments, if their citizens all embrace similar conceptions of social citizenship, the results will also be similar" (2006, 39). Echoing Simeon's ideas, Courchene declares that "despite our linguistic, cultural, legal and geographic diversity, the values that we share and the nature of the country we desire transcend all of the above differences and constitute an important part of the societal glue that attracts all of us to work toward improving the Canadian state and society" (2010, 25-6). The field of elementary and secondary education enjoys the considerable support of broad public consensus on the fundamental importance of public schooling. This ideational consensus across the Canadian public has likely contributed to the formulation of the de facto framework in education.

While effective organizations and public support are necessary conditions for learning and cooperation among the provinces, both are rendered somewhat meaningless if the provinces lack sufficient financial resources to support their various initiatives. Fiscal capacity is the linchpin in this narrative, and it reveals where Ottawa has a crucial role to play in the development of policy frameworks. The federal government made a dramatic – and yet indirect – contribution to the creation and maintenance of an education framework with the establishment of equalization in 1957. Prior to that, there were marked differences in the educational investments of the provinces (Wallner 2010). Since 1957, these discrepancies have gradually decreased and the current similarities in educational investments are quite striking. These developments signal that the federal government plays a crucial role in the formulation of policy frameworks through the effective management of the vertical and horizontal fiscal imbalances that demarcate the Canadian state (Commission on Fiscal Imbalance 2002).

EMERGING TRENDS AND RISING CHALLENGES

This chapter has considered the ways in which policy-makers in Canada respond to a fundamentally challenging question – how to reconcile the federal principle of diversity with the practical and normative need for interjurisdictional policy comparability and coordination? I argued that decision-makers use policy frameworks as a means to answer this question. Policy frameworks can install a set of basic blueprints that map out the parametres of action in pertinent policy areas, while being flexible enough to permit local innovation and diversity. The drafting of these frameworks often requires intergovernmental negotiations as policy areas frequently transcend jurisdictional boundaries, either formally in constitutional terms or informally due to the realities of interdependence. Conventional wisdom holds that Ottawa needs to be involved in these negotiations through vertical interactions, a role that the federal government has frequently played. However, due in part to embedded structural challenges and more recent changes in the policy context, Ottawa has scaled back its role in framework development, much to the chagrin of a number of observers. Using elementary and secondary education as an example, I suggested that the provinces and territories are capable of establishing meaningful and effective policy frameworks without the direct intervention of the federal government. For such cooperation and collaboration to occur, reinforced by popular support for the principles that underpin shared policy activity, provinces and territories need to maintain strong intergovernmental organizations and have access to somewhat comparable fiscal resources. This final point solidifies the fact that Ottawa has a key role to play, even when it is not directly involved in the interactions.

What emerging issues are coming into view on the horizon? A quick glimpse indicates new negotiation practices, a new organization, and new players at the table. Recently, the federal government has demonstrated a new propensity for alternative means to establish policy frameworks. Rather than bringing everyone to the negotiating table simultaneously, federal officials are negotiating bilateral deals with each of the provinces (and territories) individually. The first sustained evidence of this practice emerged during the Liberal Government led by Prime Minister Paul Martin when individual deals with each of the provinces were ratified in support of child care initiatives. Over the last few years, this practice of bilateral deals has spread outside areas of social policy. The Conservative Government led by Prime Minister Stephen Harper used this technique to institute stimulus funding in response to the economic crisis of 2008 through its Economic Action Plan.

Researchers will need to be attuned to this new practice and assess the degree to which individual agreements end up securing either a comparable or a greater degree of cohesion as was achieved in the past through multilateral processes. While multilateral negotiations are undeniably onerous and riddled with hurdles, one advantage is that they bring everyone around the table, exposing all the representatives of the governments of Canada to multiple positions and priorities. It remains to be seen if comparable dialogue and information exchanges will be able to advance through vertical negotiations that are exclusively bilateral.

On 5 December 2003, the Canadian provincial and territorial premiers announced the creation of a new intergovernmental organization known as the Council of the Federation. Its stated objectives include promoting interprovincial-territorial cooperation to ultimately strengthen Canada, and foster meaningful relations that respect the Constitution and recognize diversity, while allowing the premiers to show leadership on key issues that are of importance to Canadians. In its early years, motivated in part by the protracted health accord negotiations, the council took a prominent role on the intergovernmental stage. Recently, however, the council seems to be floundering as representatives from the provinces and territories and the council secretariat are struggling to articulate a clear role for the organization. This body nevertheless has the potential to become an effective arena for intergovernmental policy exchanges and should not be abandoned despite apparent growing pains. Much like the CMEC, the council can provide a stable forum to regularize meetings among the premiers, potentially including the prime minister, and foster interjurisdictional coordination and framework formulation.

Finally, the intergovernmental arena seems to have received new players – specifically the premiers of the territories. Historically governed explicitly under the auspices of the federal government and excluded from intergovernmental negotiations, territorial devolution has meant that representatives from the Yukon, Northwest Territories and Nunavut are now invited as de facto equal members to the intergovernmental tables. As mentioned above, internal geographic, economic, and demographic disparities among the provinces present a considerable challenge to the establishment of meaningful policy frameworks. These enduring challenges have now been increased with the inclusion of the territories, which in turn demands a new type of attention to, and recognition of, diversity in the Canadian federation.

REFERENCES

Bakan, J. 2011. "B.C.'s Child Labour Laws Are the Most Neglectful in the World" *The Globe and Mail*, 22 September. At http://www.theglobeandmail.com/news/opinions/opinion/bcs-child-labour-laws-are-the-most-neglectful-in-the-world/article2150814/ (accessed 29 November 2011).

Banting, K. 1987. *The Welfare State and Canadian Federalism* 2nd ed. Montreal and Kingston: McGill-Queen's University Press.

Bolleyer, N. 2009. *Intergovernmental Cooperation: Rational Choices in Federal Systems and Beyond*. Oxford: Oxford University Press.

Brown, D. M. 2008. "Fiscal Federalism: Searching for a New Balance." In *Canadian Federalism: Performance, Effectiveness, and Legitimacy*, 2nd ed. eds.. H. Bakvis and G. Skogstad, 63-88. Don Mills: Oxford University Press.

Burgess, M. 2006. *Comparative Federalism: Theory and Practice*. London: Routledge.

Commission on Fiscal Imbalance. 2002. *A New Division of Canada's Financial Resources Report*. Quebec: Bibliotheque nationale du Quebec.

Courchene, T. J. 1997. ACCESS: A Convention on the Canadian Economic and Social System. Working Paper prepared for the Ministry of Intergovernmental Affairs, Government of Ontario. At http://www.queensu.ca/sps/people/faculty/courchenet/Assessing_Access_Convention_Chapter.pdf (accessed 29 November 2011).

---. 2010. "Federalism, Decentralization and Canadian Nation Building." In *The Case for Decentralized Federalism*, eds. R. Hubbard and G. Paquet, 15-42. Ottawa: University of Ottawa Press.

Cutler, F. 2004. "Government Responsibility and Electoral Accountability in Federations." *Publius: The Journal of Federalism*. 34(2):19-38.

Elazar, D. 1982. "Confederation and Federal Liberty." *Publius: The Journal of Federalism*. 12 (4):1-14.

Gibbins, R. 2003. "Shifting Sands: Exploring the Political Foundations of SUFA." In *Forging the Canadian Social Union: SUFA and Beyond*, eds. S. Fortin, A. Noël, and F. St-Hilaire, 31-46. Montreal: Institute for Research on Public Policy.

Jeffrey, B. 2010. "Prime Minister Harper's Open Federalism: Promoting a Neo-liberal Agenda?" In *The Case for Centralized Federalism*, eds. G. DiGiacomo and M. Flumian, 108-136. Ottawa: University of Ottawa Press.

Kennett, S. A. 1997. *Securing the Social Union: A Commentary on the Decentralized Approach.* Research Paper No. 34. Queen's University: Institute of Intergovernmental Relations. At http://www.queensu.ca/iigr/pub/archive/researchpapers/Researchpaper34Securing thesocialunionkennett.pdf (accessed 9 December 2011)

Laski, H. 1939. "The Obsolescence of Federalism." *The New Republic.* 98(3):367-379.

Lazar, H. 2000. "In Search of a New Mission Statement for Canadian Fiscal Federalism." In *Search for a New Mission State for Fiscal Federalism: Canada: The State of the Federation, 2000,* ed. H. Lazar, 3-41. Kingston: Institute for Intergovernmental Relations, Queen's University.

Leone, R. and B. W. Carroll. 2010. "Decentralisation and Devolution in Canadian Social Housing Policy." *Environment and Planning C: Government and Policy* 28:389-404.

Maioni, A. 2002. "Health Care in the New Millennium." In *Canadian Federalism: Performance, Effectiveness, and Legitimacy,* eds. H. Bakvis and G. Skogstad, 87-104. Don Mills: Oxford University Press.

---. 2008. "Health Care." In *Canadian Federalism: Performance, Effectiveness, and Legitimacy,* eds. H. Bakvis and G. Skogstad, 161-81.. Don Mills: Oxford University Press.

Marshall, T. H. 1950. *Citizenship and Social Class.* Cambridge: Cambridge University Press.

Peach, I. 2010. "The Practical Defence of Decentralization." In *The Case for Decentralized Federalism,* eds. R. Hubbard and G. Paquet, 43-67. Ottawa: University of Ottawa Press.

Phillips, S. 2003. "SUFA and Citizen Engagement: Fake or Genuine Masterpiece?" In *Forging the Canadian Social Union: SUFA and Beyond,* eds. S. Fortin, A. Noël, and F. St-Hilaire, 93-124. Montreal: Institute for Research on Public Policy.

Pierson, P. 1995. "Fragmented Welfare States: Federal Institutions and the Development of Social Policy." *Governance.* 8(4):449-478.

Rocher, F. and M. C. Gilbert. 2010 "Re-Federalizing Canada: Refocusing the Debate on Decentralization." In *The Case for Decentralized Federalism.* Ruth Hubbard and Gilles Paquet (eds.) Ottawa: University of Ottawa Press, 116-158.

Ryan, Claude. 2000. "The Agreement on the Canadian Social Union as Seen by a Quebec Federalist." In *The Canadian Social Union without Quebec: 8 Critical Analyses,* eds. A.-G. Gagnon and H.Segal, 209-226. Montreal: Institute for Research on Public Policy.

Simeon, R. 1972. *Federal-Provincial Diplomacy: The making of recent policy in Canada.* Toronto: University of Toronto Press.

---. 2006. "Social Justice: Does Federalism Make a Difference?" In *Dilemmas of Solidarity: Rethinking Redistribution in the Canadian Federation,* eds. S. Choudhry, J.-F. Gaudreault-DesBiens, and L. Sossin, 31-41. Toronto: University of Toronto Press.

Simeon, R. and I. Robinson. 1990. *State, Society and the Development of Canadian Federalism.* Toronto: University of Toronto Press.

Smiley, D.V. 1987. *The Federal Condition in Canada.* Toronto: McGraw-Hill Ryerson.

Stilborn, J. *National Standards and Social Programs: What the Federal Government Can Do.* Political and Social Affairs Division, Parliamentary Information and Research Services. At http://www.parl.gc.ca/Content/LOP/researchpublications/bp379-e.htm#(1) end (accessed 15 November 2011).

Tiebout, C. M. 1956. "A Pure Theory of Local Expenditures." *The Journal of Political Economy* 64(5):416-24.

Wallner, J. 2010. "Beyond National Standards: Reconciling Tension Between Federalism and the Welfare State." *Publius: The Journal of Federalism* 40(4):646-71.

10

IS CITIZEN FEDERALISM CANADA'S THIRD NATIONAL POLICY?

Roderick Macdonald and Robert Wolfe

L'idée d'une « politique nationale » qui soit à la fois projet collectif et cadre d'analyse est plus indissociable de l'État canadien et de ses instruments directeurs que n'importe laquelle de ses lois constitutionnelles rebaptisées. Dans ce chapitre portant sur la troisième politique nationale du Canada (3PN), les auteurs soutiennent qu'en vertu des première et deuxième politiques nationales, le fédéralisme relevait principalement *du rapport entre des unités territoriales chargées d'exécuter des programmes par la voie d'institutions centralisées, bureaucratiques et médiatrices. À l'inverse, la 3PN promeut non pas un « fédéralisme de rang » mais un « fédéralisme citoyen » dont les instruments directeurs viennent dégrouper les programmes multidimensionnels et intègrent directement les citoyens à leur application. Les auteurs décrivent les forces idéologiques, économique et technologiques qui favorisent ce « dégroupage » des politiques publiques, puis en recensent les répercussions normatives sur nos politiques sociales. Enfin, ils donnent un aperçu des possibilités et promesses du fédéralisme citoyen s'agissant du rôle que jouera demain l'Ontario au sein du pays.*

INTRODUCTION

Experts on Canadian intergovernmental relations worry that the country is heading for an iceberg if current fiscal arrangements are not renegotiated in 2014. When we consider this risk from the perspective of citizens rather than jurisdictions, the looming crisis looks instead like an opportunity to reimagine the federation. The Canadian challenge is not rearranging the fiscal deck chairs, but how to close the gap between government and citizens. The place of Ontario in the federation is no doubt shifting as wealth and influence diffuse to other regions, but an increasing number of Canadians today care less about provincial citizenship *as such* than about personal identities and the relationships they imply: employment, familial, neighbourhood, religious, cultural, gender, and linguistic. Asking if something labeled "social policy" is a federal or a provincial responsibility does not help us understand what citizens want from their governments. One thing we know: all citizens do not want the same services from their governments any more than they want identical Swiss Army knives. The idea of federalism, just like the idea of a unitary normative order, or the notion of a multicultural state, is a metaphor for imagining how citizens conceive who they are, and how they organize the relationships through which they pursue their purposes and ambitions in concert with others across the entire range of human interaction. Reimagining the federation in the image of citizen federalism means thinking of new ways to package how government serves citizens.

Many scholars would find this to be a surprising way to characterise federalism. For them, federalism presumes the state; it is not about how citizens mediate multiple loyalties. These scholars do not consider the federal aspects of multiple sites of human association (e.g., the family, the neighbourhood or the workplace). Moreover, they see federalism only in rational structures of political decision-making, and canonical texts meant to attribute constitutional virtue. Finally, the conception of federalism held particularly by legal scholars and political scientists presumes a fixed – subject to shifting judicial interpretation – arrangement of normative institutions and jurisdictional competencies. But collective life in a country like Canada is messy, and allocation of roles and responsibilities can never be simple.

Federalism is centrally about the deduction, division and allocation of political, economic and social power; about multiple and competing sources of authority; and most importantly, about the complex and overlapping identities of citizens. This fit between pluralism and federalism is one of the great virtues of the federal principle for twenty-first century governance, when just about everything (from families to corporations to public services) can be unbundled and then reaggregated in novel ways. Governments seek to provide the aggregations or bundles of services that citizens most want. These configurations are never permanent but always in evolution. The agents who deliver services become attached to the structures that shape their working lives, but jurisdictional fights matter less to Canadians than the actual policies and programs being delivered.

Today the pace of change is extraordinary. All sorts of institutional aggregators and intermediaries have been undermined by the Internet and may be destroyed by the iPad. This is particularly true of "information industries" that deploy material vehicles and require material depositories like libraries and newspapers. But the point also applies to service industries and especially "government" service industries. For example, the nineteenth century downtown department store became part of the twentieth century suburban shopping mall. The first stage of unbundling in the retail sector was the creation of speciality suburban big box stores. Once people perfect online shopping (and even online grocery shopping) these monstrosities may disappear. Why? Because they too are aggregators, and some forums of aggregation will no longer command a premium because the services or products they offer have been successfully unbundled. Changes in the structural possibilities for aggregation have institutional implications for governments as well. The shifting configuration of municipal arrangements – from villages, towns and townships to regional municipalities and from urban villages (Forest Hill, Leaside, Swansea, Weston, Mimico, Long Branch) and historic neighbourhoods (Parkdale, the Beaches, the Junction, Cabbagetown) to mega-cities, and at least informally, back again in different guise (city vs. 905; downtown vs. "Fordburb") – show that this tendency to dis-, and then re-aggregation is not just a market or consumer phenomenon.

Constitutional scholars tend to be preoccupied with constructing the politics of Canada through its key documentary artefacts – the *Constitution Act, 1867* that provided for an allocation of legislative powers between federal and provincial legislatures, and the *Charter of Rights, 1982* that empowered courts to censure both the legislative outputs of the political process and the bureaucratic outputs of the administrative process. We see this approach as completely backwards. Political structures and institutions are the consequence of policy, not the reverse. Hence, we argue for thinking about constitutionalism and state-building in Canada in terms of agenda-setting macropolicies that frame the way in which everyday politics, both federal and provincial, are being carried out. Following the canonical expression, we call these macropolicies "National Policies" (NPs).[1] We argue that since the peace with the United States was established in the early nineteenth century, three different National Policies have been pursued in Canada.

Canada's third National Policy (NP3) is the subject of this chapter. In the next section we first explain what we mean by Canada's three NPs. We argue that both NP1 and NP2 imagined federalism *primarily* as the relationship between territorial units. By contrast, NP3 can be described as one promoting citizen agency. Were we to translate this into the structural framework of the constitution, it might also be described as a National Policy that aims at promoting "citizen federalism" instead of "place federalism." We claim that law (including constitutional law) follows policy, and policy responds to changes in the daily life of citizens. In the third section of this chapter, we describe the forces – ideological, technological, and economic – that drive the "unbundling" of public policy. We then derive what we see as the normative implications of unbundling. The fourth section applies these two concepts of "unbundling" and "citizen federalism" to a consideration of how disaggregated regulation creates the possibility of "Swiss Army knife governance." Any National Policy has many dimensions, but in the fifth section we focus on the implications of these ideas for social policy. The conclusion briefly outlines

---

[1] For the full version of our argument, with citations to the relevant literature on the idea of a "national policy," and the theoretical basis of the argument in law, politics and sociology, see Macdonald and Wolfe 2009.

the possibility and promise of citizen federalism for Ontario's place in Canada in the years ahead.

NATIONAL POLICY (NP) AS STATE-BUILDING

The National Policy is remembered as Sir John A. Macdonald's election slogan of 1879, a convenient label for a congeries of objectives meant to further building a new state. The actual policy projects comprising the National Policy clearly preceded the label, and the overall objective can be identified as early as the 1820s. That goal was to promote the commercial empire of the St. Lawrence as a vehicle for defining a country with an east-west axis. All three NPs have economic, communications, and social dimensions. The nineteenth century NP as articulated by Macdonald famously used a protective tariff, investment in railways (notably the Canadian Pacific Railway (CPR)) aggressive promotion of immigration, and the creation of the North West Mounted Police in order to sustain the transcontinental reach of federal political institutions and support domestic manufacturing in central Canada. It is significant that the rest of social policy was left largely to families and mediating institutions like churches and charities. Particularly worth noting is the absence of policies and programs aimed *directly* at citizens, understood as the atomic (and equal) political units of a liberal state.

Because NP1 was about building an east-west political community, the central policy instruments of the endeavour had largely achieved their objectives by the First World War, even though Crown business corporations like Canadian National Railways (now CN), the Canadian Broadcasting Corporation (CBC) and Trans-Canada Airlines (now Air Canada) were born thereafter. The Great Depression and, later, urbanization resulting from demobilization after the Second World War generated a second general policy framework, conventionally called NP2. By contrast with the economic and communications infrastructure aspirations of NP1, NP2 was about building a direct, local presence of government policy and services. Here we find the origins of the welfare state, beginning in the response to the dirty thirties and reaching its full flowering in the 1960s.

Although some NP1 policy reflexes continued (e.g., the Department of Regional Economic Expansion and the National Energy Program), by the 1990s, the sustaining symbols of Canada had moved from hard infrastructure (the CPR), through soft infrastructure (the CBC), to social welfare (Medicare). Health became the great national symbol, and in a 2004 CBC TV series, Tommy Douglas was voted the greatest Canadian. But just as railways retained their symbolism long after their substance was gone, so too the large, social welfare institutions of NP2 (employment insurance, public pensions, and the health care system) have retained their symbolism, even though their policy substance has been eroding for years.

To summarize, NP1 focused on territory and infrastructure, and dominated both policy reflection and the choice of governing instruments during the period from

1840-1930. NP2 focused on Canadians as recipients of government expenditure programs delivered through large, central bureaucracies and regulatory agencies. NP2 shaped both policy and instrument choice over the period 1930-80. Today important vestiges of NP1 and NP2 policies and instruments remain, although few of them are significant components of overall government policy. Or, as with some NP2 programs such as Medicare, if they are significant, their financial position is precarious and governments are seeking alternative ways to achieve the objectives of these particular programs and policies. Many analysts either lament the eroding of the NP2 institutions, or tar the alternative with the label "neoliberal." This dissonance of symbol and substance blinds them to the emergence of the third of Canada's National Policies and inhibits discussion of how to shape changing circumstances to fit normative objectives.

Commercial, social and technological possibilities influence what programs and services Canadians expect from their governments and how they expect those services to be delivered. Policy and law will follow. The central feature of NP3 is a focus on citizens as the primary target of policy. Citizens are not seen as recipients of predetermined packages of services provided by specific bureaucratic institutions (whether departments or administrative boards and commissions or Crown corporations), but instead as empowered agents who will make choices about the specific configuration of services and intensity of delivery that they desire. In such a perspective, the citizen is an active participant in making the aggregative choices we associate with federalism. "Citizen federalism" means that citizens themselves become a central unit of federalism. The *Constitution Act, 1867* imagined federalism as primarily involving provinces (s. 91, 92). Yet it also conceived federal citizenship as: linguistic (s. 133); religious (s. 93); racial (Indian status); regional (the allocation of equal representation in the Senate to the Maritimes, Quebec and Ontario); and subprovincial (the allocation of Senate constituencies by specific county in Quebec). Today, NP3 carries the implication that in addition to these traditional aggregating federalisms, there is a citizen federalism that is not dependent on ethnicity, religion or language, but is actually dependent on the self-identification of individual citizens. Many aspects of government policy over the past 30 years have been pursued through institutional design choices that reflect attention to citizens rather than bureaucracies, single-option instruments and places as the focus of public policy. Examples include providing citizens with direct input into policy-making through rights-based challenges under the *Charter of Rights and Freedoms*; facilitating individualized retirement planning through self-directed rather than financial institution intermediated Registered Retirement Savings Plans (RRSPs); enabling non-tax-distorted citizen expenditure through broad-based consumption taxes on goods and services rather than manufacturing sales taxes; enhancing citizen identity-expression by deregulating of communications networks and permitting differential services within such networks.

Consider the recent evolution of one NP2 initiative – retirement pensions. The rapid decline in agricultural population, the waning of active religious participation, the dominance of the wage-economy, and the rising life expectancy of Canadians all contributed in the mid-twentieth century to demands for governments to establish old age security and mandatory pan-Canadian portable pensions. Over the same period war-time bonds were transformed into Canada Savings Bonds (CSBs) on the payroll savings plan as a "safe retirement investment" for "ordinary" Canadians and tax regimes promoted company pension plans and RRSPs as instruments of private pension planning. Now many citizens hold, or are encouraged to hold, not CSBs, but individualized investment portfolios. Life insurance is now also marketed as a retirement product and financial services and financial products are "consumer goods." For many urban dwellers, individual reverse mortgages serve the same function as the parental life-interest in the family household in the 1930s and individual savers with investment accounts are a key part of how Canada mobilizes capital. These examples demonstrate how the single-payer, single-payee, single-program social policy tools of NP2 have been unbundled and dismembered, granting far greater discretion to citizens to select the aggregative mix they desire.

UNBUNDLING GOVERNMENT OR PUBLIC POLICY IN THE "LONG TAIL"

All institutions – governments, charities, religious institutions, neighbourhood groups, employee organizations, tenants' associations, school commissions, business associations, consumer cooperatives, and markets – involve administrative trade-offs affecting both the scope of goods and services offered, and the optimal aggregation of such services. Take some government operations as examples. For the past several decades governments have aggregated the delivery of education in three bundles: primary, secondary and post-secondary (although the line between primary and secondary has been blurred, and a national child care programme may add a fourth aggregating mode), and scholars have aggregated the transmission of knowledge by disciplinary criteria. We have aggregated health services by reference to service providers (nurses, doctors, dentists, etc.) or institutions (clinics, hospitals, hospices, etc.). We have generally aggregated transportation policy by reference to mode of transport (cars, trucks, buses, trains, subways, airplanes) rather than by distance (except interprovincially). For the most part, these aggregations have been the consequence of history and experience. As such they become anchored in consciousness as desirable (or perhaps even necessary), even though the cultural, social, political and technological rationales informing the initial choices may no longer be relevant.

Nowhere is the disaggregation or unbundling of services more visible than in the marketplace. Technology has enabled just-in-time delivery of products ranging from automobiles to laptops with customizable sets of options. Manufacturing firms are now part of complex global value chains; they are not builders of a product from start to finish. Apple, the world's most valuable company at the date we are writing this chapter, has no factories. Technology has also enabled service providers to strip a service to its essentials. Amazon and iTunes signal the end of mass-everything and the dominance of what might be called the "long tail" hypothesis, a reference to a common statistical distribution.

Imagine a graph where the horizontal axis reflects the number of products on offer, and the vertical axis reflects the number of items in stock of that product. As the number of products on offer increases, with only a few items being sold, the line on the graph that starts as a fat bulge on the left flattens into a long tail to the right. A suburban Chapters bookstore with its stacks of recent bestsellers can make money by selling many examples of a small number of things while Amazon can make money by providing individuals with access to millions of items, orders of magnitude more than any physical bookstore could stock.

Of course, the capacity of the market to function in the long tail depends first on the availability of information to purchasers about what service or product they are actually acquiring. The information intermediation of the well-read bookseller has been unbundled from her bookstore. Citizens can get information from a multitude of sources, none of which speak authoritatively. Second, the long tail market also depends on the capacity of the service provider to offer a multitude of products. Amazon can sell as it does because customers are willing to wait two weeks for delivery, or pay a premium for expedited delivery. What Amazon shoppers cannot do is pick a product up off a shelf. In other words, technology may make some products and some services more amenable to long tail delivery, while having no impact on how others are distributed.

Just as it has changed retail so will this phenomenon change government. NP2-type organizations are designed to provide a relatively small number of services on a universal basis, but out in the long tail on the right, NP3 organizations provide a few examples of a great many services. The possibility of institutional change provokes a vigorous defence from service providers, but people increasingly care about what they get, not where it comes from. In the NP3 long tail, citizens not structures can be the primary drivers of public service delivery models.

It is typical when thinking about policy instruments like Crown corporations to confuse the substantive outcomes they are meant to achieve with their instrumental form. Moreover, it is typical to think that the instruments serve only one purpose. The former Crown corporation Air Canada was generally conceived as providing a network of airline services for Canadians, but it was also a vehicle for promoting bilingualism, employment equity, best-practices for labour standards, and flying the Canadian flag in all parts of the country (including rural Quebec). Here one instrument was used to pursue several policy objectives, none of which were necessarily dependent on that instrument alone.

The same pluralities can be observed inside the mandate of a single policy instrument. For example, if one takes the primary mandate of Air Canada as providing cross-subsidized airline services to all parts of Canada, all the components of that service need not be offered on a universal basis. Some people may wish more leg room, but do not need to travel with two bags. Some may wish meals, but do not care about seat selection. Some may want the most inexpensive fare possible and be willing to fly on a space available basis on a given day. Today airlines are stripping their core services to a minimum, largely to generate more revenue, but also to permit fares to remain relatively lower for those who do not wish the extras. More than this, they are providing the extras individually; it is not necessary to buy a meal, if you only want more legroom; nor is it necessary to buy an aisle seat if all you want is to bring an extra bag.

The key idea that the airline example reveals is that it is no longer necessary for everyone to receive the same public policy "bundle." While maintenance and safety standards for personnel may be fitting targets for universal regulation, it is not clear that many of the other services provided by airlines need to be bundled together on a take it or leave it basis. Perhaps the best way of thinking about bundling and unbundling of public services is to consider the reviled cable company – the twenty-first century equivalent of the twentieth century's Ma Bell.

Apart from channels that the Canadian Radio-television and Telecommunications Commission (CRTC) orders Rogers to make available (itself a dubious requirement except insofar as one might decide that CBC-Radio Canada is – or should be – sufficiently central to every Canadian's sense of identity that carriage of its channels should be obligatory) Rogers itself makes you buy channels you do not want in order to get the few that you do. More than that, Rogers creates groupings of channels so that some channels you want to receive cannot be had in combination with others you desire. This practice is not a technological requirement. Increasingly consumers are demanding the ability to get just the bundle they want – they are creating their own, personalized aggregations – or they are finding alternatives like downloading from the Internet.

How does this market metaphor line up with the practice of NP3 public policy? The example of Air Canada, a prototypical NP2 policy realized through a now-privatized prototypical NP2 instrument (a Crown corporation), reveals how certain instruments achieve multiple policy goals. One of the risks of outright privatization is that lack of attention to these bundled goals may mean they do not survive the transfer of ownership. It is necessary to develop replacement instruments (for example, the elaboration of a detailed set of regulations, policing by a regulatory agency, the creating of new causes of action in the tort system to enhance non-government enforcement of desired policies, the negotiation of highly specific contractual commitments during the privatization process) to achieve these collateral policy goals, typically in a differentiated and reaggregated fashion.

Privatization of Crown corporations also has benefits. The private sector model often encourages unbundling the components of a policy goal, thereby enhancing citizen agency whenever specific bundled components reflect policies that are not deemed essential pubic goods. Consider the relative importance of bilingualism as compared with flying the flag of the government of Canada to every city with a significant airport. The institutions of NP2 are too often defined by operational boundaries designed for service providers not citizens: in the pre-computer universe "what is easiest to deliver universally?" was more important in designing programs than "what do citizens really want?" In NP3 citizens can and ought to be at the focus of decisions about the shape of policy instruments.

This claim might not be well received in downtown Toronto, but citizen desire for unbundling – in Etobicoke I want public money spent on my local park, not on Ontario Place; in Scarborough I want transit and roads that take me quickly to Downsview as much as I want roads and transit that take me downtown; in North York, I would rather a better local community centre than more money put into Roy Thomson Hall – may be an important part of the message in the phenomenon that made Rob Ford Mayor of Toronto in the 2010 election. Unbundling need not mean disintegration (that is, notwithstanding his own rhetoric, Ford's election does not necessarily signal the withdrawal of municipal services), but it may mean new ways of aggregating the policy bundle. In addition, it is important to note that many of the projects and instruments of NP1 were developed because markets were unable to deliver them; the goods and services provided are not public goods simply because the State once provided them. With very few exceptions, so-called public services are no more a "natural monopoly" than is telecommunications. Technology and computers now permit the State to ensure that the services people want are available to the extent they desire and at the cost they are willing to pay, without the need for these services to be directly provided by big, centralized bureaucracies providing a one -size-fits-all universal service.

The implications for government are significant. Most activity of government is oriented to services, not physical products. As a consequence, technology will permit the delivery of services from multiple local distribution points or even (like Amazon) from a remote source. In both cases, given the broad availability of information, services can be delivered at a time and place of citizens' choosing. Citizens (even in Quebec, as the Bloc Québécois discovered in the 2011 election) do not just care about constitutional jurisdiction. They care about service. If the local convenience store now performs efficiently the functions that previously required a trip to the post office citizens do not complain about privatization. Today Service Canada has close to 600 "points of service"; Service Ontario is a similar operation. Both aim to be a single window. Would citizens care if the same office and the same clerk wore two hats: one as Service Ontario provider and one as Service Canada provider? Our claim for citizen federalism addresses institutional design rather than organizational design; it addresses objectives and instruments, not structures. Governments should not confuse a "single window" for service delivery with a single structure. Do citizens care that in Alberta the federal Royal Canadian Mounted Police enforces both the criminal law and certain provincial regulatory offences? Do they care that the Ontario Provincial Police enforces not just Ontario regulatory offences but the Criminal Code as well?

Our Normative Stance – Is Unbundling a Good Thing?

One implication of our description of NP3 is that a number of cherished institutions of NP1, and especially NP2, may no longer be the optimal vehicles by which certain public policies are delivered. The government of Canada has already divested itself of several Crown corporations, and has downloaded others (airports, harbours) onto municipalities or nonproprietary local corporations. Provinces have seemed more inclined to hold onto NP1 organizations (Hydro, transportation, asbestos, potash, coal, even forest products) and NP2 institutions (universities, hospitals). But increasingly, new programs are delivered directly by governments (child care subsidies; home energy-efficiency renovation subsidies) or through the tax system. When such programs are delivered federally, the money is spent where it is needed, not where the taxes were levied, an important mechanism for ensuring that federalism serves citizens not places.

Many critics on the political left are troubled by the developments we identify as reflective of NP3 thinking because they understand these developments not primarily as governments reconfiguring the instruments by which policy objectives are accomplished, but as attempts to change what government does. Many of the arguments for privatization, Public-Private Partnerships (PPPs), indirect governance, and the wider use of the tax, subsidy and tort systems as regulatory instruments are indeed promoted by proponents of a "deregulatory agenda," which does not mean that the instruments in question are only useful to pursue a particular ideological objective; many of these instruments can serve regulatory objectives as well. In other words, we are not advocates for the ideological, technological and economic forces supposedly driving change, and we think the policy consequences are up for debate.

Here is an example. Some on the left express great regret about the advent of the *Charter of Rights and Freedoms* as a classic neoliberal instrument. People no longer work together to find common interests to move the political process and advance progressive causes. Today, according to this view, everything is driven by particularistic rights claims framed to protect the interests of the already well-endowed against government activity meant to reign in excessive individualism. And yet, despite the fact that courts and the legal profession appear to over-represent the elites of society, many have been able to use the *Charter* to discipline police and regulatory practices, to compel governments to adjust programs to advance the equality of citizens, and to ensure that the political process itself is enabled (through guarantees relating to freedom of speech and association) for all citizens.

The point of our discussion of NP3 is this: something macro is happening to the way in which public policy is being formulated and determined. These forces of change produce neither monolithic governing instruments (e.g., deregulated markets and PPPs) nor monolithic policy outcomes (neo-liberalism). Governance still requires legislatures to make substantive policy choices, and these choices will vary according to which party is in office. *Good* governance still requires selecting the optimal instrument to achieve a policy purpose, which will sometimes mean an NP1 or NP2 tool, but increasingly, governments are inclined towards instruments that were not favoured by NP1 and NP2. These instruments reflect the desires of citizens and the technological possibilities of our times. Those who wish to retain the policies now being pursued through NP1 and NP2 instruments need to reconsider whether these instruments and the particular programs they deliver are: adequate to the task; optimal given changes to communications and transportation technology; consistent with the general direction of citizen empowerment (citizen agency) reflected in important policy decisions and instruments of the past thirty years; and respectful of the enhanced capacity of citizens to make choices about their relationship to governments in the selection of the policies and programs they most desire (direct citizen federalism).

Allowing all Canadians to live rich lives of their own choosing, and ensuring the accessible provision of the essential collective services of a just society, are demanding policy objectives. But if the mandate, services, and activities of all organizations – both private sector and public sector – are in fact being unbundled, the question for policy-makers is not how to resist at all costs the structural trend, but rather how to empower citizens to guide them in deciding when any type of aggregation (as opposed to the offer of a multitude of choices) is needed, and if so, to assist them in developing a menu of reaggregations that best serve their specific interests. In the next section, we consider the implications of service unbundling and multiform agents of reaggregation for the contemporary governance agenda.

REAGGREGATING REGULATION OR SWISS-ARMY-KNIFE POLICY-MAKING

A key ingredient of the theory of regulatory agencies that dominated NP2 thinking was the belief that direct command-and-control norms had to be universal in two respects. First, they had to be non-discriminatory – applied without distinction to everyone within the target community (which, for many programs, meant all Canadians). It is in this sense that people talk about universality in Canada's health care regime. But second, universal also meant that the regulatory framework would be comprehensive; it would have no gaps. Once the policy field was identified there would be no partial opting-out. In this sense the CRTC is universal because (at least until the advent of the Internet) all forms of telecommunications fell within its mandate.

Universal regulation required the State to imagine and direct every contingency; a rule for every situation, and for every variation on every situation. The model here is the parent that thinks childrearing consists of imposing control with a rulebook in one hand, and a ruler in the other. People cannot be trusted to use their own judgement to act intelligently under a general framework of rules that are transparent about their purposes.

Take traffic regulation as an example. Today in any Canadian city, almost every lamp-post will have two, three or more signs attached to it; speed limit signs, no turn signs, no parking signs (often of three panels each), no stopping signs, snow removal signs, reserved parking for handicapped signs, school-crossing signs, slippery when wet signs, stop signs, pedestrian crossing signs, and so on. It is practically impossible for a driver to internalize all this information while driving. One has to be a resident of a neighbourhood to understand and assimilate all these meanings. And yet the argument for detailed signs setting out all contingencies is often that they are needed so that strangers to the locality will know what they can and cannot do!

Contrast the situation in many Asian cities, like Hanoi, with 300,000 motorbikes. They can often be lined up eight or ten across and 50 deep at intersections with traffic lights but no signs either for motorists or pedestrians. When the light changes the resulting scramble resembles the start of a NASCAR race. At intersections with neither traffic lights nor stop signs (that is, most intersections) everything seems to be chaos as traffic moving straight ahead in four directions vies with traffic negotiating four different sets of left turns. Two-way streets usually have no dividing line and people move in both directions on both sides of the street. Yet remarkably few accidents occur. Everyone seems to know what to do. Why? Everyone, including pedestrians trying to cross the street, follows one, double-barrelled, unwritten rule: do not do anything unexpected and do not change your mind in the middle of doing something.

Consider a second example. Some German cities that are feeling the oppression of over-regulation have reverted to the Hanoi approach to traffic signs. One city removed all traffic signs and saw traffic accidents drop by two-thirds. Without signs, drivers always have to be on the lookout for other drivers, always have to be more predictable and more rhythmic in their starts and stops and turns, and have to clearly signal their intentions. The lesson here is that creating more scope for people to manage day-to-day interaction on their own under a framework of a small number of general principles is a more effective form of regulation than bundled comprehensive regulation under the principle of universality. Unbundling universal detailed traffic regulation retaining only the necessary minimum of coordinating rules, and leaving the on-the-ground application of these general principles and detailed rules to citizens is preferable to universal regulation for all eventualities.

The move to unbundling is a recognition of what might be called the regulatory "konstant" – the sum of all regulation in a field is a constant. All that changes are the agents of regulation (the State, its direct delegates, its indirect delegates, corporations, citizens) and the mode of regulation (Crown corporation, regulatory agency, contract, tax, liability rules and adjudication, licensing). Even the so-called free market is a regulatory choice. The lesson of Hanoi and of Germany is not that the absence of prescriptive rules means the absence of regulation. The lesson is that in certain circumstances we have forgotten that other regulatory instruments – especially those that empower citizens to self-regulate (either individually or in groupings like the family) – can be a crucial part of effective regulatory governance.

Notice that this idea is not necessarily an argument for privatization and complete deregulation. Unbundled services can be unbundled to a variety of different regulatory modes and sites other than the market. In addition, for some government services – armies, police, courts – a totally bundled service and service provider is needed as the minimum backstop. But, as private security firms and neighbourhood watch groups on the one hand, and mediators, consensual arbitrators and other forms of alternative dispute resolution on the other illustrate, even some of our most obvious bundled services need not exclude other providers who offer services above the basic institutionally-bundled services provided by the State. In other words, even within the realm of traditional public services the logic of NP3 imagines a mix of public agencies, private firms, nongovernmental organizations (NGOs), and citizens, and a mix of alternative instruments like taxes, fines, and direct subsidies through which a service is provided.

The current configuration of regulatory structures came about as policy-makers addressed a substantive issue, took stock of the available instruments of governance that could achieve the desired outcome, and determined how many objectives and instruments could be combined within a particular legislative framework. Take the example of regulating network services. In the case of airline service, the policy objectives pursued might be: a minimum-level low-cost service to all parts of Canada (including remote areas); showcasing the Canadian flag; bilingualism; and stimulating local economies by cross-subsidizing airport construction. Choosing a Crown corporation as the primary vehicle to deliver this bundle meant that most objectives were achievable through the design of the corporation, although some were not. Now consider telecommunications. Given the multiple objectives of a broadcast policy for Canada, a single Crown corporation was not sufficiently supple to achieve the goals. Hence a regulatory agency oversees a Crown corporation, private broadcasters, cable companies, telephone service providers, satellite dish operators, and others.

The Swiss-Army-knife of Governance

The design choices just reviewed can be imagined based on the same logic used in the assembly of a Swiss Army knife – individualized tools for a citizen army. Not all Swiss Army knives have the same gadgets. Some have only a few. Some have a great many. Users have a choice of size, a choice of gadget, and a choice of combination. Yet no Swiss Army knife has yet been invented that can drive rivets. If the policy is one where driving rivets is desired, no matter how flexible the knife, it cannot do the job. But the analogy allows us to see that regulatory institutions can allow wide variations in their elements to suit each user.

What holds the elements of a Swiss Army knife public policy together? Government. The various tools all find connection in the political process of legitimated democratic governance. A given NP is a design decision about: what basic tools must be included in every knife; what additional tools to include in any particular knife; and the relative placement of the tools selected within the knife so that one or more are more easily accessible than the others, without at the same time either excluding other tools or making them totally inaccessible. NP3 is a particular way of thinking about the elements of the Swiss Army knife of Canadian governance rather than the fact of the knife. NP3-thinking requires a focus on the problem and the objectives, placing citizens at the centre, not a focus on creating a single, optimal regulatory tool. The instrument is not the objective.

The tools of a Swiss Army knife can be unbundled and reaggregated in infinite variations. What we already see in NP3 is that public programs are delivered through complex networks, not hermetically sealed hierarchically-managed institutions. The challenge for those who see NP3 as being fundamentally about citizen agency is to ask whether the Swiss Army knife analogy can be applied not just to certain fields of economic regulation (e.g., air travel, telecommunications) but also across the entire spectrum of social policy. Is the NP3 approach appropriate only for the kinds of policies, programs, and instruments that dominated the era of NP1, or is it equally relevant to policies, programs, and instruments that we have come to associate with NP2? Further, does it capture the expectations about service delivery that citizens have for new programs and policy that governments are now pursuing?

THREE EXAMPLES OF NP3 SOCIAL POLICY

To give a sense of the types of NP3-approaches to social policy that might be considered, we outline here three fields of action that continue to be dominated by the classical instruments of NP2; income redistribution, health policy, and immigration. In each we discuss continuing NP2 goals and policies, and then an NP3 alternative to current NP2 regimes for delivering these goals and policies.

Disaggregated Income Redistribution?

Here is one example of how rethinking the configuration of programs and services in an NP3 could be carried out by changing the instrument of program delivery. The prosperity promised by the NP1 national economy and the NP2 welfare state still has not reached large numbers of Canadians. However successful Canada has been at building a transportation and communications infrastructure, and however successful efforts to establish functioning labour, environmental and post-secondary education regimes have been, numerous social policy programs cannot be characterized as having achieved their goals. Moreover, these failures do not appear to be dependent on the particular instruments used to deliver particular social policies. To recall, programs and policies can be delivered in numerous ways. An institution can be built – a hospital, an orphanage, a school, an asylum, a reformatory, an old-age home. A particular service may be offered either by a public body (a worker's compensation board) or a private body that receives government grants (adoption agencies, doctors, families) or benefits from charitable status (food banks, religious institutions, the United Way). Finally, a contingent benefit may be conferred through a government-administered fund supported by a payroll tax (Employment Insurance (EI), Canada Pension Plan (CPP)), or through a tax-exempt voluntary contribution to a privately-held fund (RRSP, Registered Education Saving Plan (RESP)), or a simple cash transfer (Old Age Security, GST rebate), or declaring gains of capital property tax-exempt (principal residences).

The characteristic feature of NP2 is that its programs tended to have either a bricks-and-mortar physical location, or a centralized bureaucracy to administer them (EI, Workers Compensation, Welfare) or a one-size fits all revenue collection and expenditure mechanism (RRSP, CPP, RESP). In such systems, Canadians are presumed to all want the same things delivered in the same way; the only variable is that certain benefits (OAS, general welfare assistance) are means-tested.

Now imagine the Swiss Army knife metaphor for delivering social programs. In such a framework, citizens might choose some benefits, but not others; or they might choose to receive the benefits in a particular way and not in another. Even though the general policies being pursued by the state would remain the same, the way in which they would be bundled, unbundled, and reaggregated would depend largely on the choice of citizens. The new governance mantra is that social policy should be about empowering individuals, not building bureaucracies for state delivery of services, but *how* individuals are empowered matters. Of the available policy instruments deployed today, do any actually enable Canadians to select social policies they want as individuals?

Consider the following two examples. First, the financing of student participation in post-secondary education. Today we have basic loans and grants programs. Might a student prefer to defer income tax liability instead? Or to defer tuition and pay an income-tax surcharge? Second let us look at retirement planning. Why should retirement saving be available only to those who have cash resources to invest in a given tax year? Why should money invested in the purchase of capital assets such as a vacation property not be an eligible investment? Why should money borrowed and paid as tuition not be eligible for conversion to an RRSP account? In both these examples, the tax system currently provides for approximately equivalent benefits through other deductions or exemptions. Why is it necessary to make benefits available only within a single program, rather than generally available to be claimed under a range of support programs depending on the choice of the beneficiary?

The logic of these two examples can be extended across the whole field of social transfers. By far the most flexible instruments for advancing social policy are direct cash transfers. A guaranteed annual income for those without the minimum resources to spend on social programs, combined with tax deductions for designated expenditures by those with an income sufficient to be taxed, is like a Swiss Army knife for social policy: it gives people the fiscal resources to acquire the social policies they need regardless of where they live. It would reduce income inequality, enhance noncentralized delivery of social programs, and most importantly, by letting Canadians choose the exact bundle of social programs they desire, empower them as agents rather than as passive recipients of government largesse. In such a structure, State programs would only ensure universal access to an irreducible core of essential services, but even those programs would not necessarily be delivered by State bureaucracies and institutions.

Unbundling Health Policy

Perhaps the best example we can offer of the difference between an NP2- and an NP3-approach is Canada's health care system. Today, provinces have largely designed the delivery of health care around large organizations that have identical service protocols for patients regardless of the event that brought them through the doors of the institution. The paradigm of a large NP2-organization delivering a standardized product often inefficiently and inflexibly is the hospital. Failures of flexibility elsewhere in the system mean that the hospital emergency room becomes the default resource for health care users. Unnecessary wait times throughout the chain of hospital services (even in the triage room) are the inevitable consequence of failures of diversity in other parts of the system. Of course, using hospitals this way serves the interest of health care bureaucrats and politicians. It provides a leak-proof threshold for controlling costs.

Now imagine health policy (and its litmus test – wait times) not under an organization-centric (NP2) but rather under a patient-centric (NP3) delivery model. In the Swiss Army knife approach to health policy, rather than using hierarchical agencies, NP3 depends on orchestrating all nodes in a network to provide services when and where they are needed. Some problems might be solved not by internalizing all health functions in large NP2 bureaucracies, such as hospitals that must offer a standardized product with each room-night, but by the capacity to allow each part of the system to do what it does best in close collaboration with the other parts. We have all heard about patients who should be seen by a family doctor but who are instead diverted to the emergency room; the supposed result is that beds are occupied by patients who need continuing care, if not at the level of a general hospital, but the system cannot flexibly allocate resources where they are needed.

In order to reimagine health care the first step will have to be to unbundle services. Already we are experiencing pressure to unbundle, in the guise of calls to permit private health care for services currently outside of the Medicare system. If we can really unbundle health, it ought to be possible to create a core bundle of services received by everyone, while letting citizens add the other services they want. Sometimes they will add the other services by choosing acupuncture over pharmacological products, chiropractors over back surgery, midwives over hospital delivery rooms. The system can be designed so that these services might sometimes be covered by health care vouchers spent as patients wish, and sometimes private services might be only partially reimbursable by vouchers. Sometimes (e.g., most cases of cosmetic surgery) services might be covered only when a user fee is charged.

The key point is this: the current system is designed on the assumption that, generally speaking, all Canadians want the same thing from the health care system. That assumption may have been necessary prior to the revolution in communications technology, but it no longer holds. And it is no longer necessary to deliver basic social programs in the NP2 mode, because the technology available for system design when these programs were created has been far outstripped by the available administrative technology today. But, if we are to imagine unbundling payment, we must also unbundle the whole system. Pressure for a "private" option is really pressure for unbundling and multiple points of access. Tacking privatized NP3 payment onto rigid NP2 public organizations is a recipe for catastrophe.

Unbundled (Im)migration Policy

Under an NP2 approach one begins with institutions and delivers policies through them. Given the constitutional division of powers, this approach means that certain problems that are closely connected with each other may be dealt with by separate institutions – one federal and one provincial. Consider the case of population movement. If the movement occurs from an off-shore country to Canada, constitutional jurisdiction is shared between Ottawa and the provinces under section 95 of the *Constitution Act, 1867*. Given the constitutional doctrine of paramountcy, (that is, the principle that where federal legislation has "occupied a field of regulation" it will override otherwise valid provincial legislation that purports to regulate the same field) the federal government has taken the lead initiative here in all situations except, for reasons of constitutional comity, those involving Quebec. Unlike other provinces, Quebec runs its own immigration bureaucracy and develops programs to ensure the integration of immigrants into Canadian life. Other provinces have also assumed immigration responsibilities, in varying degree.

But immigration from other countries is only a part of the field of population movement. Internal migration – from province to province, or from one part of a province to another – is just as numerically important as external immigration. These internal population movements are, however, exclusively under the constitutional jurisdiction of the provinces, and are typically poorly addressed from a policy perspective.

Under an NP3 approach, which values all people and focuses on individuals, we would recognize important similarities between migrants, whether they moved to Toronto from Moosonee or Bangladesh. For decades significant numbers of Newfoundlanders spend part of the year in Fort McMurray and part on the Rock. In which province should they pay taxes, or get a health card, or be deemed a resident for purposes of drivers' licenses, equalization payments, CPP contributions, and so on? Conversely, we might ask why should there be interprovincial barriers to the movement of, nurses, teachers, social workers, lawyers, electricians, doctors and engineers.

One important feature of recognizing mobility, is that to encourage people with skills (whether migrants or immigrants) to move where their skills are most needed, we need to develop a citizen-centred policy for providing basic social services. These services must be available without qualification periods, limitations on availability, surcharges, or inordinate requalification obligations – all of which many provinces currently impose. Since people now entering the job market will, *on average*, likely hold seven or eight different jobs over their careers, policies to support (not impede) intra- and inter-provincial migration will become increasingly important.

The purpose of social policy meant to facilitate migration of those with credentials and skills across county, provincial and national boundaries is to speed their integration into the economic, cultural and political life of their new residence. This objective requires affording recognition (which we typically do well for migrants and poorly for immigrants) and a panoply of services (which we typically do well for immigrants and poorly for migrants). In an NP3 world, both migrants and immigrants would have input into the services they need in order to be most productive most quickly in their new communities.

CONCLUSION: CITIZEN FEDERALISM

This chapter uses social policy as the lens for reimagining the manner in which services are delivered by federal and provincial governments – in short, for reimagining the federation. We could just as easily have discussed productivity, where firms not industries are increasingly the focus of policy, or securities regulation, where the unbundling of financial intermediation requires subtle institutional adaptation. Four factors have contributed to federal-provincial jurisdictional conflicts in the delivery of social policy. The first is that the allocation of powers in 1867 made sense for NP1 programs and tools, but proved less amenable to sustaining NP2 instruments. Second, the centralized tools of NP2 necessarily led to conflict about which institution would take responsibility for service delivery – CPP or QPP, for example. A similar conflict can be seen in arguments about whether the 1940 constitutional amendment relating to Unemployment Insurance is broad enough to support the use of that fund as an annual income subsidy for seasonal workers. The third factor is that despite the desire of some provinces to undermine the federal spending power, no court has ever found that the federal government cannot use its power to tax and spend to promote policies that otherwise could only be pursued by provincial legislation. Fourth, for the first 100 years after Confederation, the "water-tight" compartments approach to the constitutional division of powers made it more difficult for federal-provincial program cooperation to be structured. Since the 1980s, however, the Supreme Court has taken a more flexible approach, which seeks to validate legislation and programs by both orders of government, even if they trespass on the jurisdiction of the other.

In an NP3 framework, the tools of indirect government that target citizens do not run afoul of constitutional constraints. The federal government can adopt Swiss Army knife policies, and rather than delegating tasks to provinces backed by tax points, it can keep the tax points and use a guaranteed annual income (and not just GST rebates) delivered through the income tax system as a way of empowering citizens to choose the types of social services they most desire. NP3 thinking offers a way to avoid conflict because it puts the focus on unbundled and reaggregated social policy and allows citizens to select services without reference to the particular government that offers them. More radically, it might (in the manner that students may seek post-secondary education anywhere in Canada) even permit citizens of Ontario to purchase certain social services from Nova Scotia or British Columbia. NP3 thinking allows a focus on citizens and their choice of services, not on residence in a particular place and mandatory predetermined aggregations of discrete services.

This shift has a number of obvious tax implications including that resources should flow to the order of government best able to accomplish broad redistributive goals within a particular policy field and that forms of taxation which focus on wealth are less efficient than those that focus on consumption. This means, for example, shifting a percentage of the income tax burden onto a Value Added Tax (i.e., the GST). Income taxes are created in the image of the single bureau NP2 institution. Consumption taxes are the ideal NP3 tax, because their collection point and target is disaggregated. The advantage is that consumption taxes enable citizens to see the policy choices and consequences that lie behind their spending decisions. For example, the normal VAT would be hidden in the price of goods and services, but where one is dealing with luxury goods, or goods that produce social externalities (e.g., tobacco, alcohol, gambling) the additional VAT would be visible. In the same fashion, a visible carbon tax or metered garbage and effluent charges are information rich. If the tax is levied by the federal government close to the source of the carbon emission, it would provide the necessary resources for equalization. As for other forms of wealth taxation, the requirement that municipalities finance their expenditures by taxing real estate places the burden on certain taxpayers without reference to the extent they actually consume those services, whereas allocating a percentage of reduced provincial income taxes to municipalities would slow down urban sprawl.

In NP2, the aggregation of policies into particular programs was both centralized and top-down. In this governance model, everybody has to want the same thing, and the same thing has to be delivered equally well to everybody – hence the need for big, bureaucratized, expensive command-and-control organizations. In business today, anything that can be digitized can be unbundled (i.e., "outsourced"). Extracting energy from the oil sands necessarily takes place in northern Alberta, but the back office does not have to be in Fort McMurray. Why should government be different?

If, as we argue, the large "N" National Policy is the "real" constitution, then debate over how to provide social programs is about the relation of parts of the country to each other, and the relation of Canadians to the world. From the start, Canadians have used social policy to serve the integrative purposes of the National Policy. Questions about who is responsible, therefore, turn not only on the division of powers in the written constitution, but on the country Canadians wish to create. When the focus is on the provision of services through provincially-financed NP2 institutions, Ontario rightly worries about its fiscal capacity to deliver the services its citizens have a right to expect. If the focus is instead on unbundled services chosen by citizens and financed through direct federal transfers to individuals, then the place of residence affects life choices less.

Our fundamental hypothesis is that the distinctive feature of NP3 is its enhanced focus on citizens. Citizens constitute the state, and they do it to serve their individual and collective purposes. NP3 will be characterized by policies that aim to facilitate citizen agency, that unbundle programs, and that reaggregate policy goals now largely managed by centralized bureaucracies (both public and private). Together these policies will be implemented in ways that enhance the ability of citizens to lead self-directed lives in concert with others, surely the litmus test for a liberal democracy.

REFERENCE

Macdonald, R.A. and R. Wolfe. 2009. "Canada's Third National Policy: The Epiphenomenal or the Real Constitution?" *University of Toronto Law Journal* 49 (4):469-523.

V

A Federal Partner for the New Ontario

11

THE FUTURE OF THE FISCAL ARRANGEMENTS

Matthew Mendelsohn

Les mutations économiques et politiques ont placé l'Ontario dans une situation budgétaire unique qui nécessite de repenser les accords ayant traditionnellement redistribué la richesse ailleurs que dans la plus grande province du pays. Les vastes transferts qui composent l'essentiel des transferts financiers intergouvernementaux – péréquation, Transfert canadien en matière de santé (TCS) et Transfert canadien en matière de programmes sociaux (TCPS) – ont été conçus quand l'Ontario connaissait une certaine prospérité. Toute réforme aux accords fiscaux qui viennent à échéance en 2014 devrait ainsi prendre en compte plusieurs nouvelles réalités, notamment le fait que l'Ontario est maintenant bénéficiaire de la péréquation, l'importance grandissante des économies fondées sur les ressources naturelles et une redistribution de fonds qui continue de négliger cette province.

INTRODUCTION

Canada's system of fiscal transfers was established to ensure that all provinces and territories have a comparable fiscal ability to provide public services to their residents. Historically, this meant the redistribution of funds, by the federal government, from the Ontario tax base (as well as the tax bases in Alberta and usually British Columbia) to provincial governments in other provinces. The fact that Ontario now collects Equalization payments is an enormous shock to the country's system of fiscal redistribution. The reason and meaning for this shift have been poorly understood. This shock necessitates a principled debate over how best to reorganize the system of federal transfers to the provinces and territories in order to accommodate Canada's new political economy. That is the goal of this chapter.

Canada's system of fiscal transfers was not designed for the current economic realities. The most important of these realities are the growing fiscal disparities between provinces, fuelled by differences in provincial endowments of natural resources and a federal government that is doing less than ever to moderate these inequities (Figure 1). The evidence shows that Canada's system of fiscal transfers is broken in fundamental ways. Canada's fiscal arrangements have evolved numerous times over the past half century in response to changing circumstances. Circumstances are again changing and further evolution is again necessary. This chapter outlines options showing how a new system might look.

Commodities increasingly drive fiscal disparities in Canada, however, our fiscal arrangements do not redistribute commodity wealth, in part because of provincial ownership of natural resources. These realities place Ontario in a unique situation: lacking the natural resources of the oil and gas provinces, while being significantly more prosperous than the traditional Equalization-receiving provinces. In practice, this means that funds continue to be redistributed away from Ontario at a time when its fiscal capacity is below the national average.

How is it possible that a province receiving Equalization is in fact a net fiscal contributor to the program? Residents of Ontario, like residents of other provinces, pay federal taxes that pay for federal programs like Equalization. Ontarians pay the share of taxes to be expected given its population (approximately 40 percent), but receive a relatively small Equalization cheque. In other words, Ontarians get far less out than they put in, despite having a below average fiscal capacity. This is unsustainable. This redistribution undermines Ontario's ability to provide comparable levels of public services to its residents and undermines its ability to invest in its competitiveness, its prosperity, and the transformation toward Ontario's Next Economy.[1] Given the huge contribution Ontario taxpayers make to the program in return for the relatively small Equalization payment their provincial government receives back, the program is certainly not in the fiscal interests of Ontario or its residents. The most fiscally profitable response for Ontario would be the elimination of the Equalization program, or at least a radical reduction in its size. However, eliminating the program would violate Ontarians' sense of solidarity with other Canadians and place undue hardship on Canadians in other regions. The far better solution is a reform of the fiscal arrangements that would result in Ontarians carrying a burden of redistribution that is more in line with the principle of equity and would allow the transfers to achieve their intended purpose.

A principled and productive debate requires an acknowledgement of these new realities and an exploration of new fiscal arrangements, along with a new discourse and new narratives. Labels like "have" and "have-not" distort the debate. A province

---

[1] The Next Economy is defined as an innovative, knowledge- and export-driven economy centred in metropolitan areas. It is characterized by networked regional economies that cross international borders (Mendelsohn et al. 2011, p.8-9).

Figure 1: Evolution of Provincial Governments' Fiscal Capacity Compared to National Average, 1972-1973 to 2010-2011

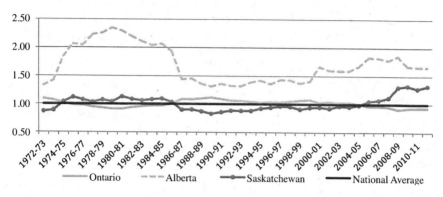

Source: Author's calculations

Note: National average = 1

can be prosperous and collect Equalization. Collecting Equalization is a relative measure of fiscal capacity, not an indicator of poverty, or a lack of entrepreneurial spirit. For example, Manitoba will not have a higher fiscal capacity than Alberta or Ontario in the conceivable future, regardless of how well its economy is performing, or how hard its people are working. The equivalence in Canadian political discourse between "poor," "have not," and "Equalization-receiving" perverts our national debate. More importantly, it has become clear that for the foreseeable future, those provinces endowed with natural resources that are demanding high prices on world markets will have higher fiscal capacities than other provinces. Whether Ontario or Saskatchewan receives Equalization ten years from now will depend largely on the internationally determined price for commodities like oil and potash. It is, therefore, far more useful to think of two coalitions of provinces: prosperous provinces with commodities demanding high prices on international markets, and less prosperous provinces with less natural resource income. Under the current system of redistribution, the latter group will receive Equalization regardless of how well their economies perform. Ontario, however, does not fit neatly into either category. Some commentators have argued that Ontario must decide whether it is part of the "wealth creating west" or "wealth consuming east," but the question is based on faulty premises (Coyne 2012; Ibbitson 2012). Ontario is neither a rich petroleum province, nor a less-rich non-petroleum province. Ontario shares interests and characteristics with both groups and faces its own unique challenges. British Columbia, a relatively prosperous province that is not overly reliant on royalties for its revenue base, is one province that shares Ontario's interests.

This chapter will introduce options for the principled reform of Canada's fiscal arrangements, particularly the Canada Health Transfer (CHT), Canada Social Transfer (CST), and Equalization. It will first outline the new political and economic realities for which our current system was not designed. It will then highlight problems with the current system that impact Ontario more severely than elsewhere and scope out possible changes to overcome these problems. Table 1 outlines current entitlements for each province in each of the three major transfers.

Canada's current regime of per capita transfers, supplemented by Equalization as currently designed, is failing and is punitive in practice toward Ontario. The Ontario tax base carries an enormous share of the burden to ensure that the governments of Manitoba, Quebec, and the Maritimes have comparable levels of fiscal capacity at a time when Ontario's own fiscal capacity has fallen below that of provinces with significant oil and gas revenues. Ontario currently has the largest per capita deficit in the country, but spends less per capita on just about every public service than any other province, with its per capita spending tied for last place, alongside PEI. Continued redistribution away from Ontario is not sustainable. The goal of this chapter is to propose reforms that respond to these new realities

CURRENT CONTEXT AND REALITIES

Equalization and other fiscal transfers are the primary way we ensure that many of the social benefits of Canadian citizenship are enjoyed by residents of all regions, including those that are less prosperous. This is a very worthy goal. Without federal fiscal transfers of some kind, many Canadians would see the ability of their provincial governments to invest in public services significantly curtailed. To achieve their intended objective, fiscal arrangements must be aligned with the economic realities of the country. A significant reason for the current misalignment is that the tax base to which the federal government has access, closely mirrors the Ontario tax base. The federal government relies disproportionately on this tax base for all of its spending, including spending to help less prosperous provinces. This fact does not change during a commodity boom when the major contributor to growing imbalances between provinces is the different endowments of natural resources. Although this arrangement determines the redistributive pressure of fiscal transfers, it is one from which Ontario derives almost no benefit.

Identifying new models for fiscal transfers requires clarity about what we are trying to achieve and an understanding of why our transfer system is no longer working as designed. A number of crucial observations are outlined below.

Canadians' commitment to Equalization (such that schools in small town New Brunswick will be able to provide the same quality of education as schools in suburban Vancouver) remains strong and widely embraced. Our commitment to the principle that all Canadians should have access to comparable public services is ingrained in our understanding of the role of government and has a variety of

Table 1: Total Major Federal Transfers to Provinces (Including Other Payments), 2012-2013 (millions of dollars)

	NL	PEI	NS	NB	QC	ON	MB	SK	AB	BC	Canada[a]
Canada Health Transfer	472	123	797	637	6,770	11,390	1,062	909	2,287	4,032	28,569
Per Capita Allocation (dollars)	927	842	843	843	843	843	843	851	595	869	820
Canada Social Transfer	173	50	322	257	2,735	4,601	429	365	1,309	1,581	11,859
Per Capita Allocation (dollars)	340	342	341	340	341	340	340	342	340	341	340
Equalization		337	1,268	1,495	7,391	3,261	1,671				15,423
Per Capita Allocation (dollars)		2,306	1,341	1,978	920	241	1,326				443
Total Transfer Protection				103	362		201				680
Per Capita Allocation (dollars)				136	45		159				20
Offshore Accords			458								458
Total Major Transfers	645	510	2,859	2,492	17,258	19,252	3,363	1,273	3,597	5,613	56,531

Source: Finance Canada 2012

Notes: Ontario amounts in the table are on an entitlement basis and may not match Ontario public documents.

[a]Canada totals for CHT and CST include Territories.

Total Transfer Protection was paid in 2010-2012, 2011-2012 and 2012-2013. Finance Minister Flaherty has stated it will not be continued by the federal government in 2013-2014.

Per capita numbers based on June 1st, 2012 Statistics Canada estimates.

Numbers may not add up due to rounding.

virtuous public impacts. Few suggest that we do away with equalization of some kind. Canada's debate focuses instead on how and whether or not we are properly achieving our Constitutional commitment (*Subsection 36(2)*).

Canada no longer lives under the umbrella of the protected internal markets of John A. Macdonald's National Policy. Equalization was part of a larger, implicit national bargain, whereby Ontario benefited from a greater concentration of manufacturing and other provinces received some share of the wealth generated by the sector in the form of federal fiscal transfers. Today, businesses, provinces, and cities compete with their peers globally. Those that produce export and trade oriented goods and services – particularly in geographically mobile sectors like manufacturing and services – are less able to afford a redistributive tithe (Courchene 2008).

The uneven concentration of natural resource wealth has exacerbated differences in fiscal capacity across the country to an extent never before seen. As pointed out by the Manitoba government, "the uneven distribution of natural resources is the single most important source of fiscal disparities among provinces. While the natural resource base is small (only five percent of total revenues subject to Equalization), it is responsible for approximately one-third of total Equalization entitlements in 2012/13" (Manitoba Ministry of Finance 2012). Alberta and Saskatchewan have fiscal capacities far greater than most other provinces and have an ability to provide more generous public services at lower rates of taxation. The extent to which Alberta and Saskatchewan are more prosperous than other provinces dwarfs the historic difference between prosperous Ontario and other provinces. Even at times of relative Ontario prosperity, Ontario's fiscal capacity was barely above the national average. In addition, natural resources are owned by the provinces. The royalties extracted from them belong to provincial governments and are not re-distributed to other provinces or the federal government.

The growing importance of the resource economy in general and the oil sector in particular, coupled with the relative economic decline of the United States and the increasing strength of emerging economies, will put great pressure on many of Ontario's traditional sources of economic strength in the manufacturing sector. Ontario will have below average fiscal capacity for the indefinite future, so long as the price of oil remains high. In 2009-10, Ontario officially became an Equalization-receiving province. In its first recipient year, the province received $347 million. Ontario's entitlements have rapidly increased and are set to reach $3.26 billion in 2012-13. Though growth in the size of Ontario's Equalization entitlement has been steep (now second only to Quebec in total dollar amounts), the per capita value is by far the lowest in Canada – approximately $241 per Ontarian. (Finance Canada 2012)

Overall federal spending continues to re-distribute funds away from, rather than toward Ontario. Ontarians contribute approximately 39 percent of federal revenues but receive only 34 percent of federal expenditures. "The net result of this revenue and spending pattern on a per capita basis is worth about $12.3 billion or 2.1 percent of Ontario's 2009 GDP" (Drummond 2012, 450). For 2009, the Mowat Centre estimates that this amount totaled approximately $11 billion (Zon 2013).

The inter-regional redistributive principle, which should be a core principle of the fiscal transfer system, is no longer operative. While once there was a principled re-distribution from richer to poorer, our system of fiscal federalism has largely broken down (see Figure 2).

Despite these realities, which should, *prima facie*, provide the impetus for significant reforms to the current transfer system, a serious discussion about re-forms has not happened. Such a conversation faces the following hurdles. Historic resentment in many parts of the country toward Ontario's economic and political power remains strong. Raising legitimate, evidence-based concerns or questions is often greeted with dismissal rather than principled engagement with the facts or arguments being highlighted. The legacy of the National Energy Program makes it difficult to have reasoned discussions about the impacts of the oil and gas sector on other parts of the country. The Western Canadian resource boom is having a significant impact on the Canadian economy but even raising these issues is sometimes treated as an attack on Alberta and Saskatchewan. A checkered history

Figure 2: Equity in Treatment of Provinces in Fiscal Arrangements, 1983-2009

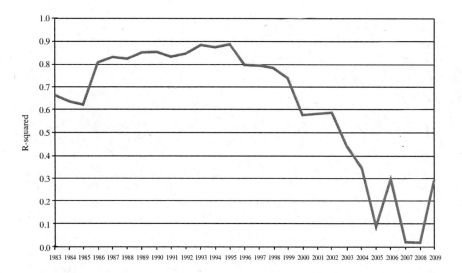

Source: Mendelson 2012

Note: Results in the figure represent an evolution in the correlation coefficient between provincial GDP and federal transfers per capita. One (1.0) reflects a perfect correlation between a province's GDP and its share of federal fiscal transfers. Zero represents a complete lack of correlation.

of *ad hoc* and politically driven adjustments by the federal government to the fiscal arrangements has fostered a lack of trust between governments, along with a zero-sum competition both horizontally (between the provinces who compete for shares of federal transfers) and vertically (between the provinces and the federal government who compete for shares of the aggregate tax base). The fiscal arrangements are complex and technical, making principled or evidence-based discussion of them in the political and public realms extraordinarily difficult. The politicized nature of fiscal transfers means provincial claims are greeted with skepticism and eye-rolling from the commentariat who shrug and say, "here we go again." The technical and complicated nature of transfers makes it far easier for observers to avoid the difficult work of engaging with the substances of critiques and simply lump them all into the same category of "more provincial whining."

Any change will produce provincial winners and losers. Provinces are capable of figuring out from a strictly fiscal position whether they would benefit or be hurt by changes. They tend not to accept principled changes that impact their own bottom line and they are always ready to explain to their own residents how a proposal will disadvantage them. Debates about design and objectives are self-interested and rhetorical, with residents of all provinces ready to believe their provincial government when they're told they're getting a raw deal. The Ontario government, for its part, has often complained about federal fiscal transfers but has offered no systematic critique of Equalization. Ontario has articulated no public views on the details of the Equalization formula, unlike other provinces that have had clear objectives on preferred changes to the fiscal arrangements. Ontario barely wants to acknowledge that it now receives Equalization for fear that this will communicate the wrong message about the health of the Ontario economy. Now that Ontario is a recipient of Equalization, its traditional agnosticism will need to end.

Although it will be difficult, Ontario must be prepared to lead an evidence-based and principled national conversation. Such a conversation would begin by recognizing that the sources of differing fiscal capacities are not what they once were and the ability of the Ontario tax base to fund redistributive efforts is lower than it once was. This should lead to a new conversation about how to design a principled system grounded in the Canada of today. The key question is how do we achieve the principle of Equalization in this new Canada, so that all provinces have the fiscal capacity to provide reasonably comparable levels of public services at reasonably comparable levels of taxation?

Ontario's emergence as a recipient province has led to some concern about the affordability of the program. It has also led to concerns among the other five recipients about the potential "crowding out effect" of Ontario. That is, the other recipient provinces are concerned their equalization entitlements will decrease now that Ontario is also a recipient. The concerns about affordability are not well founded. If the federal government wished to increase the size of the Equalization program, this could be offset through a reduction in per capita or other non-equalized transfers, or through program spending. Fiscal transfers are clearly affordable – the issue is determining the relative allocation and distribution between various transfers. A revenue-neutral growth in transfers designed to equalize fiscal capacity would simply need to be offset by a decline in other transfers. Affordability concerns are a red herring.

As part of this conversation it is important to consider not just Equalization, but other fiscal transfers as well – all of which should be properly understood as performing an equalizing function. Per capita transfers like the CHT and CST provide all provinces with the same per capita share (regardless of the richness of their tax base), thus representing significant transfers of wealth from places with higher per capita personal and corporate income (such as Ontario and Alberta) to others. We must think much more carefully about the interaction of all the various federal programs and transfers.

The Impact of Increasing Natural Resource Revenues on Equalization

The rise in importance of resource royalties for some provincial coffers has been matched by a relative decline in the manufacturing sector, historically centred in Ontario. Although the extent of the impact remains open to debate, there seems to be little doubt that there are some negative effects on Canadian manufacturing from a booming oil and gas sector, most notably the increase in the value of the Canadian dollar (Lemphers and Woynillowicz 2012). We will not revisit the discussion of "Dutch Disease" here, except to note that the impact of the resource economy on manufacturing in Canada is unique. In the Netherlands, the resource boom benefited national coffers, while the decline in the manufacturing sector was likewise national. In Canada, our particular challenge is that the benefits of the resource boom and the damage to the manufacturing sector are both experienced regionally.[2] Although the country's overall fiscal and economic positions are helped by diversified economic activity (including strength in both the manufacturing and resource sectors) significant strength in one can have negative effects on the other.

Increased provincial revenues from natural resources in non-recipient provinces put pressure on the Equalization program to grow by raising the national average standard (NAS) fiscal capacity. High oil prices (reaching over $100 per barrel)

---

[2] The fact that oil and gas revenues have not been saved in a sovereign wealth fund (as in Norway), has contributed to the rise of the Canadian dollar and the decline of Ontario's exports (Lemphers and Woynillowicz 2012).

were not considered when the current formula was designed and have contributed significantly to the program's growth. In fact, the Expert Panel on Equalization and Territorial Formula Financing, commonly known as the O'Brien Report, estimated a $60 per barrel high (2006, 33). A growth in any revenue source could put pressure on the program and natural resource wealth is no exception. What makes the commodity boom so challenging for the Equalization program, however, is threefold. The wealth is concentrated in a small number of provinces that do not receive equalization; natural resource royalties have grown very quickly in the past decade; and the federal government – which pays for equalization – has only marginal access to revenues from natural resources.

By removing natural resource fiscal capacity from the data, we see what many might suspect about the relative prosperity of provinces (prior to federal transfers). Alberta shows higher than average fiscal capacity, followed by British Columbia, Saskatchewan, and then Ontario, with all other provinces trailing (Figure 3). Canada's Equalization program and formula can do a great deal to correct for these differences. However, the current formula can do very little about the differences in natural resource revenues, as seen in Figure 4. These differences are becoming a more important source of varying fiscal capacities in the country. The question for Canadians is what to do about this, if anything.

Figure 3: Provincial Fiscal Capacity, Excluding Natural Resource Revenues, 2011-2012

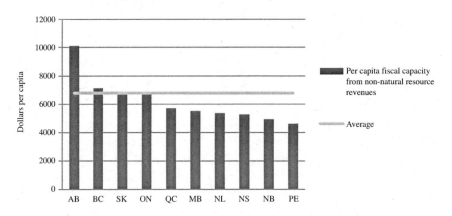

Source: Finances Quebec 2011

Figure 4: Provincial Fiscal Capacity from Natural Resources, 2011-2012

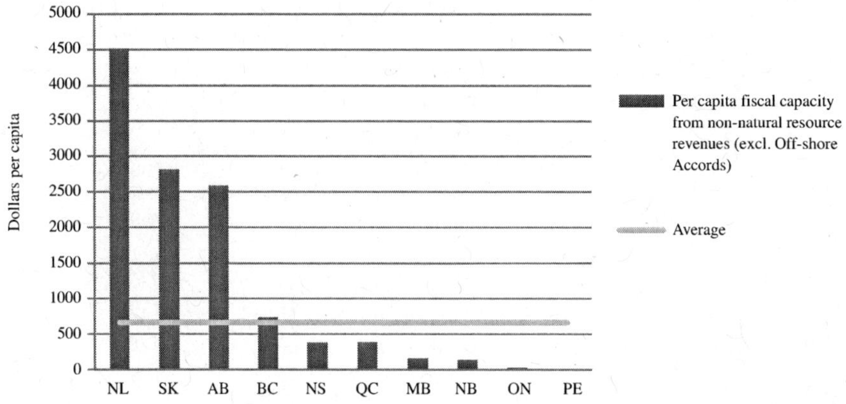

Source: Finances Quebec 2011

FISCAL CAPACITY

The major government studies of the mid 2000s – the O'Brien Report and the provincially led report of the Council of the Federation's Advisory Panel on Fiscal Imbalance – did not directly address the question of whether or not fiscal transfers ensured that provinces have comparable abilities to provide public services. Instead, these reports focused on technical debates acknowledging the constitutional commitment without measuring the success of the program. So we begin with this key question: Do provinces have the fiscal capacity to provide reasonably comparable levels of public services at reasonably comparable levels of taxation?

Prior to the inclusion of natural resource revenues (e.g., royalties, payments for exploration rights, profits remitted from provincial electricity utilities, etc.) and federal transfers, Ontario's fiscal capacity is fourth highest in the country (Figure 3). Ontario remains a relatively prosperous province with broad access to corporate, personal, and consumption tax revenues.

Once the value of natural resource fiscal capacity is included in overall provincial fiscal capacity, however, Ontario slides to fifth, below that of the four provinces with above average resource royalties as seen in Figure 5 (British Columbia, Alberta, Saskatchewan, and Newfoundland and Labrador). This is due to Ontario's very low level of resource revenues.

Figure 5: Provincial Fiscal Capacity Including 50 Percent of Natural Resources, 2011-2012

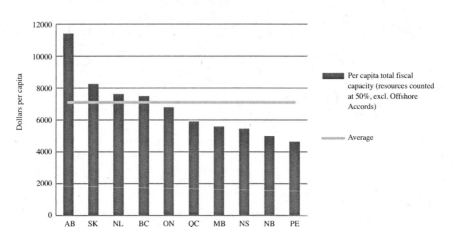

Source: Finances Quebec 2011

By including the value of federal transfers in measures of provincial fiscal capacity, we see that Ontario's ability to deliver public services is nearly tied for last, just a few dollars above that of PEI (Figure 6).

Other Federal Spending

The numbers presented above include the major federal transfers only, not other federal spending. They therefore understate the federal role in reducing Ontario's fiscal position relative to the other provinces. In the Final Report of the Commission on the Reform of Ontario's Public Services, Don Drummond estimated a $12.3 billion difference between Ontarians' contribution to federal revenues and the benefit to Ontarians from federal spending on transfers and services (assuming a balanced federal budget) (Drummond 2012, 450). Many federal programs represent significant transfers from the Ontario tax base to other provinces and are simply better designed for other provinces than they are for Ontario. For example, the Employment Insurance (EI) program does a far better job supporting the unemployed in other provinces. Figure 7 shows that EI coverage rates across the country are inconsistent and that unemployed Ontarians are the least likely to receive regular EI benefits, which may place pressure on other provincial programs (Mowat Centre EI Task Force 2011, 11).

Figure 6: Total Per Capita Provincial Fiscal Capacity after Federal Transfers, 2011-2012

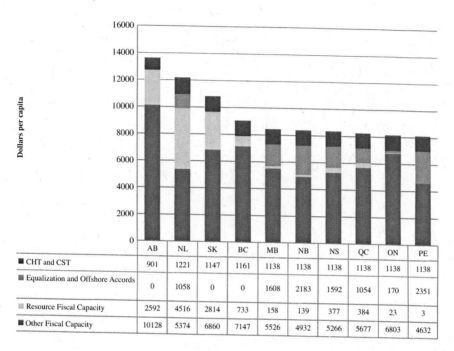

	AB	NL	SK	BC	MB	NB	NS	QC	ON	PE
■ CHT and CST	901	1221	1147	1161	1138	1138	1138	1138	1138	1138
▨ Equalization and Offshore Accords	0	1058	0	0	1608	2183	1592	1054	170	2351
▨ Resource Fiscal Capacity	2592	4516	2814	733	158	139	377	384	23	3
■ Other Fiscal Capacity	10128	5374	6860	7147	5526	4932	5266	5677	6803	4632

Source: Drummond 2012

The federal government has moved towards per capita transfers in many areas, but continues to operate random allocation formulae in other areas such as active labour market measures (through Labour Market Development Agreements (LMDAs)), economic development funding (through federal agencies), infrastructure funding, and social housing. To highlight one example, federal allocations for active employment measures (i.e., training) are based on decades-old assessments of what unemployment rates are expected to be in the future. As seen in Table 2, Ontario is the only province whose share of national unemployment exceeds its share of the federal allocation for active labour market measures.

Over time, these and other programs have taken their toll. Ontario, a relatively prosperous province, spends less per capita than other provinces but also has the largest per capita deficit in the country. Ontario's spending on just about every public program is lower than in other provinces, contributing to the growing income inequality in Ontario (Ontario Common Front 2012, 5). Regardless of

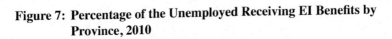

Figure 7: Percentage of the Unemployed Receiving EI Benefits by Province, 2010

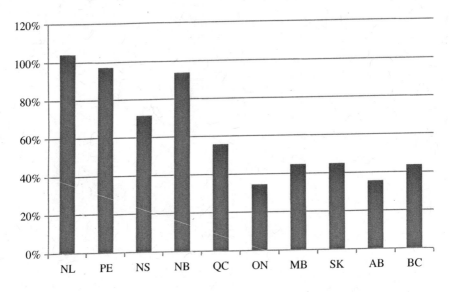

Source: Statistics Canada 2010

Note: The data expressed above can over- and under-count the percentage of the unemployed receiving support. Some EI beneficiaries are not counted as unemployed (e.g., those working while receiving EI). As a result, more than 100 percent of the unemployed can appear to be receiving benefits. Additionally, those counted as unemployed and not receiving EI may receive other benefits such as social assistance. Still, this figure provides a powerful comparison of the operation of EI across provinces.

whether one's long-term goal in Ontario is to reduce taxes or to increase spending (or both) failing to deal with the federal fiscal transfer system will make it difficult to see significant movement on either of those agendas. It should also be noted that while Ontario spends less than other provinces, its taxes are about average (McMillan 2012). When compared to other provinces, Ontario is a moderate tax, low spending jurisdiction. Ontario's deficit is the result of many factors, including a significant economic downturn, but a major contributor is the operation of fiscal federalism. These Ontario realities form the backdrop for a necessary redesign of the country's fiscal arrangements.

Table 2: **Transfers to Provinces for Active Employment Measures and Provincial Share of Unemployed, 2009-2010**

Province	Total Allocation ($000s)	Share of Total Allocation	Share of Canada's Unemployed	Total Allocation Per Unemployed
NL	$162,806	5%	3%	$4,889
NS	$120,306	4%	3%	$3,208
NB	$125,181	4%	3%	$3,737
PE	$36,072	1%	1%	$4,294
QC	$909,317	29%	27%	$3,006
ON	**$1,046,196**	**33%**	**42%**	**$2,244**
MB	$81,249	3%	2%	$3,066
SK	$67,563	2%	2%	$3,114
AB	$209,414	7%	7%	$2,720
BC	$424,425	13%	10%	$3,862

Source: Mowat Centre EI Task Force 2011, 58

Note: Includes LMDA, new LMDA allocation, Strategic Training and Transition Fund, and Labour Market Agreements (LMAs); totals may not add up to 100 percent due to rounding.

A PRINCIPLED APPROACH

Negotiations around fiscal arrangements have historically been among the most acrimonious in Canadian federalism. They have been characterized by a zero-sum climate and self-interested position taking, with little room for principled debate about provinces' relative abilities to provide public services. Myriad changes to programs and formulae have been adopted by successive federal governments in an effort to appease angry provinces, creating a confusing hodgepodge. It is very difficult for even the engaged policy expert – let alone the average citizen – to understand why provincial governments receive the amounts they receive. Many, in fact, have an interest in confusing rather than clarifying the issues. This chapter takes a different approach. It will focus on the key principles that should animate reform efforts. Fiscal arrangements should, to the best extent possible, provide provinces with comparable fiscal capacities with which to deliver provincial programs and services at comparable levels of taxation.

A return to principles, with an appreciation of new realities, is necessary. In 2010, the Mowat Centre issued a report card on Canada's fiscal arrangements and identified the principles that should guide reform efforts. A focus on three of these key principles – adequacy, equity, and provincial autonomy – seems most appropriate for dealing with this key challenge to the Canadian federation. The other principles – predictability, transparency, efficiency, and accountability – will also be brought to bear on an assessment of the options outlined in the following section.

REFORM OPTIONS FOR THE NEW CANADA

This section presents three types of reforms. The first group includes small changes within the current architecture that would improve the operation of Canada's existing fiscal arrangements and bring them closer to achieving their constitutional purpose. The second group represents larger, more ambitious changes that could be more contentious and difficult to operationalize but would still leave the overall structure of fiscal transfers intact. The third group of reforms is transformative in nature and responds to the growing imbalances driven by differences in natural resource endowments. These transformative proposals are sufficiently flexible and are designed to be responsive to changes in macroeconomic conditions, including a sudden or sustained downturn in the natural resource sector or an intensification of the commodity boom. They are designed to moderate, not accentuate inter-regional tension due to differences in economic activity and regionally differentiated economic cycles.

All of these reforms would increase the transparency of the country's fiscal transfer system and reduce opportunities to advance distortionary rhetoric about the fiscal arrangements. This would allow citizens to more easily hold their governments to account for policy decisions. Many of these reforms could be undertaken together. For example, removal of the GDP growth constraint, movement toward a need-based system, and an independent reporting mechanism could all be undertaken within the structure of either of the two transformative reform proposals.

Type 1: Incremental Fixes

A. Elimination of the GDP Growth Constraint

The federal government imposed a cap on the growth of the Equalization program in its 2009 budget. The cap was set at the rate of growth in the national economy. This unilateral change was enacted without consultation with the provinces and it violated the commitment made to provinces to return to a formula-driven program. In particular, it broke the bargain to which Ontario had agreed: that a movement toward a formula driven Equalization program would be coupled with a movement toward per capita transfers. Unilateral tinkering with a formula that has been accepted by all governments, albeit grudgingly, clearly violates the principles of transparency and predictability. More importantly, the imposition of the cap violates the core principle of revenue adequacy. The rate of national GDP growth is not a relevant measure for a program designed to address differences in provincial fiscal capacity. GDP growth could be flat, while fiscal disparities could be growing. Under such a situation, provinces receiving Equalization would have inadequate fiscal capacity to meet their responsibilities and Canada would move further away from achieving the spirit of its constitutional commitment.

As illustrated in Figure 8, all provinces that receive Equalization have taken a fiscal hit due to the imposition of the cap. The federal government has offered neither a compelling rationale for the cap, nor a compelling rationale for its decision to operationalize the cap by clawing back approximately 25 percent of Ontario's entitlement and only 7.5 percent from the other five recipient provinces. A full 55 percent of the entire federal claw back comes from Ontario. The arbitrary federal decision will deny Ontario approximately $1.1 billion in Equalization entitlements in 2012-13. Ontario's struggle to bring down its deficit is made more difficult when the federal government disproportionately constrains its transfers to Ontario in particular.

Figure 8: Impact of GDP Growth Cap on Equalization Payments, 2012-2013

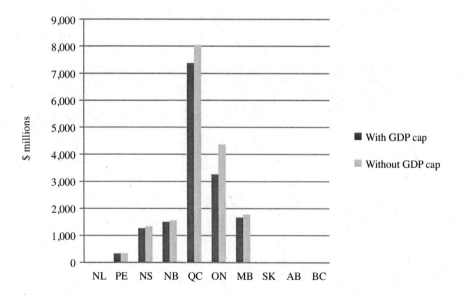

Source: Author's calculations

B. Adjusting Fiscal Capacity to Include Measures of Cost of Living (i.e., wages and salaries)

The Equalization formula only measures differences in fiscal capacity among provinces. It does not include any measure of variations in the actual costs to provide services. If we are serious about trying to achieve our constitutional commitment, both sides of the balance sheet must be considered. For example, both Ontario and British Columbia have higher than average costs. It is simply more expensive to provide services in Toronto or Vancouver than in Winnipeg or Saint John. Relying on a narrow measure of fiscal capacity, with no reference to the higher cost of providing public services in Ontario and British Columbia in particular, results in an over-equalization of those lower-cost recipient provinces (Courchene 2008, 1).

The evidence to support this proposed change is compelling. Wages and salaries represent the majority of provincial and local government expenditures and those provinces that receive Equalization (not counting Ontario) have the lowest wage and salaries in the country (Gusen 2012). A simple adjustment to allocations would account for differences in wages. Using the average private sector wage in a province, rather than focusing on public sector wages, would prevent gaming of the system and would ensure that provinces do not have fiscal incentives to drive up public sector wages.

C. Inclusion of a Different Percentage of Natural Resource Revenues in the Calculation of Fiscal Capacity

In 2007-2008, the federal government began to exclude 50 percent of natural resource revenues to measure fiscal capacity. This was largely a political compromise rather than a principled fiscal decision. Previously, 100 percent of resource revenues had been included in measures of provincial fiscal capacity (although this was under the previous five-province standard). Given that natural resource royalties are responsible for growing fiscal imbalances across the country, counting them in their entirety would increase the national average fiscal capacity and, in turn, increase the size of entitlements. Table 3 shows the likely outcomes of 100 percent inclusion. With no cap on payments, the size of the program would grow significantly, highlighting again how the Equalization program is doing a remarkably poor job at equalizing fiscal capacities across provinces. Alternatively, a percentage in between 50 and 100 could be used.

Table 3: Impact of 100 percent Natural Resource Revenue Inclusion in the Equalization Formula, 2012-2013 ($ billions)

	Ontario's Entitlement	*Total Value of Program*
With GDP growth cap	$3.7	$15.4
Without GDP growth cap	$8.6	$24.6

Source: Author's calculations

However, as discussed, the federal government does not receive resource revenues and so any increases in entitlements arising from this change would come from general federal revenues. This would put significant pressure on federal finances and would probably have to be offset elsewhere through reductions in other federal expenses or transfers to provinces.

A principled case could be made to exclude resource revenues entirely if these revenues are treated by provinces as assets rather than as revenue that is indistinguishable from other revenue. This debate has arisen in Alberta where sheltering more resource revenues was recommended by the Premier's Council for Economic Strategy (2011, 101-3). However, so long as provinces use their resource royalties to pay for ongoing current expenses, the case for excluding resource revenues is very weak. Removing natural resource revenues from the formula entirely is a principled option, so long as provinces are sheltering and saving these revenues in sovereign wealth funds, for example. Such an approach would have the added benefits of moderating the impact of commodities on the value of the dollar and inflation.

D. Inclusion of Hydroelectricity Revenues at Market Prices
Provinces' entitlements under the Equalization program are dependent on federal decisions about how to treat various forms of revenue. They are also dependent on provincial behavior. Under most circumstances, provinces do not adjust their behavior as a result of federal decisions regarding the Equalization formula. But, there are exceptional and narrow situations in which federal definitions regarding the treatment of various forms of revenue can have an impact on provincial entitlements and, hence, can influence provincial behavior.

If a province under-prices its hydroelectricity, it is passing up revenues it could have collected. This makes these provinces look poorer than they are and entitles them to higher Equalization payments than they deserve. Provinces should not be able to boost their Equalization payments by refraining from reasonable revenue-raising effort and artificially deflating their measured fiscal capacity. Manitoba and Quebec both offer their residents discounted electricity rates through their provincial utilities. Thus, their measured fiscal capacities are less than they would be if market rates were applied. From an equity perspective, provinces should not be able to game the system by deflating their reported fiscal capacity. Such a process also provides these provinces with revenues that are not in fact necessary, measured against the adequacy principle.

The issue of under-pricing hydro power has been noted by others for some time (FCPP 2012). In 2012-13, the issue may be more theoretical than real, given the decline in international prices for hydroelectricity and hence the convergence of what provinces charge to their own residents compared to what they charge outside their borders. The impact on entitlements of a change toward real market rates for hydroelectricity might therefore be quite small today.

This convergence of domestic and international prices may, in fact, be an opportunity to move toward a measure of real potential hydro revenues because the impact on entitlements will be small at the moment. However, should there ever again be divergence, equalization entitlements will be a better reflection of the real fiscal capacities of provinces.

E. Including Debt Servicing in Measured Fiscal Capacity

Equalization is designed to provide provinces with comparable abilities to provide public services. The system clearly fails to do this by completely ignoring the fact that provinces have very different debts and debt servicing obligations. Funds used to pay interest on debt are clearly not available for spending on public services. Provinces with higher debts therefore have less ability to provide public services than their measured fiscal capacity suggests. If Equalization entitlements were adjusted to account for public debt flows, more equitable and adequate payments would result. The moral hazard inherent in this proposal may disqualify it from further consideration. Nonetheless, highlighting the issue serves to once again underline how poorly our current arrangements achieve their stated purpose.

F. Inclusion of Imputed Value of Other Federal Transfers

For decades, Ontario has expressed concern about the structural inequities in federal spending decisions and the impact this has had on Ontario. Although there have been evolutions over time, the core issue remains: the federal government disproportionately extracts funds from Ontario and disproportionately spends and transfers them elsewhere. The reasons for this are complex, often unintended, and difficult to change. Rather than overturn deeply-seated and structural revenue and spending patterns, an alternative way of approaching this issue is to simply account for federal spending and transfers as part of provincial fiscal capacity.

Because the federal EI program makes far more funds available for active labour market measures in other provinces, Ontario will have to use its own source revenues to provide comparable levels of training programs. Recalculating measures of fiscal capacity and adjusting entitlements to account for these and other federal spending patterns would allow the program to more effectively achieve its objective. Provincial fiscal capacity is not a complete measure of a province's ability to provide comparable levels of public services as other provinces. Federal spending must be added to provincial fiscal capacity to have a more accurate measure of a province's ability to deliver programs to its residents. Failing to include federal transfers and spending inflates equalization entitlements to those provinces that have traditionally received both equalization and higher than average transfers in other areas of federal spending.

Type 2: Ambitious Changes
(maintaining the existing architecture of the transfer system)

A. Need-based Equalization
An expenditure need-based Equalization formula (herein referred to simply as "need-based") would consider the expenditure side of the public services equation in addition to Equalization's current focus on fiscal capacity. Such an approach is similar to, but much broader than, the option discussed above to add a measure of the cost of wages and salaries. Under a comprehensive, need-based approach, the formula would consider a full range of indicators including demographic and geographic indicators that influence the cost of providing comparable levels of services in each province. Equalization cannot adequately fulfill its constitutional responsibility without considering the very different needs of the country's diverse regions and populations (Gusen 2006; 2012). Atlantic premiers have been asking for such a change. They point to the rising costs associated with their growing senior citizen population as evidence of the need to consider costs (*The Globe and Mail*, 16 May 2011). This is reasonable, so long as a principled approach is adopted and the full range of variables that affect need are considered, rather than any attempt to cherry-pick measures of need that benefit one's own province.

A comprehensive need-based formula would account for how different work load, unit cost, and geographic circumstances impact the provision of public services across the country (Gusen 2012). Work load refers to the expenditure outlay mandated by the volume of service requirements in each recipient jurisdiction. For example, the size of the senior citizen population. Unit cost refers to the relative cost of providing the services mandated by the work load, including the cost of labour. Finally, geographic realities such as remoteness and climate result in varying levels of cost. Providing health care in far-flung communities may cost more than in an urban setting.

A need-based formula is used by Australia's Commonwealth Grants Commission (CGC), but other federations employ variations of it, as do provincial governments in Canada when computing grants for their school boards, hospitals and municipalities. The need-based approach has attracted attention for its capacity to deliver equity in a federation. If each province were transferred the exact amount of resources it required to provide a standard level of services, the country would conceivably achieve its constitutional commitment. Some have argued that transparency could suffer under a need-based transfer. Calculating need is often criticized as being extremely complex. In Australia's case there are 39 different expenditure categories, each with a sub-set of indicators meant to capture a detailed picture of each state's need profile (Gusen 2006, 5-7). The argument can also be made, however, that complexity does not have to interfere with transparency. Although the details of a formula may be difficult to understand, this does not mean that the essential features of its operation cannot be clearly explained. Moreover, Canada's current systecks transparency and it is not at all evident that a move toward a need-based system would produce less transparency. It is also possible to achieve greater transparency through other mechanisms, discussed below.

B. Creation of an Independent Commission

The creation of an independent commission that would be responsible for moni-toring Canada's major fiscal transfers was a reform considered by the O'Brien Commission in 2006. The O'Brien Report ultimately chose to recommend a softer version of this option, stating that "a more rigorous process should be put in place to improve transparency, communications, and governance" (2006, 65). The creation of such a rigorous process was the one element of the O'Brien Report that the government chose not to accept initially. The federal government should revisit this decision. A permanent commission would have the ability to assess the impact of the transfer arrangements, providing governments with a view on the downstream consequences of reforms. Although politics cannot be entirely removed from debates over fiscal arrangements, neutral public reporting on fis-cal capacity and other issues could help provide basic factual information which governments and other stakeholders would need to consider before launching fantasy-based arguments regarding perceived injustices in the fiscal arrangements. As Daniel Béland and André Lecours note, Canada has used this model before. For example, the CPP Investment Board was established during the last major reform of the Canada Pension Plan in the mid- to late-1990s. It has since invested over $140 billion on behalf of Canadian pensioners with little political interference. The Canadian Institute for Health Information (CIHI) has similarly been providing expert and neutral healthcare information and guidance to Canadian governments since 1994 (2012, 2). Arm's length governance *is* compatible with the Canadian policy context. One of the current challenges of the transfer system is that there is no way to measure the success of the transfers at achieving their intended outcomes. An independent body could assist in measuring these outcomes. An annual report to Parliament would be appropriate.

Type 3: Transformational Changes

It may be that the structure of our fiscal arrangements is so inconsistent with the nature of our national economy that more fundamental reform is necessary. If our objective is indeed to respond to the changes outlined in section one (a sustained commodity boom, global competition for manufacturing and service firms, etc.) while coming closer to achieving our constitutional commitment, there are at least two better ways of achieving this.

These two options are fundamental in nature, but they are practical, achievable, and would require no more than legislative changes. They are flexible and could accommodate a variety of different macroeconomic, regional, and fiscal evolutions. Neither one is fanciful or overly theoretical and both could be achieved in a relatively short time. The fundamental nature of the changes that have taken place in Ontario, Canada, and the world over the past three decades are such that our system of fiscal federalism also requires fundamental change.

A. One Health and Social Transfer

There is nothing natural or inevitable about Canada's current arrangement – i.e., one major equalizing transfer and two major per capita transfers. In fact, the size and number of these transfers is *ad hoc*, a result of a variety of political deals made over the past two decades. All three transfers serve an equalizing function and all come with virtually no strings attached. They also serve the purpose of ensuring that the federal government makes a significant contribution to provincial revenues that are used to achieve social purposes, like the provision of publicly funded health care and education. They are intended to give provinces the ability to provide services at comparable levels of taxation.

Bundling all three major transfers into one equalized Health and Social Transfer, with more prosperous provinces receiving less per capita and less prosperous provinces receiving more, would do a better job of meeting the principles and objectives outlined earlier. The new Canadian Health and Social Transfer (CHST) would include an equalizing element, which in practice would mean that provinces with lower fiscal capacities would receive more per capita dollars than those with higher fiscal capacities. The difference in fiscal capacity between the least and most prosperous province could be open to discussion and the extent to which the federal government equalizes through its transfers would be a decision for the federal government. A reasonable starting point for discussion would be to equalize 90 percent of the difference in fiscal capacity between each province and the national average.

Figure 9 presents a graphical depiction of how such a system would work. Such a system does a far better job than Canada's current system (see Figure 5) in achieving equity while also maintaining incentives for provincial economic growth.

The data in Figure 9 are the result of combining all three major transfers into a single transfer that has an Equalization component (measured using 100 percent of natural resource revenues and no GDP growth cap) that grants provinces below the NAS, 90 percent of their fiscal capacity deficiency, and has a per capita element that is adjusted downward for provinces with above average fiscal capacity to 90 percent of their entitlement.[3] The result is that provinces with below average fiscal capacity receive more and provinces with above average fiscal capacity receive less.

---

[3] Under the current transfer scenario, the total amount paid out to the ten provinces ($55.7 billion) is the sum of the existing CHT cash transfer ($28.5 billion) + CST cash transfer ($11.8 billion) + Equalization ($15.4 billion). Under the single transfer scenario, the total

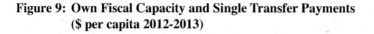

**Figure 9: Own Fiscal Capacity and Single Transfer Payments
($ per capita 2012-2013)**

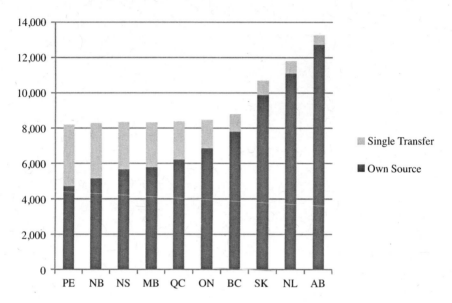

Source: Author's calculations

The attractiveness of such a system is that it meets the objectives of the program and advances the principles of autonomy, equity, transparency, and adequacy. It also does not suffer from most of the flaws that critics – on both the left and right – have identified with current arrangements. For example, some have said there is little financial incentive for provinces receiving equalization to generate wealth because this results in lower equalization payments, leaving them no better off (Courchene 2004). Although this is likely an overstatement, and provinces do

---

amount paid out to the ten provinces would be set at the same value as under the current system ($55.7 billion), however the Equalization portion of the transfer would be the sum of the amounts received by eligible/recipient provinces ($19.8 billion) and the total amount paid out under the per capita component would be $36 billion ($1038 per capita), with provinces with above average fiscal capacity receiving 90 percent of their entitlement. These are illustrative examples and the parameters of such a transfer system could be adjusted to achieve either more or less horizontal equity.

indeed have other incentives for becoming more prosperous, the fact remains that increasing prosperity for a province receiving equalization will result in no net new dollars for the provincial government because of shrinking equalization payments.

The system proposed here would eliminate this disincentive to wealth creating activities. Provinces would not be brought up to the national average fiscal capacity but instead would receive a percentage of their entitlement (e.g., 90 percent), therefore, provinces with greater fiscal capacity prior to equalization payments would still be better off after inclusion of equalization payments. This contrasts with the current system which provides fully equalized entitlements to any province below the national average – regardless of relative fiscal need – and no equalizing element to any province above the national average – regardless of how prosperous. A single, equalized CHST could still maintain the weak conditionality of the current transfer system, such as the obligation to maintain a single-payer public health care system. It would therefore be consistent with the principle of provincial autonomy. It would also be more explicit and thus more transparent in identifying how much of the disparity in fiscal capacity it was seeking to redress. It would moderate some of the interprovincial differences in fiscal capacity being driven by natural resource wealth, without the federal government making any attempt to access those revenues. And it would bring the contribution of Ontarians and what Ontario receives more in line with principles of equity and adequacy.

B. Remove Natural Resource Revenues from the Equalization Formula; Create a New Transfer

Some have argued that natural resource royalties should be removed entirely from the calculation of provincial fiscal capacity. However, if one were to do that, the interprovincial differences in post- equalization fiscal capacity would grow even greater and the imbalances between the resource-rich and the resource-poor would grow even more. The situation would be entirely inconsistent with Canada's constitutional commitment. There is, however, an elegant solution to this challenge. Natural resource revenues could be removed entirely from the calculation of provincial fiscal capacity, while at the same time the federal government could create a new transfer out of general revenues to equalize natural resource related differences in fiscal capacity. This would enable the federal government to better meet its constitutional commitment to the principle that all provincial governments should have the ability to provide their residents with comparable levels of services at comparable levels of taxation. At the same time, this would be consistent with provincial ownership of the resource, a lack of federal access to the revenues, and the understanding that natural resources are a depleting asset. Provinces with higher levels of natural resource royalties would receive no or little funds from this second transfer. Those with lower resource revenues would receive more.

Much like the creation of a single equalized Health and Social Transfer, this approach accomplishes three goals simultaneously: it moderates fiscal disparities between provinces; it leaves natural resource wealth entirely in provincial hands;

and it moderates the unfair burden placed on the Ontario tax base. Similar to a single equalized transfer, the federal government would have some discretion in determining how much of the differences in fiscal capacity it seeks to erase through fiscal transfers.

CONCLUSION

Canada's Equalization program as designed, is no longer working. Under the current economic realities of the federation, Canada's fiscal transfer system no longer does a good job of achieving its stated goals. Currently, our system comes up short, placing increased pressure on the Ontario tax base to shoulder the responsibility for inter-regional redistribution driven by a commodity boom from which it derives little benefit.

A simplified form of fiscal transfers is best, and that system should be designed in such a way that wealthier provinces receive less than poorer provinces. This leads us to the conclusion that the transformative changes discussed above, particularly the proposal for one simplified equalized transfer, merit the most serious consideration. In the meantime, as transformative changes often require time and consultation, the federal government should move immediately to change its most unprincipled practices, such as the application of the GDP cap to claw back Ontario's entitlements.

We have just begun to explore these and other new options. It is clear that our system of fiscal federalism was not designed for our current economy and that the current fiscal arrangements are unintentionally punitive toward Ontario. Any principled redesign would either provide Ontario with more or take less from the Ontario tax base. This only reflects the fact that the system serves Ontario so poorly, to the benefit of other provinces. The solutions are even less clear than the problems and are likely to be complex and divisive. However, the proposals offered here provide a good, principled, and credible place to start a national conversation on how to redesign the system from the ground up.

REFERENCES

Alberta Ministry of Finance. 2011. *Budget 2011*. Edmonton: Government of Alberta.

Béland, D. and A. Lecours. 2012. *Equalization at Arm's Length*. Toronto: Mowat Centre.

Courchene, T. 2004. "Confiscatory Equalization: The Intriguing Case of Saskatchewan's Vanishing Energy Revenues." *Choices 10 (2): 1-39.*

Courchene, T. 2008. "Fiscalamity! Ontario: From Heartland to Have-not," *Policy Options* June: 46-54.

Coyne, A. 2012. There is a method to Thomas Mulcair's "Dutch Disease" madness. *National Post*, 18 May. At www.google.ca/url?sa=t&rct=j&q=&esrc=s&source=web&cd=1&ved=

0CC0QFjAA&url=http://fullcomment.nationalpost.com/2012/05/18/andrew-coyne-there-is-a-method-to-thomas-mulcairs-dutch-disease-madness/&ei=C_rFUOTYCfH22QXxi4H ADQ&usg=AFQjCNFaQGIktOeJYtal8SyG4Am_-ddE6Q (accessed 10 December 2012).

Drummond, D. 2012. *Final Report of the Commission on the Reform of Ontario's Public Services*. Toronto: Government of Ontario.

Frontier Centre for Public Policy (FCPP). 2012. *Artificially Cheap Hydro Power*. Winnipeg: Frontier Centre for Public Policy. (http://www.fcpp.org/publication.php/4216)

Finance Canada. 2012. Federal Transfers to Provinces and Territories. Government of Canada. (www.fin.gc.ca)

Finances Quebec. 2011. Update on Federal Transfers. Quebec City: Government of Quebec.

Gusen, P. 2012. *Expenditure Need: Equalization's Other Half*. Toronto: Mowat Centre.

Ibbitson, J. 2012. The Collapse of the Laurentian Consensus: On the westward shift of Canadian power - and values. The Literary Review of Canada, 1 January. At http://reviewcanada.ca/essays/2012/01/01/the-collapse-of-the-laurentian-consensus/ (accessed 10 December 2012).

Lemphers, N. and D. Woynillowicz. 2012. *In the Shadow of the Boom*. Calgary: The Pembina Institute.

Manitoba Ministry of Finance. 2012. *Budget Paper D: Update on Transfer Arrangements*. Winnipeg: Government of Manitoba.

McMillan, M. 2012. *Alberta and Equalization: Separating Fact from Fiction*. Toronto: Mowat Centre.

Mendelsohn, et al. 2011. *The Vital Commons: a policy agenda for the Great Lakes century*. Toronto: Mowat Centre.

Mendelson, M. 2012. *Is Canada (Still) a Fiscal Union?* Toronto: Caledon Institute of Social Policy.

Mowat Centre EI Task Force. 2011. *Making It Work: Final Recommendations of the Mowat Centre Employment Insurance Task Force*. Toronto: Mowat Centre.

O'Brien. 2006. *Achieving A National Purpose: Putting Equalization Back on Track*. Ottawa: Department of Finance Canada.

Ontario Common Front. 2012. *Falling Behind: Ontario's Backslide into Widening Inequality, Growing Poverty and Cuts to Social Programs*. (www.weareontario.ca)

Ontario Ministry of Finance. 2005. *Ontario Budget: Investing in People, Strengthening our Economy* Toronto: Government of Ontario.

Premier's Council for Economic Strategy. 2011. *Shaping Alberta's Future*. Edmonton: Government of Alberta.

Statistics Canada. 2010.CANSIM Tables 282-0087; 276-0001. Ottawa: Statistics Canada

The Globe and Mail. 2011. Atlantic Premiers Make Plea for More Transfer-Payment Cash. 16 May. At: http://m.theglobeandmail.com/news/politics/atlantic-premiers-make-plea-for-more-transfer-payment-cash/article579921/?service=mobile (accessed July 2012).

Tremblay, J. 2012. *Fiscal Problems, Taxation Solutions: Options for Reforming Canada's Tax and Transfer System*. Toronto: Mowat Centre.

Zon, N. 2013. *Filling the Gap: Measuring Ontario's Balance with the Federal Government*. Toronto: Mowat Centre.

12

A NEW INTERGOVERNMENTAL AGENDA FOR THE NEW ONTARIO[1]

Matthew Mendelsohn, Joshua Hjartarson, and James Pearce

Les gouvernements fédéral et provinciaux-territoriaux du Canada sont trop souvent engagés de façon improductive dans le même espace politique, notent tout d'abord les auteurs de ce chapitre. Et bien qu'il soit parfois indispensable aux deux ordres de gouvernement de collaborer dans un même domaine, le pays ne peut plus se permettre des chevauchements qui, de surcroît, servent de moins en moins les intérêts de l'Ontario. Cette analyse identifie donc les domaines politiques dans lesquels les recommandations des auteurs – dévolution, prise en charge et rationalisation/séparation des rôles et responsabilités gouvernementales – viendront renforcer les trois principes clés d'efficience, d'efficacité et de responsabilisation, tout en proposant des priorités intergouvernementales qui favoriseront les progrès dans ces domaines. L'application d'une telle stratégie pourrait engendrer d'importantes économies et une réelle amélioration du service public. Fondamentalement, il s'agit de départager intelligemment les domaines qui seraient mieux servis tantôt par le gouvernement fédéral, tantôt par les provinces et territoires.

---

[1] This paper is largely based on "Saving Dollars and Making Sense: an agenda for a more efficient, effective and accountable federation" written by the same authors and published in 2010 by the Mowat Centre for Policy Innovation

INTRODUCTION

For much of the twentieth century, Ontario was content to have the federal government be involved in areas of provincial jurisdiction. Canadians in general, and Ontarians in particular, were likewise perfectly happy to have both orders of government involved in the same policy space.

Some have made a virtue of this practice. Many Canadians believe in the important nation-building role for the federal government, which has implicitly benefited Ontario. Having two governments involved in the same policy space also appeals to citizens as a way to check the power of either order of government (Mendelsohn and Cutler 2000). Some academics have seen artistic merit in this overlapping exercise of powers, thereby turning a reasonable observation about the need for multilevel governance in a global age of Canadian federalism into a national virtue (Gibbins, Maioni, and Stein 2006). However, the federal government is increasingly interested in removing itself from areas of social policy. It is possible that this element of Canadian federal-provincial life is coming to an end?

Small provinces worry about these developments and Ontario has usually spoken out against them. However, it is possible that Ontario will withdraw its long-standing support of an interventionist, nation-building federal government because those efforts still mean taking money from Ontario residents and sending it elsewhere, particularly at a time when Ontario's economy is struggling. It is unlikely that Ontario will join Quebec and Alberta in their traditional opposition to federal nation-building efforts, but it is possible that Ontario will take steps in that direction. More Oliver Mowat, less Leslie Robarts.

Federal-provincial competition within the same policy areas results in dueling program offerings that vie for the loyalty of voters, and which governments may simply no longer be able to afford. Ontario certainly cannot afford this overlap and will likely look for greater clarity in "who does what."

The analysis in this paper begins with the observation that the federal and provincial-territorial governments in Canada are too often, and unproductively, involved in the same policy space. While there is at times a compelling logic for both orders of government to be active in a particular policy area, overlap and duplication can no longer be afforded and is increasingly outside of Ontario's interest.

We argue that some combination of reducing this duplication while ensuring that the government is best able to provide a service will help governments return to fiscal sustainability. Governments that choose to compete with one another to provide services or programs in each other's areas of responsibility are engaged in a conceit that is no longer affordable. This competition also weakens service delivery due to fuzzy accountability, and in the process it decreases rather than increases citizens' confidence in government and their ability to provide public goods and services.

Devolution, uploading, and streamlining roles and responsibilities are elements of a larger strategy that will improve service delivery and clarify accountability. Such a strategy will free up resources and better align the source of policy solutions with the site of policy problems. For example, well-intentioned federal efforts to address unique and widely divergent social housing needs across the country would fall just as flat as provincial efforts to engage in national defence. Governments that maintain a presence in areas outside their expertise are making poor fiscal choices, ultimately providing sub-optimal services and leaving citizens with less rather than more confidence in their governments.

Beyond balancing budgets, a reform agenda could help tear down the barriers to constructive citizen engagement imposed by the country's federal system. The logic of intergovernmental negotiations makes it extraordinarily difficult for citizens to have a direct say in outcomes when more than one government is involved in a policy field. When a single government is responsible it can more easily ensure citizen engagement and public preferences can be more clearly incorporated into decision-making. In short, having more than one government involved in a policy area thwarts Canada's ability to fulfill its democratic promise.

Constitutional changes are not necessary to realize the reform agenda articulated in this chapter. Governments must simply agree to work together constructively, to clarify their areas of responsibility, and to agree that they should all have more independence to manage their own policy areas.

Increased provincial responsibility in social program design and delivery does not need to undermine Canadians' common citizenship so long as the federal government retains its constitutional role in equalizing differences of fiscal capacity across the country.

It is possible to build a broad federal-provincial consensus around a fundamental transformation agenda that reflects the desire for effective government. The federal government promised such a rationalization of "who does what" in 2006 (Speech from the Throne 2006). This would require the federal government to remove itself from some aspects of social policy. Moving forward on this overall agenda will help improve fiscal positions, service delivery, policy development, and governance within the Canadian federation.

Increasingly, Ontario will be less likely to object to this agenda than it has over the past half century. On the one hand, the nation-building role of the federal government was funded by an Ontario tax base that can no longer afford it. On the other hand, budget constraints within the Ontario and federal governments will make the desire to spend money to compete with one another less possible and less attractive politically.

This agenda, if pursued properly, does not weaken Canada. Canadians' sense of national identity is still strong, but Canadians are less likely to define themselves through attachment to social programs delivered by the federal government than they once were. So long as the federal government plays an important role in equalizing fiscal capacity across the country, Canada's promise of common social citizenship can be realized. The federal government creates the opportunity for provincial experimentation and difference that reflects the diversity of the country when it cuts cheques and gets out of the way. By working together, provinces can likewise advance a common Canadian social space.

THE NEXT FOUNDATIONAL INTERGOVERNMENTAL DISCUSSION

The 1970s and 1980s featured lengthy constitutional discussions culminating in the patriation of the Constitution and eventually the failed Meech Lake and Charlottetown Accords. The 1990s witnessed ongoing negotiations on how governments could better manage interdependence, concluding in 1999 with the Social Union Framework Agreement (SUFA), which identified how governments could better manage shared policy space. These efforts have run their course. There is no serious interest in re-engaging in macro-level constitutional discussions while the spirit of cooperation that is crucial to SUFA is often absent.

To date, discussions about roles and responsibilities in the federation have been driven by national unity concerns. Devolution was usually presented as part of a larger political strategy to confront western alienation or Quebec nationalism. In other instances, conversations took place on an *ad hoc* basis or in a siloed manner focusing on one issue at a time, such as labour market training or immigrant settlement services. This research takes a different approach by providing a careful analysis of government participation in relevant policy fields and outlining recommendations on which level of government is best placed to most effectively develop and deliver the required policies and programs in each field.

Devolution is not an end in itself, nor is uploading responsibility to the federal government. Instead, however, this analysis highlights where policy and service delivery can be improved and made more affordable by shifting responsibilities between governments. This is about making government work better for Canadians. This approach differs from Tom Courchene's full ACCESS model, which would transfer full responsibility for much of the social and economic union to the provinces. The ACCESS model is ambitious and would require the "conversion of the [federal] cash transfers into equalized tax-point transfers" (Courchene 1996, 87), thereby removing Ottawa's role in many key policy areas including health care and education. This approach might overlook opportunities for policy improvement, such as the cost-savings achievable through federal pharmaceutical procurement. In contrast, the animating spirit of the agenda presented here re-focuses in a principled way on the areas which are best delivered by the federal government and those which the provinces-territories should address.

Much progress has been made in recent decades. The federal government has devolved many policy areas that are better delivered by provinces, and cooperative agreements have been reached in many policy fields that have led to real savings and efficiencies. The Immigration Agreements between the federal and both BC and Manitoba governments had been success stories until the federal unilateral termination of the agreements with these two provinces in 2012. So too is the 2006 Agreement between the Governments of Canada and Ontario to upload corporate tax collection. By creating a single point of contact and collection, this agreement generates savings of up to $100 million in annual compliance costs for Ontario businesses and creates administrative efficiencies by eliminating a duplicate layer of tax authority.

There is no doubt that overlap will inevitably be necessary in some policy fields. However, Canadian governments have been too prepared to accept and manage this overlap and its resulting incoherence. The burden of proof should be reversed: governments should devote their energies to avoiding duplication wherever possible unless there are good, principled reasons for overlap that advance the public interest. Governments should get their own houses in order before venturing into the constitutional domains of the other order of government. Simply put, governments need to get out of each other's way.

Federal involvement in areas of provincial jurisdiction can undermine the ability of provinces to plan and deliver the services and programs for which they are responsible. When the federal government moves in and out of social policy and programs it too often disrupts provincial plans and leaves provinces on the hook financially for the programs it abandons. Federal decisions to not renew funding for the HPV vaccine and childcare spaces are two recent examples. Jumping into a policy field for three years to offer up "boutique" programs and then abandon them is not an efficient, effective, or accountable method of long-term policy development and program planning. Provinces that try to run their own parallel and competitive foreign policies are no less disruptive to the federal government. A new strategy is needed – one that takes a hard look at "who does what" and why.

Existing arrangements often produce unacceptable outcomes. The federal government's passage of the Crime Bill in 2011, under their responsibility for criminal law, will impose costs on provincial governments who operate jails. Even an example of federal-provincial cooperation such as the agreement between the federal and Ontario governments on harmonized corporate income tax collection – widely supported by Ontario businesses – may be called into question. The unilateral federal tax decisions enabled by this agreement affect Ontario's portion of revenues, which has significant fiscal implications for the Ontario government and precludes provincial control over the policy decisions that could lead to fiscal harm.

A NEW STRATEGY

The goal of this chapter is to identify policy areas where one of three recommendations – devolution, uploading, streamlining/disentangling of government roles and responsibilities – will improve on three basic framework principles of efficiency, effectiveness, and accountability. This will be followed by a recommended intergovernmental agenda to move forward in these areas. The application of this strategy could result in significant cost savings and public service improvements.

Three Recommendations

1. Devolving

Devolution would grant provinces-territories sole responsibility over the policy area. This may require that the federal government vacate the policy space, including program delivery. It could also mean the removal of national standards and conditions attached to funds that are transferred to the provinces-territories in order to allow them the full scope of decision-making over program design and implementation. Reasons to devolve are:

- to capitalize on provincial knowledge about provincial needs and preferences and to enable provinces to tailor programs to suit local conditions (Experts often refer to this as the "principle of subsidiarity");
- to promote innovation, experimentation, and policy learning across the provinces and territories;
- to capitalize on economies of scale in policy and program administration thereby improving efficiency and generating cost-savings when the bulk of program activity is already located at the provincial level;
- to facilitate better integration with related provincial programming;
- to improve accountability and service delivery.

2. Uploading

Uploading gives the federal government sole responsibility over a policy area. This may require that the provincial government vacate the policy space. In areas where the federal government chooses not to act, the provinces could band together to create provincially administered programs that are national in scope and achieve greater efficiency and effectiveness without federal involvement. One example is the Ontario-led effort to set up a pan-Canadian pharmaceutical purchasing alliance through the Council of the Federation. However, this would be a second-best outcome to active federal leadership. Reasons to upload are:

- to preserve the pan-Canadian social safety net and ensure Canadians have equitable access to social services;
- to promote the efficiency of the economic union where provincial and territorial oversight disrupts the free flow of people, goods and services;
- to generate economies of scale and administrative savings by removing overlap and duplication across two orders of government and/or across provinces-territories;

- to take advantage of the federal government's core competency in a policy area thereby enhancing program effectiveness;
- to respond to global challenges;
- to promote consumer safety and enhance regulatory standards by closing regulatory gaps and eliminating coordination challenges.

3. Streamlining/Disentangling
Streamlining/disentangling involves coordinating government actions in the same policy space to ensure minimal overlap and duplication. While both levels of government may wish to maintain a presence, there is no need for each to perform the same tasks. Reasons to streamline/disentangle are:

- to improve efficiency and service delivery in policy areas where there are compelling reasons for both orders of government to be present;
- to enhance accountability and provide citizens with a clear understanding of "who does what";
- to ensure effective, coordinated efforts take place when crises arise.

Three Framework Principles

1. Efficiency
Efficiency in the context of this chapter means value for money. Which order of government can most efficiently deliver a given program or service based on administrative economies of scale, existing competencies, and a better understanding of local conditions? The concept of a single service provider is gaining traction as current budget deficits make the search for efficiencies all the more urgent. Canada's Premiers have taken note, deciding that it makes more sense to pool their pharmaceutical purchases in order to save money and administrative resources. According to one former federal official, "[w]hen one government is in charge, it can make the hard choices necessary to most efficiently deliver a public service; when more than one is involved, both have other incentives and may also not fully understand the overlapping activities of the other government." (Clark 2010). In areas where there is no justification for both federal and provincial-territorial involvement, efficiencies can be easily achieved by simply eliminating the overlap.

2. Effectiveness
Effectiveness is linked explicitly to policy outcomes. Can government policy be effective in addressing substantive challenges (Skogstad and Bakvis 2008)? In the context of federalism, overlap, duplication and the failure to coordinate activities among orders of government can lead to policy incoherence, program incompatibility, and ultimately second- or third-best outcomes.

In areas where both orders of government are active, decision-making is subject to joint decision traps whereby each government can veto change. This causes decision making to be slow and unable to keep up with societal and/or economic changes. It has taken years (and sometimes decades) for Canadian governments to harmonize policies and make seemingly easy fixes, such as a single standard for advertising the cost of bank and credit union loans, the size of truck tires, and even the colour of margarine. In worst-case scenarios, Canadians are stuck with antiquated programs and rules because jurisdictions cannot agree on reforms, or how to move forward. There are many examples in Canadian public policy where there are simply too many cooks in the kitchen. There is a real price to pay in terms of performance when roles and responsibilities overlap or are unclear and when decision-making is dispersed across 14 jurisdictions (Cameron 2010).

One of the advantages of being a federation is that responsibilities are, in theory, divided according to competencies. It does not make sense for the provinces to be responsible for defending our national borders. Similarly, it does not make sense for the federal government to help immigrants integrate into local labour markets or run one-size fits all training programs in Kitchener-Waterloo, Swift Current or Cornerbrook. Governments must simply avoid meddling in jurisdictions where they have little policy expertise.

3. Accountability
Governments are accountable to citizens for the funds they spend and the programs they deliver. A core democratic principle is that governments must publicly account for their decisions, providing citizens with an opportunity to reward or punish governments based on their performance. Accountability in federal states can be especially complicated because the lines of responsibility for a given program are often unclear. This lack of clarity can encourage "blame avoidance" behavior among governments and diminish the incentives for public servants and elected officials to strive for maximum program efficiency and effectiveness (Weaver 1986).

The recommendations made in this chapter, if adopted, would provide citizens with a clear understanding of which order of government is responsible for policy successes and failures, and limit governments' ability to pass the buck.

Sectoral Analyses

The following section will consider the most promising opportunities to devolve, upload, and streamline/disentangle government programs and services. The policy areas discussed below represent just a few of the best options to employ this new strategy. If pursued, these recommendations stand to improve the efficiency, effectiveness and accountability of governments across the federation.

Devolution

Maintaining federal involvement in a policy sector for the sake of political appearances is detrimental to policy effectiveness and can no longer be justified. Ontarians should join Canadians elsewhere in objecting to federal-provincial dabbling where they have no business.

Active Labour Market Programs

Responsibility for all remaining federal training programs should be devolved to the provinces and federal transfers to provinces for training should be made unconditional.

Labour market training programs are designed to help unemployed Canadians gain the skills they need to find employment. The existence of a coherent set of accessible training programs to support self-sufficiency is critical to Canadians. Most training programs were devolved to the provinces beginning in the mid to late 1990s. This occurred because both orders of government recognized that the provinces were much better situated to deliver effective and efficient labour market programs. Provinces are better placed to tailor training policies to local market conditions. A good training program in Windsor may not work in Fort McMurray.

Yet the job is not complete. The federal government still runs a number of smaller, specialized training programs aimed at youth, older workers, and persons with disabilities. Continued federal government activity in providing labour market services/programs has led to duplication and inefficiencies in administration and gaps in programming and services.

> New federal-provincial labour market agreements have increased funding for the social assistance stream, but ... [o]verall, employment supports remain a patchwork of uneven access [and] quality and [are] for the most part not delivered in an integrated way, thereby creating gaps, duplication and instability (Social Assistance Review Advisory Council 2010, 12).

In its 2007 budget, the federal government acknowledged that there was more work to be done and that the devolution of all labour market programming would be in the best interest of Canadians (Government of Canada 2007). The federal government has not followed through on a commitment to review the feasibility of devolving its remaining programs. Moreover, while the provinces now deliver most labour market training for unemployed workers, the federal government continues to define eligibility for these programs through the Employment Insurance (EI) program and apply "tests of similarity" across training programs to uphold national standards.

Federal tests of similarity and the requirement that funding flow directly to clients act as barriers to achieving economies of scale and are unnecessarily prescriptive. For example, provinces cannot buy classroom space in bulk to support provincial training programs for the unemployed. These spaces must be purchased through individual programs, costing the taxpayer more money (Government of Ontario 1996, s. 63; Governments of Canada and Ontario 2005).

The case for devolution: Provinces are, quite simply, better suited to run active labour market programs. They have a better understanding of local economies, closer relationships with local stakeholders, and the ability to seamlessly integrate training programs with the full range of provincially run education services.

Social Housing

Responsibility for social housing should be devolved, with federal financial support provided to the provinces through a single unconditional transfer. Provinces should report publicly on how their social housing funds are spent and with what impacts.

In Ontario alone, total government spending (federal, provincial, and municipal) on social housing totaled close to $2 billion in the 2008-2009 fiscal year. Federal funding is currently provided through several separate allocations for the various federal housing programs (Social Housing Agreements, Affordable Housing Initiatives, etc), which are cost-shared with the provinces.

The terms of this federal funding impose fragmentation on the policy sector and limit provincial flexibility to design programs that suit local needs. For example, federal conditions limit the type of expenditures that can count toward provincial cost sharing. Specific funding streams must also be segregated and spent on particular population groups such as seniors, First Nations, and disabled persons. Further, the federal government imposes time-consuming and costly administrative requirements by, for example, imposing different reporting obligations for each funding stream.

The provinces are closest to the social housing policy area. They have long-standing relationships with municipalities, local housing providers and citizen advocacy groups. They are much better placed to make decisions on how the pool of funds should be allocated. If the federal government vacated this policy space and eliminated the conditions attached to funding, the provinces could do a better job. More resources would be spent on the ground to meet local needs. Moreover, the provinces would be better able to integrate social housing policy with provincially and locally administered social assistance programs.

Some progress has been made. The federal government recently agreed to allow provinces greater flexibility in spending federal funds through a series of bilateral agreements (CMHC 2011). More provincial control over spending decisions will ensure that taxpayers get the most value for their money.

The case for devolution: Social housing policy, if integrated with the suite of provincially administered social programs, could be more flexibly administered. Experts agree that provinces-territories are best placed to determine the appropriate allocation of housing funds and to craft programs that suit local circumstances.

Immigrant Settlement
Responsibility for immigrant settlement services should be devolved to the provinces.

Canada is experiencing an intense competition for immigrants. The population is aging and we face labour shortages that must be addressed. Developing a well planned, forward-looking immigration strategy is critical to Canada's ability to remain competitive and prosperous. The federal government rightly takes a lead role in selecting immigrants. They should reassert their leadership in this regard. This is an important component of nation building. At present however, there are three models of federal-provincial immigrant settlement services employed in Canada.

First, Quebec has operated its entire immigration strategy including selection, independent of Ottawa since 1991. In the second model, provinces work with the federal government on settlement services through intergovernmental agreements. This model is in place in Alberta, Saskatchewan, Ontario, and the Altantic provinces. In British Columbia and Manitoba there had been a third model where settlement services were been devolved to the provincial level allowing them to develop an integrated set of programs that address the specific needs of their immigrant communities. Devolution in both of these provinces had led to innovative program design and positive economic outcomes for new immigrants.

The success of the British Columbia/Manitoba model, while it lasted, is unsurprising. Provinces typically have closer ties to service provider organizations (SPOs), the third party organizations that deliver most of Canada's immigrant settlement services. Also, in a devolved model, SPOs have to follow only one set of rules and file one set of forms to receive grants and fulfill reporting requirements (Seidle 2010). This eliminates bureaucratic overlap and ensures that more resources are available to be delivered on the ground. This model reflects an international trend toward greater devolution and multilevel governance as is increasingly practiced in the United Kingdom, Australia and Germany (Siematycki and Triadafilopoulos 2010).

The savings associated with devolution are particularly important given that the federal government has announced unilateral national cuts to spending on settlement services of $53 million for 2011-2012 and $59 million for 2012-2013. Ontario alone will see a reduction of $43 million – 80 percent of the planned funding cuts (OCASI 2011).

Not surprisingly, the federal government has not devolved settlement programs to the other provinces. The federal government denied a request for devolution made in Ontario's 2011 budget (Government of Ontario 2011). Continued inflexibility makes program delivery unresponsive to the needs of local communities. Immigrants that acquire citizenship for example, automatically have their access to federally-funded language training cut off. This negatively affects some categories of immigrants, such as family class entrants, who traditionally take longer to transition to the work force and cannot benefit from federal services when they need them.

At a time when new Canadians are performing worse in the job market than previous generations of immigrants, tiresome federal-provincial conflicts and battles to take political credit should end. Settlement and integration services should be performed by the government that can best perform these functions.

Settlement services is one of the best examples of "free-for-all federalism" where the federal government makes separate deals with different provinces and the quality of a provincial deal depends on a wide variety of political factors.

The case for devolution: Devolution is the more efficient option. Current federal involvement siphons vital resources that could help immigrants successfully integrate (Seidle 2010). Moreover, provincial governments are better placed to respond effectively to local immigrant needs.

Early Learning
Responsibility for early learning services should be devolved to the provinces-territories.

Canada suffers from relatively poor quality childcare services (OECD 2006; UNICEF 2008). There are two problems: lack of integration with provincial education systems and inadequate supply. Provincial governments, who have the lead responsibility for this issue, have undertaken a variety of strategies to deal with these problems. For example, Quebec has seven-dollar-a-day daycare while British Columbia and Ontario have introduced all-day kindergarten.

Childcare used to be viewed as babysitting until children accessed the school system. This mindset has changed. Today daycare is viewed as an opportunity for early learning and a head start in building human capital. To childcare experts, a holistic approach to early learning is a key driver of economic competitiveness and social justice (Friendly 2004).

Provincial-territorial governments are innovating to help kids learn more effectively by integrating early childhood programs with provincially-territorially run school systems. Ontario's recent Early Learning Report recommended all-day kindergarten to facilitate better educational outcomes, prompting the province to implement this change.

> This comprehensive model applies logic, best practice, and evidence to the way we organize, manage, deliver, and account for services for children. It reflects what literally thousands of parents and practitioners told me – to make effective use of the facilities and resources we have, eliminate bureaucratic duplication, and respond to the needs of modern families, in order to benefit children (Pascal 2009, Chap. 1).

Devolution (by way of transferring money to the provinces through the childcare expense deduction and the universal childcare benefit) would allow provinces – which have the tools and the capacity in this policy field – to make their own choices about how to use funds for childcare and ensure that these choices are responsive to local preferences and integrated with other services delivered by provinces, municipalities, and schools.

The case for devolution: Education is within provincial jurisdiction. Daycare is now considered to be education and early learning. The effectiveness of daycare programs, like active labour market programs, would be improved if fully integrated into provincial education systems.

Uploading

Provincial-territorial policy actions that complicate Canada's regulatory landscape and impose additional costs on businesses and consumers will prevent Canada from competing globally.

Pharmaceuticals
Responsibility for regulating, administering, delivering, and funding a new, single, national prescription drug plan should be uploaded to the federal government.
    The existing public, single-payer health care system is unsustainable unless efficiencies and new models of service delivery are implemented. Health care costs continue to rise at a rate faster than government revenues and constitute the single largest provincial expense, typically greater than 40 percent for all provincial budgets (Reuters, 31 May 2010; *Calgary Herald*, 5 August 2010).
    When Medicare was first introduced, intergovernmental agreements were negotiated to ensure that the federal government would cover approximately 45 percent of health care costs. Over the years this has declined dramatically despite the importance of the Canada Health Act and the public's strong belief that all Canadians should have access to good quality health care services wherever they live. The federal government now contributes between 20 and 23 percent of health care expenditures (Ontario Ministry of Finance 2010, Finance Canada 2010). Beyond this shrinking contribution, current federal involvement such as entering the debate on wait times only to withdraw soon after, exacerbates intergovernmental tensions and fails to serve a useful role in sustaining the publicly-funded health care system over the long-term.
    What role is left for the federal government to meet Canadians' desire for a strong national health care system? As the second most expensive element of health care budgets, pharmaceuticals represent an opportunity for considerable cost-savings. The federal government needs to take serious action to address these rising costs. Canada is notable among its international peers for its lack of universal drug coverage (Gagnon and Hébert 2010, 56-7). By creating a federal pharmacare program, the federal government could carve out a unique and important role for itself in

the area of health care, an area where the public expects the federal government to be involved.

Uploading pharmaceutical coverage would also gain support from the provinces. The issue has been on the Council of the Federation's agenda for the past two years. The economies of scale achieved through national purchasing are encouraging the provinces to cooperate on this issue, spurring the development of a pan-Canadian approach to joint procurement in 2010 (CBC News, 31 May 2011).

The case for uploading: Huge administrative efficiencies (valued at up to $1.4 billion) and purchasing power could lower pharmaceutical prices if procurement responsibilities were consolidated federally (Gagnon and Hébert 2010). Provincial-territorial cost-savings could be reinvested in other areas of the health care system, thereby increasing the effectiveness and efficiency of the system.

Financial Institutions Regulation
Regulation of all financial entities should be uploaded to the federal government.

The stability and performance of the Canadian banking system is the envy of the world. However, the non-bank financial sectors are plagued by an inefficient regulatory landscape, characterized by overlap, duplication, and harmful regulatory competition, that hinders their growth and competitiveness. This problem is well documented in the securities sector. It is also rife in the credit union and mortgage sectors, which are regulated by the provinces, and in the insurance and pension sectors, which are regulated jointly by the provinces and the federal government.

Fragmentation along provincial lines has limited the ability of credit unions and mortgage brokers, for example, to expand into other provinces, thereby undermining potential economies of scale in the industry and preventing the development of an even stronger national brand in financial services. Efforts to create a single market for these entities (where for example, a mortgage or insurance broker licensed in one province can service other markets) have been slowed by joint decision traps. Harmonization is also occurring at a snail's pace. It has taken Canada's insurance regulators years to harmonize some basic forms.

Provinces have varying capacities to regulate their sectors. In many provinces, the legislation governing financial entities is woefully out of date. Financial regulation is among the federal government's core competencies whereas many provinces just dabble in this policy area.

Financial regulation is operated on a cost-recovery basis. Industry participants and, ultimately, consumers pay for inefficiencies. What are the compliance costs when there are approximately 3000 pages of overlapping federal and provincial statutes for the insurance sector in Ontario alone? What are the compliance costs if a firm has agents across the country that are subject to 12 other sets of idiosyncratic rules and regulations? Why does Canada, with a population of 33 million, have

14 or more prudential regulators while the United Kingdom, with a population of over 61 million, has one?

The Canadian Bankers Association (CBA) has warned against further fragmentation of banking regulation. Provinces have begun attempts to edge their way into credit card regulation, which could lead to inconsistently applied credit card fees and regulatory tinkering subject to provincial political pressures that are incompatible with industry needs. "[T]he effort to grab power from Ottawa runs counter to 'international standards that require strong and coherent bank regulatory regimes at the national level'" (National Post, 26 May 2011).

Ultimately, federal regulation of these sectors could enhance the efficiency of the economic union and boost competition in Canada's highly concentrated financial services sector (where the banks are dominant and consumers lack choice). A financial regulation upload could be examined as part of the recently announced review of federal financial regulation legislation.

The Supreme Court's unanimous decision to block the creation of a national securities regulator has set back efforts to strengthen the economic union through federal leadership. It is our view that the court's decision interprets the trade and commerce clause far too narrowly, over-relying on the Judicial Committee of the Privy Council's 1881 decision, which restricted the applicability of the clause.

The case for uploading: Uploading would improve the economic union by reducing regulatory barriers across the country and boosting competition in the financial sector. Consumers and businesses across the country would benefit from administrative efficiencies and a higher standard of protection.

Food Safety
Responsibility for food regulation and safety should be uploaded to the federal government.

The health of every Canadian depends on access to high-quality, safe, and affordable food. While the jurisdictional overlap in agriculture has typically been managed well, due to strong intergovernmental cooperation and strong stakeholder pressure, agricultural product safety issues have caused considerable policy challenges and may be one of the exceptions to the rule.

Food and animal product safety, including management of food-borne emergencies, is handled by both orders of government. However, a lack of effective coordination has meant that accountability is unclear. The uncertainty among government officials and the public as to who was ultimately responsible for dealing with the listeriosis outbreak of 2008 or the Bovine Spongiform Encephalopathy (BSE, or mad cow disease) outbreak of 2003 exemplifies the confusion over accountability.

The federal government is responsible for safety inspections of exported goods, while the provincial government inspects goods that are produced and sold in local markets. Theoretically, a single national standard would clarify accountability and reduce the likelihood of food-borne emergencies resulting from inconsistent inspection and enforcement.

There is some concern that onerous federal standards will make compliance for small producers (who are selling locally) too costly. Some industry experts believe that a second tier of federal regulation for locally sold products that does not impose additional standards would effectively eliminate duplication and take advantage of greater federal resource capacity.

In an effort to save approximately $4 million a year the federal government has recently taken steps to back out of food safety inspections in three provinces: British Columbia, Saskatchewan, and Manitoba. This move met with criticism from these provinces who argue that the decision merely downloads the costs to provincial governments where capacity will need to be strengthened to match the federal level (Windsor Star, 10 August 2011).

The case for uploading: Current fragmentation of governmental responsibilities creates gaps in regulation and weakens accountability in the sector. It is unclear to Canadians who is responsible for the safety of food. Uploading would create efficiencies and save businesses and consumers money.

Temporary Unemployment Assistance and Disability Support
Responsibility for programs that support individuals who do not qualify for EI or who cannot work due to disability should be uploaded to the federal government through the creation of a Temporary Unemployment Assistance program and an income support system for persons with disabilities.

The integration between income support programs for working age adults is virtually non-existent. The lack of coordination between federally administered EI and provincially administered social assistance creates huge gaps in the system and an incoherence that cannot be justified on principle. It also produces a regional patchwork where EI plays a very different role in income security in different regions of the country.

Currently, federally administered EI is a temporary support system for the unemployed that is not means-tested and not available to all Canadians, including the self-employed. After EI, the next (and last) resort for EI "exhaustees," or those who do not qualify, is usually means-tested provincial social assistance. However, to access this provincial support individuals are required to have little to no income or assets, leaving a service gap for individuals at the in-between stage of the EI-social assistance spectrum.

Further, the limited scope of EI does not adequately account for the changing needs of a modern labour force. Many Canadians are increasingly self-employed or working multiple part-time jobs; they fall outside of the EI umbrella and thus do not have access to regular EI supports. A federally administered Temporary

Unemployment Assistance program (TUA) structured as a forgivable loan would fill this gap in the income security landscape and help Canadians stay attached to the labour market during times of economic change (Mowat Centre 2011).

TUA could significantly ease the burden on provincial social assistance. This could offset some of the additional federal spending needed to administer the program especially in Ontario where the number of people relying on welfare has increased by 25 percent since 2007 (Mowat Centre 2011). The inclusion of cost-recovery elements (e.g., repayable loans) would also lessen the additional taxpayer burden.

The federal government should also create a federal income support system (similar to the current system for seniors) for persons with severe disabilities or other working-age adults who cannot participate in the labour market. This would alleviate the growing cost of disability caseloads in all provinces due to aging populations and enable provinces to focus on training and income assistance for potential workers.

The case for uploading:[2] Vesting the federal government with the responsibility to provide more robust EI supports will ensure that Canadians are better protected in the event of job loss and keep them attached to the labour market. Improved federal supports will lessen the burden on provincial social assistance programs. It will also produce a more coherent, integrated income security system for working-age adults with fewer gaps and fewer anomalies.

Streamlining/Disentangling

When both orders of government need to be involved in a policy area, their actions must be coordinated. Overlap is costly and ineffective.

Inspections, Investigations, and Enforcement (II&E)
Overlap in II&E should be eliminated through a combination of uploading and devolving.

Canadians rely on governments to make sure the water they drink is clean and the food they eat is safe. However, it is incumbent upon government that inspections, investigations, and enforcement be conducted efficiently and do not impose unnecessary costs on businesses and consumers. Canadian producers are subject to global competition and undue regulatory burdens can undermine their ability to succeed. Unfortunately, many of Canada's industries are burdened with unnecessary costs due to overlapping federal and provincial II&E mandates. A crowded

---

[2]See *Making it Work: Final Recommendations of the Mowat Centre Employment Insurance Task Force* for a complete rationale of the recommendations made here.

regulatory framework increases the costs of doing business in Canada as industries are forced to spend significant amounts of time and money to navigate multiple layers of regulations.

Unnecessary administrative burdens have an impact on public confidence and trust in government. Complaints about two orders of inspections take a toll on citizens' evaluations of government. There is no reason for having two sets of inspectors performing the same job. In some cases, the provinces are more knowledgeable and sophisticated regulators; in other cases it is the federal government. On a case-by-case basis, the federal and provincial governments should work together to decide which level is better placed to conduct II&E functions.

For example, the regulation of effluent from Canada's pulp and paper mills is crowded with different provincial and federal regulatory standards. The federal regulatory framework imposes a lower standard and the presence of two regulatory processes depletes industry resources. According to industry analysts, a more appropriate regulatory strategy would be to have strict national standards enforced locally by provincial regulators. This disentangling strategy would allow both levels of government to maintain a presence in the sector without imposing additional industry costs.

Environmental Assessment (EA) is a good example of successful government coordination. In order to balance the tension between retaining oversight and streamlining processes for businesses, Ontario and the federal government entered into an agreement on EA cooperation. The 2004 Canada-Ontario Agreement created an administrative mechanism to coordinate the EA process whenever projects are subject to simultaneous review by both jurisdictions. Although both orders retain their legislative and decision-making responsibility, decisions are based on the same body of information and the timing of approvals and announcements is coordinated. This may be a potential model for II&E coordination in other sectors.

It is our assessment that governments should take their existing program reviews and expand upon them, turning them into "whole-of-government" or "vertical" program reviews, meaning that the federal and provincial governments would work together to identify areas of possible duplication and then make decisions about who should vacate the space.

The case for streamlining/disentangling: Coordination between the different orders of government will close gaps in regulation and improve efficiency, which will better protect public health and safety while reducing industry costs.

Corrections
Responsibility for offenders sentenced to six months or more should be uploaded to the federal government. Responsibility for offenders sentenced to less than six months should be devolved to the provinces (as recommended by the Changing Face of Corrections Task Force (CFCTF)).

Effective correctional services are essential for maintaining the safety of Canadian communities and successfully rehabilitating offenders. Unfortunately, the system is confusing and complicated by an arbitrary distribution of responsibilities between governments. The "two-year" rule dictates that sentences of two or more years must be served in federal penitentiaries, while sentences that are less than two years are served under provincial jurisdiction.

The *Constitution Act of 1867* allocates responsibility for "penitentiaries" to Parliament and gives provinces jurisdiction over "prisons and reformatories," but does not detail the differences between the two. The two-year rule was an *ad hoc* attempt to clarify this ambiguity but it no longer reflects sentencing patterns in Canada (CFCTF 2009). As noted by the CFCTF report, the rule creates an "artificial barrier to efficient and effective programs and deprives large numbers of offenders programs that could benefit them and enhance public safety" (CFCTF 2009, 24). The result is the duplication of programs and services, which impedes the effectiveness and efficient administration of Canadian corrections and creates tension over cost sharing (Griffiths 1998). Expert consensus converges on the need to redraw the line "between long-term programs aimed at criminal behaviours and short-term programming aimed at issues that can be addressed – or at least started to be addressed – in a very limited time frame" (CFCTF 2009).

The case for streamlining/disentangling: Clearly assigning responsibility for corrections services based on a distinction that makes sense will minimize duplication, thereby improving the sector's efficiency while upholding the functional division of responsibilities within Canada's constitutional framework. Further, uploading responsibility for offenders sentenced to longer than six months would make the federal government responsible for the cost of their own "tough on crime" legislation, which is estimated to increase provincial costs from $2.2 billion in 2009-2010 to $5.3 billion in 2015-2016 (Rajekar and Mathilakath 2010, 12).

Municipal Project Governance
The federal government should remove itself from decision-making processes where it does not serve a vital need and where the legitimate interest is local and/or provincial rather than national.

In its 2010 Speech from the Throne the federal government committed to eliminate unnecessary appointments to federal agencies, boards, commissions, and Crown corporations. This commitment should be extended to a broader examination of federal participation in decision-making within areas of clear provincial jurisdiction. In these areas inaction often prevails due to joint decision traps and conflicting aims, goals, and disputes over funding. This is particularly true in the urban development field.

For example, the complexity of governance relationships at play in the development of Toronto's Downsview Park project has significantly undermined policy outcomes. "In general, the more fragmented power and agendas were, the poorer the eventual policy outputs of a given policy initiative were" (Horak 2009). When the federal government involves itself in the governance of municipal policy-making, significant time and resources are devoted to lobbying and bargaining, resulting in lengthened project timelines and reduced political will to achieve desired policy ends (Horak 2009).

Similar challenges have faced the development of Toronto's waterfront. Years of broken commitments and disputes between all levels of government have plagued the development of what should be a widely celebrated and enjoyed public space in downtown Toronto. Although the number of government bodies involved in the development of Toronto's waterfront has been gradually reduced due to the forma- tion of Waterfront Toronto – a joint federal, provincial, and municipal development agency – problems persist. Despite being granted legal autonomy under its own provincial legislation, the corporation still cannot mortgage assets, acquire land, or borrow money without the express consent of all three levels of government. Instead, however, revenues flow from contribution agreements negotiated behind closed doors by the three governments on a project-by-project basis.

This arrangement has left Waterfront Toronto vulnerable to bureaucratic and political delays replicated at each level of government. Over the last decade, at the federal level alone, the agency has worked with five different cabinet ministers across six different departments and under three different political administrations. Such instability precludes the long-term outlook necessary for successful redevel- opment (Eidelman 2011).

Canada used to have the luxury of indulging intergovernmental conflicts for decades before municipal projects were built. The world is moving along. The time for this self-indulgence is over.

The case for streamlining/disentangling: Removing an order of government will speed the pace of decision-making processes and facilitate better policy outcomes. There is legitimate federal interest in some issues related to the use of federal crown lands, whereas there is no legitimate national interest on others.

Non-Profit
Responsibilities in the non-profit sector should be streamlined/disentangled to ensure complementarities between provincial social enterprise strategies and the Canada Revenue Agency (CRA). A federal-provincial-territorial working table should be established to clarify responsibilities.

The non-profit sector is growing both in size and importance in Canada. The sector is vast, accounting for $106.4 billion and seven percent of the Canadian economy (Statistics Canada 2010). Ontario alone has 46,000 not-for-profit orga- nizations, which generate revenues of $29 billion and employ 16 percent of the province's population (Eakin and Graham 2009).

There have been many intergovernmental initiatives to eliminate barriers to the smooth functioning of Canada's economic union (e.g., the Agreement on Internal Trade) and its social union (e.g., the Social Union Framework Agreement). There remain, however, many intergovernmental barriers to the smooth functioning and growth of the non-profit sector.

Provinces maintain constitutional jurisdiction over charitable and non-profit entities and have engaged in efforts to strengthen the sector. For example, Ontario has attempted to loosen provisions to allow greater autonomy in generating revenues through its *Good Government Act* (Bill 212) while New Brunswick, British Columbia and other provinces-territories have moved forward with aggressive and innovative strategies to support the growth and entrepreneurship of the sector.

However, the federal government, through the Canada Revenue Agency (CRA) and the Income Tax Act (ITA), maintain jurisdiction over the charitable status and taxation issues related to the sector. Strict federal interpretation of charitable and tax-exempt activities is often in direct contradiction with provincial strategies for the sector.

The result of shared jurisdiction is a lack of coherence in the non-profit sector. The issue has become even more important because governments are increasingly looking to the sector to be a partner in program delivery. Across provinces and territories there is broad consensus that charities and non-profits need more opportunities to generate revenue in order to occupy the space vacated by governments, but the CRA is an obstacle. Other countries such as the UK, are finding ways to support the growth of the sector by creating space for social enterprise including more freedom to generate revenue. Canada needs a mechanism to help clarify the fragmented regulatory landscape.

The case for streamlining/disentangling: The lack of federal-provincial-territorial coordination is a barrier to improving effectiveness and to the emergence of a nationally integrated, entrepreneurial non-profit sector. Streamlining federal-provincial-territorial legislation will eliminate interprovincial barriers and enable the sector to maximize administrative efficiencies on a national scale.

CONCLUSION

Canada's federal system of government has been a success story. It has permitted the accommodation of diversity, the building of national projects, and the exercise of local autonomy to respond to local preferences. These successes have made us complacent. We have been too quick to congratulate ourselves for our ability to manage a diverse federation rather than acknowledge that much can be improved. Most who work in government know this but work in a system that is difficult to change.

The way Canada's federal system works is too costly, too inefficient, too closed to public engagement, and it hinders innovation in policy-making and service delivery. It is slow in a world that is quick. It is also too unaccountable because when more than one government jostles in the same policy space it is difficult for citizens to know who is in charge – often because everyone is, or no one is.

This chapter has made recommendations that will improve policy development and program delivery. The recommendations do not presume that Canadians care which government delivers a particular service. In fact, Canadians care about governments delivering public services efficiently more than they care about "who does what." This is another reason why it makes sense to look for opportunities to upload, devolve, or streamline roles.

This chapter has provided the scope for a broad reform agenda. Individual observers will no doubt disagree with any number of the specific recommendations, worrying that they either weaken the federal government or strip sub-national governments of their autonomy. But it is important to note that the recommendations strike a balance between a strong federal presence in those areas where the federal government can play a useful and productive role – both strengthening the economic union and reinforcing Canadians' common citizenship – and a strong provincial-territorial role where these governments are better able to develop, design and implement programs and services to suit their local circumstances.

However, there are two crucial observations. First, Ontario is going through a period where it will have few fiscal resources and will welcome opportunities to clarify roles and responsibilities. Spending that can be removed from either the provincial or federal books will be well received by both governments. Second, Ontario may not have the fiscal capacity or desire to invest in a strong, active federal government with an interest in inter-regional redistributive social policy. Although some worry about a weakening federal role, we believe that Canada and the Canadian identity are stronger than any particular constitutional, jurisdictional, or programmatic role for the federal government.

REFERENCES

Cameron, D. 2010. *Author Interview*. Toronto: Mowat Centre for Policy Innovation.

CFCTF (Changing Face of Corrections Task Force). 2009. *Task Force Report*. Toronto: CFTCF.

Clark, I. 2010. *Author Interview*. Toronto: Mowat Centre for Policy Innovation.

CMHC (Canadian Mortgage and Housing Corporation). 2011. *Affordable Housing Framework 2011-2014*. Ottawa: CMHC. http://www.cmhc.ca/en/corp/nero/nere/2011/2011-07-04-0930.cfm

Courchene, T.J. 1996. ACCESS: A Convention on the Canadian Economic and Social Systems. Working Paper, School of Policy Studies. Kingston: Queen's University.

Cutler, F., and M. Mendelsohn. 2000. "The Effect of Referendums on Democratic Citizens: Information, Politicization, Efficacy, and Tolerance." *British Journal of Political Science* 30:685-701.

Dean. T. 2010. *Efficiency and Effectiveness in the Federation Interview*. Toronto: Mowat Centre for Policy Innovation.

Eakin, L., and H. Graham. 2009. *Canada's non-profit maze: A scan of legislative and regulation impacting revenue generation in the non-profit sector*. Toronto: Wellesley Institute. http://wellesleyinstitute.com/files/Canada's%20Non-Profit%20Maze%20report.pdf.

Eidelman, G. 2011. "Who's in Charge? Jurisdictional Gridlock and the Genesis of Waterfront Toronto." In *Reshaping Toronto's Waterfront*, edited by G. Desfor and J. Laidley, 263-286. Toronto: University of Toronto Press.

Employment Insurance Act, SC 1996.

Fitzpatrick, M. 2011. "Canada's health-care promises not yet met," CBC News, May 31. http://www.cbc.ca/news/health/story/2011/05/31/pol-health-accord-report.html

Friendly, M. 2004. "Strengthening Canada's social and economic foundations: next steps for early childhood education and childcare." *Policy Options* 25 (3):46-51.

Gagnon, M., and G. Hebert. 2010. *The Economic Case for Universal Pharmacare: Costs and Benefits of Publicly Funded Drug Coverage for all Canadians*. Ottawa and Montreal: Canadian Centre for Policy Alternatives and Institut de recherche et d'informations socio-économiques.

Gibbins, R., A. Maioni, and J.G. Stein. 2006. *Canada by Picasso: The Faces of Federalism*. Ottawa: The Conference Board of Canada.

Government of Canada. 1996. *Employment Insurance Act*. Ottawa: Parliament of Canada.

Government of Canada. 2006. *Speech From the Throne*. Ottawa: Parliament of Canada.

Government of Canada. 2007. *Budget 2007: A Stronger, Safer, Better Canada*. Ottawa: Parliament of Canada.

Government of Canada and Government of Ontario. 2005. *Canada-Ontario Labour Market Development Agreement*. Ottawa and Toronto: Parliaments of Canada and Ontario.

Government of Ontario. 2011. *Annual Budget*. Toronto: Parliament of Ontario.

Greenwood, G. 2011. "Banks push back against provinces; 'Federal' matter." *National Post*, May 26. http://www.cba.ca/contents/files/cba-in-the-news/int_20110526_post_regulate_bil.pdf

Griffiths, C.T. 1988. "Canadian Corrections: Policy and Practice North of 49°." *The Prison Journal* 68 (51):51-62.

Horak, M. 2009. Multilevel Governance in Toronto: Overcoming Coordination Challenges in the "Megacity." Working Paper, Department of Political Science. London: University of Western Ontario.

Ibbitson, J. 2011. "Without any fanfare, Canada has grown up." *The Globe and Mail,* September 4. http://www.theglobeandmail.com/news/politics/without-any-fanfare-canada-has-grown-up/article627076/

Klassen, T. 1999. "Job Market Training: The Social Union in Practice." *Policy Options* 20 (10):40-44.

Mowat Centre. 2011. *Making it Work: Final Recommendations of the Mowat Centre Employment Insurance Task Force*. Toronto: Mowat Centre.

Mallea, P. 2010. "Harper's "tough on crime" bills costly, counterproductive," Canadian Centre for Policy Alternatives, last modified March 16, 2010. http://www.policyalternatives.ca/publications/commentary/harpers-tough-crime-bills-costly-counterproductive

OCASI (Ontario Council of Agencies Serving Immigrants). 2011. *Background Information on CIC Cuts*. Toronto: OCASI. (http://www.ocasi.org/downloads/OCASI_CIC_Cuts_Backgrounder.pdf.)

Ontario Ministry of Finance, and Finance Canada. 2010. *Federal Transfers as a Percentage of Health Spending 2010-2011*. Toronto and Ottawa: Ontario Ministry of Finance and Finance Canada.

OECD (Organisation for Economic Cooperation and Development). 2006. *Starting Strong II: Early Childhood Education and Care*. Paris: OECD.

Pascal, C. 2009. *With Our Best Future in Mind: Implementing Early Learning in Ontario*. Toronto: Parliament of Ontario.

Pierre, N. 2007. *A Safer Haven: Innovations for Improving Social Housing in Canada*. Ottawa: Canadian Policy Research Network.

Rajekar, A. and R. Mathilakath. 2010. *The Funding Requirement and Impact of the "Truth In Sentencing Act" on the Correctional System in Canada*. Ottawa: Office of the Parliamentary Budget Officer.

Schmidt, S. 2011. "Federal gov't to quit inspecting provincial slaughterhouses." *Windsor Star*, August 10. http://www.windsorstar.com/Federal+quit+inspecting+provincial+slaughterhouses/5235872/story.html

Seidle, L.F. 2010. *The Canada-Ontario Immigrant Agreement: Assessment and Options for Renewal*. Toronto: Mowat Centre for Policy Innovation.

Sibonney, C. 2010. "Soaring costs force Canada to reassess health model," *Reuters*, 31 May. http://www.reuters.com/article/2010/05/31/us-health-idUSTRE64U3XO20100531

Siemiatycki, M., and T. Triadafilopoulos. 2010. *International Perspectives on Immigrant Service Provision*. Toronto: Mowat Centre for Policy Innovation.

Skogstad, G., and H. Bakvis. 2008. "Canadian Federalism: Performance, Effectiveness, and Legitimacy." In *Canadian Federalism: Performance, Effectiveness, and Legitimacy*. Toronto: Oxford University Press.

SARAC (Social Assistance Review Advisory Council). 2010. *Recommendations for and Ontario Income Security Review*. Toronto: SARAC.

Statistics Canada. 2010. "Satellite account of non-profit institutions and volunteering," last modified 5 July 2011, accessed December 2010, http://www.statcan.gc.ca/daily-quotidien/101217/dq101217b-eng.htm

UNICEF. 2008. *The Child Care Transition, Innocenti Report #8*. Florence: UNICEF Innocenti Research Centre.

Weaver, R.K. 1986. "The Politics of Blame Avoidance." *Journal of Public Policy* 6 (4):371-398.

Queen's Policy Studies
Recent Publications

The Queen's Policy Studies Series is dedicated to the exploration of major public policy issues that confront governments and society in Canada and other nations.

Manuscript submission. We are pleased to consider new book proposals and manuscripts. Preliminary inquiries are welcome. A subvention is normally required for the publication of an academic book. Please direct questions or proposals to the Publications Unit by email at spspress@queensu.ca, or visit our website at: www.queensu.ca/sps/books, or contact us by phone at (613) 533-2192.

Our books are available from good bookstores everywhere, including the Queen's University bookstore (http://www.campusbookstore.com/). McGill-Queen's University Press is the exclusive world representative and distributor of books in the series. A full catalogue and ordering information may be found on their web site (http://mqup.mcgill.ca/).

School of Policy Studies

Navigationg on the Titanic: Economic Growth, Energy, and the Failure of Governance, Bryne Purchase 2013. ISBN 978-1-55339-330-6

Measuring the Value of a Postsecondary Education, Ken Norrie and Mary Catharine Lennon (eds.) 2013. ISBN 978-1-55339-325-2

Immigration, Integration, and Inclusion in Ontario Cities, Caroline Andrew, John Biles, Meyer Burstein, Victoria M. Esses, and Erin Tolley (eds.) 2012. ISBN 978-1-55339-292-7

Diverse Nations, Diverse Responses: Approaches to Social Cohesion in Immigrant Societies, Paul Spoonley and Erin Tolley (eds.) 2012. ISBN 978-1-55339-309-2

Making EI Work: Research from the Mowat Centre Employment Insurance Task Force, Keith Banting and Jon Medow (eds.) 2012. ISBN 978-1-55339-323-8

Managing Immigration and Diversity in Canada: A Transatlantic Dialogue in the New Age of Migration, Dan Rodríguez-García (ed.) 2012. ISBN 978-1-55339-289-7

International Perspectives: Integration and Inclusion, James Frideres and John Biles (eds.) 2012. ISBN 978-1-55339-317-7

Dynamic Negotiations: Teacher Labour Relations in Canadian Elementary and Secondary Education, Sara Slinn and Arthur Sweetman (eds.) 2012. ISBN 978-1-55339-304-7

Where to from Here? Keeping Medicare Sustainable, Stephen Duckett 2012. ISBN 978-1-55339-318-4

International Migration in Uncertain Times, John Nieuwenhuysen, Howard Duncan, and Stine Neerup (eds.) 2012. ISBN 978-1-55339-308-5

Centre for International and Defence Policy

Afghanistan in the Balance: Counterinsurgency, Comprehensive Approach, and Political Order, Hans-Georg Ehrhart, Sven Bernhard Gareis, and Charles Pentland (eds.), 2012. ISBN 978-1-55339-353-5

Institute of Intergovernmental Relations

The Democratic Dilemma: Reforming Canada's Supreme Court, Nadia Verrelli (ed.), 2013.
ISBN 978-1-55339-203-3

The Evolving Canadian Crown, Jennifer Smith and D. Michael Jackson (eds.), 2011.
ISBN 978-1-55339-202-6

The Federal Idea: Essays in Honour of Ronald L. Watts, Thomas J. Courchene, John R. Allan,
Christian Leuprecht, and Nadia Verrelli (eds.), 2011. Paper ISBN 978-1-55339-198-2
Cloth ISBN 978-1-55339-199-9

The Democratic Dilemma: Reforming the Canadian Senate, Jennifer Smith (ed.), 2009.
Paper ISBN 978-1-55339-190-6

Canada: The State of the Federation 2009: Carbon Pricing and Environmental Federalism,
Thomas J. Courchene and John R. Allan (eds.), 2010. Paper ISBN 978-1-55339-196-8
Cloth ISBN 978-1-55339-197-5

Canada: The State of the Federation 2008: Open Federalism and the Spending Power,
John R. Allan, Thomas J. Courchene, Marc-Antoine Adam, and Hoi Kong (eds.), 2012.
Paper ISBN 978-1-55339-194-4 Cloth ISBN 978-1-55339-195-1

Canada: The State of the Federation 2003: Reconfiguring Aboriginal-State Relations,
Michael Murphy (ed.), 2005. Paper ISBN 1-55339-010-5 Cloth ISBN 1-55339-011-3

Our publications may be purchased at leading bookstores, including the Queen's University Bookstore (http://www.campusbookstore.com/) or can be ordered online from: McGill-Queen's University Press, at **http://mqup.mcgill.ca/ordering.php**

For more information about new and backlist titles from Queen's Policy Studies, visit http://www.queensu.ca/sps/books or visit the McGill-Queen's University Press web site at: **http://mqup.mcgill.ca/**

Mowat Centre Publications

Emerging Stronger 2013
Mowat Centre & The Ontario Chamber of Commerce, 29 January 2013

Back to Basics: The Future of the Fiscal Arrangements
Matthew Mendelsohn, 20 December 2012

Integrating Human Services in an Age of Fiscal Restraint: A Shifting Gears Report
Jennifer Gold & Josh Hjartarson, 11 December 2012

Homelessness: Closing the Gap Between Capacity and Performance
James Hughes, 6 December 2012

Moving Toward Voter Equality: Mowat Centre Report on the Proposed Federal Electoral Boundaries for Ontario
Michael Pal & Melissa Molson, 15 November 2012

Smarter and Stronger: Taking Charge of Canada's Energy Technology Future
Tatiana Khanberg & Robert Joshi, 6 September 2012

Fiscal Problems, Taxation Solutions: Options for Reforming Canada's Tax and Transfer System
Jean-François Tremblay, 14 May 2012

Workers Left Outside the EI Umbrella: Explanations and a Simple Solution
Mary Davis, 16 April 2012

Alberta and Equalization: Separating Fact from Fiction
Melville L. McMillan, 28 March 2012

Equalization at Arm's Length
Daniel Béland & André Lecours, 18 March 2012

Energy Security for Ontario
Robert Joshi, 7 February 2012

Expenditure Need: Equalization's Other Half
Peter Gusen, 5 February 2012

Emerging Stronger: A Transformative Agenda for Ontario
Mowat Centre & The Ontario Chamber of Commerce, 25 January 2012

Fiscal Sustainability and the Future of Public Services: A Shifting Gears Report
Jennifer Gold & Matthew Mendelsohn & Joshua Hjartarson, 23 November 2011

Making it Work: Final Recommendations of the Mowat Centre Employment Insurance Task Force
Mowat Centre Employment Insurance Task Force, 18 November 2011

Fiscal Sustainability and the Transformation of Canada's Healthcare System: A Shifting Gears Report
Will Falk & Matthew Mendelsohn & Joshua Hjartarson, 31 October 2011

Putting Canada on Track: A Blueprint for a National Transit Framework
Joshua Hjartarson & Kelly Hinton & Michael Szala, 24 October 2011

Voter Equality and Other Canadian Values: Finding the Right Balance
Matthew Mendelsohn & Sujit Choudhry, 17 October 2011

Postal Code Lottery: Canada's EI System Compared
Vuk Radmilovic, 14 April 2011

The New Economics of the NHL: Why Canada Can Support 12 Teams
Tony Keller & Neville McGuire, 11 April 2011

Strengthening the Third Pillar of the Canadian Union: An Intergovernmental Agenda for
Canada's Charities and Non-Profits
Elizabeth Mulholland & Matthew Mendelsohn & Negin Shamshiri, 10 March 2011

Shifting Gears: Paths to Fiscal Sustainability in Canada
Matthew Mendelsohn, 09 December 2010

Is 70 the New 65? Raising the Eligibility Age in the Canada Pension Plan
Martin Hering & Thomas Klassen, 15 November 2010

A Report Card on Canada's Fiscal Arrangements
Joshua Hjartarson & James Pearce & Matthew Mendelsohn, 10 November 2010

Saving Dollars and Making Sense: An Agenda for a More Efficient, Effective and
Accountable Federation
James Pearce & Joshua Hjartarson & Matthew Mendelsohn, 15 October 2010

Help Wanted: How Well did the EI Program Respond During Recent Recessions?
Matthew Mendelsohn & Jon Medow, 08 September 2010

One Economic Market or a Collection of Jealous Rivals? Ensuring the Effectiveness of
Securities Reform in Canada
Joshua Hjartarson, 13 July 2010

Toward a Transformative Agenda for FedDev Ontario
Neil Bradford & David A. Wolfe, 29 June 2010

Regional Economic Development Agencies in Canada: Lessons for Southern Ontario
Neil Bradford, 29 June 2010

From Entanglement to Alignment: A Review of International Practice in Regional
Economic Development
David A. Wolfe, 29 June 2010

International Perspectives on Immigrant Service Provision
Myer Siemiatycki & Phil Triadfilopoulos, 28 May 2010

The Canada-Ontario Immigration Agreement: Assessment and Options for Renewal
Leslie Seidle, 27 May 2010

Some are More Equal than Others: Canadian Political Representation in Comparative
Context
Matthew Mendelsohn, 23 March 2010

The Principle of Representation by Population in Canadian Federal Politics
Andrew Sancton, 22 March 2010

The New Ontario: The Shifting Attitudes of Ontarians toward the Federation
J. Scott Matthews & Matthew Mendelsohn, 23 February 2010